EDWINA

*The Biography of The Countess Mountbatten
of Burma*

Portrait of Edwina Mountbatten by Salvador Dali. Reproduced by
kind permission of the artist

EDWINA

The Biography of
The Countess Mountbatten of Burma

BY

MADELEINE MASSON

London
Robert Hale Limited
63 Old Brompton Road, S.W.7.

Printed in Great Britain by Richard Clay and Company, Ltd.,
Bungay, Suffolk

For
MY SON

ACKNOWLEDGEMENTS

I am indebted to Alan Campbell Johnson and his publisher for permitting me to use his book, *Mission with Mountbatten* as background material for my chapters on India; to Mrs. Georgiana Blois for material and photographs; to J. S. McDowell of the London Library for interest and help; to the publishers of *Edwardian Hey-Days* by George Cornwallis-West and *Things Past* by Vittoria Colonna for permission to quote from those books; to my husband for his unremitting patience and to all those who assisted me during the preparation of this book.

CONTENTS

LIST OF ILLUSTRATIONS

Facing page

PREFACE

It is not usual, I know, for a biographer to preface a work which should flow smoothly and impersonally from the cradle to maturity with every scrap of data neatly tabulated and woven into a pattern. This style is in the grand tradition and as such is to be admired and emulated. Equally successful is the approach of the biographer who was an intimate or lifelong friend of his subject; a Boswell shadowing his Johnson, or an Eckerman dedicated to his Goethe.

Nothing of this kind can be said to apply to my relations with Lady Louis, the heroine of this book. I had read of her, seen many photographs of her in fashionable poses at fashionable places, and was no more interested in her than I was in any other great mondaine of our time. Some years ago, when travelling in East Africa, I happened to spend the night on a farm near Mombasa, and in the shabby, friendly living-room I came across a tattered copy of a magazine. I leafed through it until my attention was arrested by an article entitled 'The Angel of Mercy'. It was an overplayed piece starred with adjectives and was illustrated with many photographs of Lady Mountbatten visiting the sick and wounded in Malayan prison camps and hospitals. Here indeed was a new angle on a lady of fashion. For a long time I stared at the pictured face of the woman in uniform. Something about the widespread eyes and mobile witty mouth captured my imagination, and I determined that sooner or later I would find out for myself why this immensely wealthy heiress should have stepped down from her gilded pedestal into a mundane and suffering world, and if the article were true, have dedicated her life to the service of humanity.

I met Lady Louis and after an hour spent with her I knew that I must attempt to write her biography. This was not easy. Lady Louis loves people, but she does not care for publicity, and since she is a woman of reticences and of great sincerity, she could not assist any curious writer to pry into

her past and private life.   Nor I imagine did she care for the
idea of playing Guinea Pig under the scalpel of my curiosity.
For the time being, therefore, the project was abandoned.

Many years passed, when, owing to a combination of
circumstances, I saw a good deal of Lady Louis.   During that
time we had many talks together, and the more I saw of her,
the more fascinated I became in a character which had apparently inexhaustible depths and reserves.   During this time,
too, I made it my business to meet her friends and colleagues,
and since all of them—apart from a common devotion—
presented me with a different facet of her personality, my resolve
was strengthened to write a book about this remarkable woman,
who has long been engaged in a spiritual search.   If at times
the goal has been obscured, the search has continued, intensified, bitter and at times almost unbearable.   For this reason,
perhaps, there is much in her character and evolution that is
inexplicable to the casual observer.   Even those who know
her well will testify to the solitary and hermetic quality which
baffles and sometimes misleads.   But all who have ever come
in contact with her remember always her fire and her wit, her
humility and the quality of mercy which gives her spirit wings.

M. M.

Lady Louis's Descent from Edward IV and Henry VII

Elizabeth, daughter of Edward IV *m.* 1486 King Henry VII

Mary, daughter of Henry VII *m* Charles Brandon, Duke of Suffolk
(widow of Louis XII of France)

Eleanor, daughter of the Duke of *m.* Henry Clifford, Earl of Cumber-
Suffolk land

Margaret, daughter of the Earl of *m.* Henry, 4th Earl of Derby
Cumberland

Alice, daughter of Sir John Spencer *m.* Ferdinando, 5th Earl of Derby
of Althorp

Frances, daughter of 5th Earl of *m.* John, Earl of Bridgewater
Derby

Elizabeth, daughter of the Earl of *m.* David, Earl of Exeter
Bridgewater

Frances, daughter of the Earl of *m.* Anthony, 1st Earl of Shaftesbury as
Exeter his second wife

Here follow the 2nd, 3rd, 4th, 5th and 6th Earls of Shaftesbury

Emily, daughter of Peter Leopold, *m.* Anthony, Lord Ashley, 1830, after-
5th Earl Cowper wards 7th Earl of Shaftesbury

Sybella Charlotte, daughter of Sir *m.* 1866, Hon. Evelyn Ashley, second
Walter Farquhar, 3rd Bart. son of above

Amelia Mary Maud, only child of *m.* Wilfrid William Ashley, 1901,
Sir Ernest Cassel, G.C.B. eldest son of above

Edwina, Mary,
born 1901 born 1906

CHAPTER I

DEATH OF A MILLIONAIRE

THE GREAT company knelt in prayer. With hands
reverently folded they listened attentively to the Requiem
Mass which was being said for the repose of the old man's
soul. For a while they listened devoutly, impressed by the
deep solemnity of the occasion, and by the death of one whom
they had looked upon as almost immortal, so long had he
dwelt in their midst, and so firmly entrenched had he been
in the vast web of his success. Then their thoughts began to
stray, and snuggling deep into their furs, for it was September,
and chilly in the church, a few great ladies glanced in the
direction of the family who were standing close together.
Huddled almost, and leaderless, now that the Patriarch was
dead. Dubious, kindly, and speculative glances rested on
the chief mourners. To many, an aura of gold encompassed
them. The old man had been so rich, so immensely rich.
On whom would the mantle of his wealth now fall? The
worldly, match-making mothers before hurriedly returning to
their prayers singled out a slight, angular figure for closer
inspection. Yes, that was she—his favourite, the eldest Ashley
girl. Shrewd eyes studied her. It was rumoured that she
was in love with a penniless young Naval officer. Had she
told her grandfather of this attachment? Had he approved
her choice?

Edwina, pale and composed, was not conscious of the
appraising glances of the congregation. She was thinking of
her grandfather, whose end had been unexpected, swift, and
lonely. He had died as he had lived, she thought, in loneliness. A quick remorse flashed through her that she had failed
him at the end. He had died sprawled across his desk in that
great echoing house from which she had escaped into the light:
into the blinding light of the revelation of love; and he, the
old man, had known nothing of this revelation. He who had
listened often to her views on life, on people, would never now

15

know that she was happy. It would have comforted him, she thought, to know that she was so happy that even in this moment of solemnity and silence, tremors of excitement shot through her heart. She wrenched her mind back from those last sunlit days in Scotland. Music was beating through the church. It was all as he would have liked it. Pomp and circumstance, and everything arranged on a magnificent scale. She glanced at the family, at his family near her. Auntie Grannie gave her a tremulous smile. Strangely enough, already the memory of Ernest as the head of the house had faded and she remembered only the small boy he had been before he left Cologne, before he became so rich and so remote —and so difficult. Kind he always was, but he had become stern, and it was impossible to know what he was thinking. He had done so much for the family—she drooped in her Russian sables—so much for everybody, and he had not been happy. Only twice in his life had he had a small measure of happiness. When he married and when Maud was born. Poor Maudie, to die so young; poor Ernest; poor Edwina. . . .

Sitting at the back of the church, as far away as possible from the well-clothed, perfumed throng, was Chaim Wasserman. His feet in their broken boots were cold, as was his heart. In Yiddish he murmured the prayers for the dead, establishing in death, as he had in life, a bond with his friend. For Chaim had been Ernest Cassel's *alter ego*, a shadowy figure who, unknown to those who shared so much of the financier's public life, had been his closest contact with his past and with reality.

Born in the same year and in the same city of Cologne, he and the pale-faced son of Jacob Cassel had been friends. To him Ernest Cassel had outlined his plans and ambitions for the future, and together they had walked and talked. But already, even in their adolescence, Chaim had known that Ernest would succeed and that he would fail. Lost to his religion, lost to us, mourned Chaim, dismally contemplating the gold spears of candle-flame flickering before the altar, and yet he was truly one of us, and only great love made him renounce us. Look, he never forgot us. Chaim remembered the many occasions on which he had come to his friend for succour for his co-religionists. Not for great charities—there was always someone to bring those to his notice—but for those humble outcasts of society who had failed in their small enter-prises—tailors, dabblers in commerce—failures, failures like himself.   And Ernest had never refused to receive him, not once, not even when the presence in his house of his King might have barred all approach to that study in which Ernest trans-acted so much of his business; that room in the heart of the marble mansion which was, thought Chaim, so like a tomb. But now he was dead and there was no one left, no one to whom an old man could talk, remembering a past in which two boys had planned to conquer the world, and how one of them only had succeeded.

Ernest Cassel was buried in Kensal Green Cemetery, and on his simple grave was laid a wreath sent by Queen Alexandra. Across the broad ribbon was an inscription 'In sorrowing memory of Sir Ernest Cassel, the kindest and most generous of men, and a great personal friend of my beloved Husband, King Edward. Now Comes Rest. Alexandra.' . . . The mourners dispersed, returning to their homes, to toast their feet in front of the fire and, in the majority of cases, to forget, as rapidly as possible, that death had walked amongst them.

But he, among all his contemporaries, would not so soon be forgotten.   The good that he had done during his lifetime would live on in the generations to come.   Spurred by the memory of his own personal tragedy and inability to cure the sufferings of his wife and daughter, he had given vast sums to medicine.   In memory of his daughter, Maud Ashley, he gave large sums to the King Edward VII Hospital Fund for London. He also helped build and endow the great King Edward VII Sanatorium for tuberculosis at Midhurst, and he supplemented this later on by starting the Papworth Industrial Colony for Consumptives.   He contributed generously to the buying of radium for cancer research.   He founded and endowed a sanatorium for nervous disorders originally established at Pens-hurst in Kent and still functioning now at Ham Common. Among his other munificent gifts was the sum of £500,000, which was placed in the hands of trustees for educational purposes, including adult education, scholarships for workmen and their children, the higher education of women, the study

B

of foreign languages, and the establishment of a Faculty of Commerce in the University of London.

Ernest Cassel was born on March 3rd, 1852, in Cologne, the youngest son of Jacob Cassel and his wife Amalia. When Ernest was a year old, his father was elected a representative of the Jewish community of Cologne, in which town he conducted a banking business of local and minor importance. Jacob Cassel fostered in his Benjamin a precocious talent for chess and for the violin, but as Ernest reached manhood family conferences were held to decide his future. It was thought that he might do well as a professional chess-player, though his mother, an incurable romantic, inclined towards a musical career. Ernest, however, then as always, had ideas of his own, and at his request his father apprenticed him to the firm of Elzbacher and Co. in Cologne. Ernest absorbed all he could from this excellent firm and then, with their approval, decided to gain experience away from his native land. Shortly after his sixteenth birthday, armed with a carpet bag and his violin, he arrived in Liverpool, and for a short time worked in the firm of the commission merchants Blessig, Braun and Co.

Soon, however, he was again on the move and this time he went to Paris, where he became a clerk in the Anglo-Egyptian Bank. This was work he enjoyed, and his future might have been in Paris had not the outbreak of the Franco-Prussian War convinced him that it was in England that he must build his financial empire. For, even then, England and all things English attracted him, and hearing that the senior partner of the firm of Bischoffsheim and Goldschmidt in London were looking for a confidential clerk, with great aplomb he applied for the post. Mr. Bischoffsheim, having received an avalanche of otiose letters filled with self-praise, was in despair. He read young Cassel's brief communication, 'Dear Sir, I apply for the position in your office and refer you to my former chiefs Messrs. Elzbacher, Cologne. Yours sincerely, Ernest Cassel' . . . Handing the letter over to his secretary, old Bischoffsheim said, 'That's our man!'

He was indeed their man. With them his main activities lay in the financing of railways and the straightening out of existing, but not very profitable, undertakings in which the firm was interested, and when he had successfully negotiated and settled a complicated engagement in connexion with Nicaragua, Henry Bischoffsheim sent for Cassel and told him that in recognition of his services the firm would raise his salary from £200 to £500. . . . 'You mean £5,000, Mr. Bischoffsheim,' said Cassel drily. 'Quite so, quite so,' retorted the elderly gentleman; 'I meant £5,000.' Cassel was worth this sum to his firm, for from the day he took over the management of the branch which dealt with lawsuits, an inevitable hazard of railway building, not a single case more was settled in court. He was a relentless adversary, showing himself ruthless and unbending until the breaking point, when, always on the strength of some crucial point in his favour, he won the day. His speciality was to become railway financing. Unlike some of his showier rivals in the railway boom, he was not a speculator. He was 'an economic imperialist, with the whole world as his empire'.[1]

Cassel's dreams of becoming a successful financier were fast achieving reality. He began to look forward to a time when he could prove to his parents that their youngest son had become a man of substance, but a series of tragic deaths cut short any plans he may have made for the welfare of his family. The death of his mother in 1874 was shortly followed by that of his father and eldest brother Max. Only his sister was left to witness the rise of Ernest Cassel. He made arrangements for her to come to London to keep house for him and, not being a man to parade his private griefs, he buried his dead, and once again immersed himself in work. The house of Bischoffsheim and Goldschmidt came to depend more and more upon the razor-sharp mind of young Cassel.

One of his more spectacular successes for his firm was the reconstruction of the Erie Railway, which had failed in 1875. In connexion with this transaction he came into close contact with Kuhn Loeb and Co. in New York, and their partner, Jacob H. Schiff, who, towards the turn of the century, was reaching heights which Cassel hoped to emulate. Schiff had a warm regard for Cassel, a regard which, after an episode one summer at Chamonix, where they were all holidaying *en famille*, turned to deep and lasting gratitude and friendship. It was on this occasion that Schiff's small daughter Frieda

[1] *Manifest Destiny*, by Brian Connell (Cassell).

slipped and fell into a crevasse several hundred feet deep. Without an instant's hesitation Cassel flung himself after the child and was able to drag her back to safety from the bush which had miraculously broken her fall.

In the rising industries of Sweden, Cassel was to find scope for his original creative methods. In the early seventies his firm had become interested in the Swedish Central Railway and had tied up enormous sums which paid no dividends. Cassel studied the situation and, realizing that the undertaking was destined to remain sterile unless it were possible to increase the output of a nearby iron mine (the ore of which contained a large amount of phosphorus) to an extent which would make freights from the mine provide the railway with continual and remunerative employment. With this in mind, he took a keen interest in a new process invented by Sidney Gilchrist Thomas of eliminating phosphorus from pig-iron, thus enabling phosphoric ores to be used. This process had been disregarded in England, but Cassel, certain of its value, introduced the Thomas process in the iron mine (in which he took a large participation) and, as he had anticipated, the mine prospered.

So successful was his project, in fact, that in order to have complete control of the railways from the mining district to the coast, he merged with the Swedish Central, the Royal Swedish Railway, and the Oxalosund Railway into one vast concern. His ever-increasing interests in Sweden were to lay the foundations of his fortune, which, in 1881, before he was thirty years old, amounted to some £150,000.

In 1877 Cassel met Annette, daughter of Robert Thompson Maxwell, of Crofts Hall, Croft, Darlington. He fell instantly in love with the gentle, affectionate girl, whose fragile charm quickly penetrated the armour of reserve with which he had girded himself to joust against life. His marriage to Annette was celebrated a year after their first meeting. To add to the joy of marrying the woman he loved, he became a naturalized British citizen, thus realizing two of his major ambitions. For a brief period, happiness flowered within him and, to the surprise of his friends, he became gay and even loquacious. The birth of a daughter, Amelia Mary Maud, gave him a greater incentive than ever to provide his small and beloved family with all the material benefits that could be heaped upon them.

Cassel was to pay a high price for his happiness. His wife fell ill and within three years of their marriage she was dying of tuberculosis. Powerless, he witnessed her long-drawn agony, and the sight of her suffering penetrated him so deeply that no material triumph was ever to efface this memory. As it became apparent that her illness was fatal, so did her anxiety about her husband and child increase. She was a devout Roman Catholic and could not bear the knowledge that Cassel would not be able to be with her in the hereafter. She implored him to become a convert, and because he cared for her so profoundly, he prepared himself to enter the Catholic Church. So, secure in the belief that she, her husband, and child would be again united in a better world, Annette Cassel died.

The death of his wife changed Cassel from an ambitious but thoughtful husband into a man of stone, in whose heart was rooted one obsession. He was determined to endow his motherless daughter with a vast fortune. She should enjoy all that he had not been able to give her mother. Maud became the centre of his existence. The child was cared for by his sister, who 'brought up little Maudie with as much love and tender care as she gave her own children, even more, because she was so delicate'.

In 1884 Cassel started on his own. In the small, simply furnished office at No. 21 Broad Street, which were his head-quarters until 1910, when he retired from active business, he set about consolidating his fortune. Hard work, good in-formation, and instinct were the basic principles which guided him. In time he was to become the most powerful financier, who, in two continents, was to acquire a unique personal position. 'He was to combine the art of a finished diplomatic *negociateur* with the gift of a never failing visionary.'

His first big coup undertaken on his own was the reorganiza-tion of the Louisville and Nashville Railway Company in 1884. This undertaking was carried out with the co-operation of Kuhn, Loeb and Co. Mexico was the next venture. He raised capital for the Mexican Central Railways. From rail-ways, he turned to Government finance, and though his negotiations with the Mexican Government were unfruitful, he raised loans to China and to Uruguay. Cassel was always

careful and conscientious in his business dealings and he himself
studied every detail before entering into negotiations with any
country.

In 1890 the finances of Argentina collapsed, and assistance
had to be given by the Bank of England to the great Bishopsgate
House whose name was so closely linked with the River Plate.
Cassel, who was already regarded by the 'inner cabinet' of
the city as a cool and sagacious adviser in matters of finance
with practical experience in difficult reorganizations, was
selected to negotiate and to straighten out a perilous situation.
This he did successfully, himself acquiring large interests in
the Argentine.

In 1895 Ernest Cassel became interested in a project of the
Electric Traction Company, which, with his backing, began
the underground construction of the Central London Railway,
connecting the Bank with Shepherd's Bush. Opened in 1900,
it was popularly known as the 'Twopenny Tube' and was one
of Cassel's few unprofitable investment schemes. As he himself
drily remarked after the opening, it was evident that the surest
way to have made money on it would have been, not to build
it, but to let someone else do so, and to buy land at its western
terminal.

It was due to Cassel's contacts and diplomacy that, in 1897,
the fusion took place between the Naval Construction and
Armament Company of Barrow-in-Furness, Messrs. Vickers
Sons and Co., and the Maxim-Nordenfelt Guns and Ammuni-
tion Company. This amalgamation became the world-
renowned firm of Vickers Sons and Maxim (later, in 1911, to
be known as Vickers Ltd.).

.   .   .

Quietly and unostentatiously, as he did all things, Cassel
was making his way, not only in the world of finance, but also
in the social world, and particularly in that circle which
gravitated about Edward, Prince of Wales. Frowned upon
by Queen Victoria and the Palace, the Marlborough House
set represented a glamour and a glitter which, until the Prince
finally came to the throne, were to cause raised eyebrows and
pursed lips. Deprived of his State duties by his august mother,
the Heir Apparent dedicated his life to a seeming frivolity,
which in the final analysis was to stand him in good stead,

for, 'from the wisdom of business men and the wit of beautiful women, he learnt how to deal with men'.[1]

Cloistered in her widowhood, Queen Victoria had no inclination to rule over any particular section of English society. It was sufficient for her that she ruled England. Her son, by virtue of his intelligence, charm, and *joie de vivre*, exercised a total sovereignty over those he chose to gather about him. But he brought to this rarified coterie, ossified in its antique traditions, a breath of something new and revolutionary. He chose his friends not by virtue of their birth alone, but simply because of their personal qualities and because they amused him. Having little taste for intellectual pursuits and disliking solitude, he gathered about him those who could best foster and share in his particular interests. Foreigners, Americans, sportsmen, and men of business were welcome at his table. And, *mirabile dictu*, Jews were not only *persona grata* with the Prince, but were admitted to his close friendship. Three of the Sassoon brothers were members of the Prince's inner circle. The Rothschilds were entertained at Marlborough House, and Baron Maurice de Hirsch, Bischoffsheim's brother-in-law, was the Prince's banker and private adviser. Hirsch was an admirer of Cassel's brilliant brain and had often mentioned his spectacular exploits in the financial field to the Prince. When, in 1896, Hirsch died, Cassel became his executor. This led, perforce, to a meeting with the Heir Apparent, an encounter which was to have momentous consequences, for not only did Cassel become the Prince's banker and financial guide, but he was, in the course of time, to become one of the Prince's closest friends.

According to Sir Felix Semon, Cassel was 'of medium height, very thick set, of distinctly Jewish type, with an almost bald head, a short full beard, big nose, rather small eyes, carefully but not ostentatiously dressed, anything but a *causeur*, usually taciturn, not a public speaker'.[2]

He had none of the suave polish and almost professional charm which so endeared the Portuguese diplomat, the Marquis de Soveral, to the Prince, but in Cassel were qualities of loyalty, discretion and a profound understanding of the nature

---

[1] *The End of a Chapter*, by Shane Leslie.
[2] Sir Felix Semon's Autobiography. Jarrolds.

of princes, and of the needs of this Prince in particular. The future Edward VII respected the man of whom he once said, 'he has the cleverest head in England', and in the blunt, almost puritanical little Jew he reposed unbounded trust and confidence. Cassel, together with Lord Farquhar, a banker, and later Master of the King's Household, unravelled the Prince's somewhat tangled finances and made certain that the Prince would never again find himself embarrassed, and so diligently did Cassel—'Windsor' Cassel, as he was nicknamed—direct the Prince's finances, that Sir Dighton Probyn, as Keeper of the Privy Purse, the official manager of the King's finances, was able to report to the usual Commission to inquire into the financial position of the new Sovereign, that Edward VII had ascended to the throne 'unencumbered by a single penny debt'.

On Tuesday, January 22nd, 1901, the curtain fell on the sixty-four years reign of a legendary woman who had united in her person the roles of Queen of England, Empress of India, and sorrowing widow. The great Queen was dead, and at her passing her son, the Prince of Wales, aged fifty-nine, became Edward VII. The gloom, stiffness, and boredom of Victoria's Court were to be replaced by an era of opulence and glitter.

'Those were wonderful days [wrote George Cornwallis-West in his memoirs], taxation and the cost of living were low; money was freely spent, and wealth was everywhere in evidence. Dinners were gargantuan affairs, far too long, Champagne, Port, and brandy were the order of the day. . . . Women's dresses were very elaborate and quantities of jewellery were worn. These were the days of tiaras and stomachers. The blaze of jewels at the Opera was really amazing.' [1]

The King reigned supreme over his Court. He was the arbiter of fashion. He liked cards, good food, and the company of pretty, but not intellectual women. He loved a good race-meeting, amusing stories, and unmalicious gossip. He was courteous, benevolent, and, in spite of his seeming simplicity, autocratic. Though he permitted his intimates a cer-

[1] *Edwardian Hey-Days*, by George Cornwallis-West (Putnam).

tain degree of familiarity, he had a curt and caustic way of snubbing the overbold. From his mother he had inherited many traits: her smile, her common sense, and her fanatical punctuality and love of order. Every clock at Sandringham was kept fast, by his orders. In spite of his grasp of and intense interest in domestic, foreign, and empire affairs, his private life was planned down to the last detail.

The friendship of the Prince of Wales was a privilege, that of the King of England a rare honour. Edward VII, on his accession to the throne, did not forget Cassel. In 1901, immediately after his accession, Cassel was made a K.C.V.O., and in the following year he obtained the distinction of being called to the Privy Council. Cassel was firmly entrenched in the King's intimate circle, who, if they did not care for him personally, knew the weight his opinion carried with their King, and were impressed by the qualities which had made him one of the wealthiest men in England. Cassel was cited as a model for the gilded youths who, having run through their inheritance, now sought to supplement their meagre incomes by becoming connected in some way with leading financial or industrial firms. But few of them had the Midas touch. Some of them, when job-hunting, sought an interview with Cassel, or broached the subject over the dinner-table. The advice he gave them was sound, if not encouraging; but, as they generally discovered, he was a shrewd judge of character and refused to help anyone unless he thought they had within themselves the stuff to succeed.

Even those who did not like Cassel were glad enough to avail themselves of his magnificent—if slightly overwhelming —hospitality and of his generosity. But few men knew him really well, and though he had many acquaintances he had few close friends. George Cornwallis-West wrote of him thus:

'I was friendly, but never intimate, with him. I doubt if many men ever were intimate with him. His was not a personality to invite intimacy; but with his cold, hard headed business nature, he had many kindly feelings. I believe that neither money nor social position meant anything to him beyond the power they gave him. Power meant everything to him. His friendship with King

Edward VII was, so far as he, Cassel was concerned, founded on his love of power; it helped to that end.   In his speech he was curt and to the point.   I never heard him speak on any subject with which he was not thoroughly conversant, but when he did talk he was inclined to lay down the law and resent argument.   To a woman, if she were pretty, and he liked her, he was suavity itself.   He never forgot a slight, and like many of his race he was extremely sensitive.' [1]

By now he had made his first million, and was living in considerable state at 48, Grosvenor Square, to which he had moved from 2, Orme Square, Bayswater.   Ascetic by nature, and of a frugal habit, he was nevertheless engaged in a perpetual struggle against obesity.   The fear of getting fat obsessed him and was, in part, responsible for much of his irritability.   Also, as his power grew so did he become more despotic in his home.   His devoted sister Bobbie, who loved and admired him, generally bore the brunt of his ill humours, though there were times when he became impatient with his beloved daughter should she in any way thwart his wishes.   And Maudie was no puppet.   She stated, very firmly, her views, and if Cassel flared up temporarily, he was secretly amused by her audacity and independence, as he would later be by that of his granddaughter Edwina.

His friendship with the Prince and his contact with the Prince's circle made him aware that there were certain lacunae in his way of life.   He now began to take a more sustained interest in entertaining and in the decor of his house.   Without having any specialized knowledge of pictures, silver, or *objets d'art*, he none the less set himself to collect them, and as he was as shrewd in his choice of artistic advisers as he was in matters of business, it was not long before he had built up a unique collection of pictures, silver, and jades.

Among these treasures were the 'Bacon' Silver-Gilt Cup and Cover, one of the three made in 1574 from the Great Seal of England;   the Commonwealth Blacksmith's Cup;   the 'Wolsey' Henry VIIth Silver Beaker, made in 1496;   and the 'Cunliffe Salt' made in 1580.   The collection included some magnificent pieces of furniture, notably an Empire table from

[1] George Cornwallis-West, *op. cit.*

Napoleon's collection, and Empire chairs by Bellangé. No less important were the pictures, masterpieces by George Romney, Sir Henry Raeburn, Sir Joshua Reynolds, Franz Hals and Van Dyck. Most of these pictures were purchased for Sir Ernest by Joseph Duveen.

But it was his collection of jade which gave Cassel the greatest satisfaction. The cool beauty of jade, which depends for its value on play of colour and quality of surface, appealed to him as much because of its antiquity as by its icy purity. Ernest Cassel's tragic spirit, sealed within its shell, shied from all lusty and sensual warmth. He was essentially a solitary, seeking inspiration in silence. His happiest moments were spent alone among the Alpine snows. Mountaineering was his favourite relaxation; whenever he could get away, he went to Switzerland, finally acquiring a mountain residence in the Riederfurke Alps, on the south-eastern side of the Aletsch Glacier. The surrounding peaks were a challenge, and, doggedly, the short, stocky millionaire conquered them, one after the other, finding in this achievement an exaltation which no financial triumph could give him.

CHAPTER II

THE MIDAS TOUCH

WHILE SIR ERNEST CASSEL was building up his glittering monument to Mammon in the world of Society and the world of finance, his daughter Maud was growing up as he had hoped she might, in an atmosphere of opulent luxury. For her sake he cultivated assiduously men and women with whom, fundamentally, he had nothing in common. When she came out, the stately homes of England must be open to her, and for her sake, and also to entertain the King and his friends, he rented and bought country estates in which he played squire, learning with courage to ride, shoot, and fish, though none of these pursuits appealed to him. His only real interest in his country estates was the growing of flowers, which he loved and with which he surrounded himself. For a number of years he rented Lord Willoughby de Broke's castle, Compton Verney. Here, as at Moulton Paddocks, he entertained on a lavish scale, watching with a certain ironic satisfaction his severest critics gathered in his dining-room, where he regaled them with the choicest viands and the finest wines, partaking himself of severe little dishes, of vegetables cooked in water, and grilled meats washed down with copious draughts of still water.

Maud was the jewel enshrined in the various settings. Pampered and spoilt, she remained essentially sound. Nothing had tarnished the fine qualities which she had inherited from her mother. Like her, she had deep religious convictions, unshakeable loyalty to her friends, and a desire to help others less fortunate than herself. But all that Cassel demanded of her was that she should be gracious, feminine, and well versed in the roles she would later be called upon to play when she became a wife and a great hostess. Maud, however, was both intelligent and wilful. She was also avid for life and experience, and impatient of the delicate constitution which constantly betrayed her fiery spirit. Forced to curb her physical activities, Maud read widely and carefully, concealing from her father her intellectual bent, determined when she married to have a literary salon in which she hoped to gather writers, poets, artists, and even great actresses. In the meantime, she led the life of a carefully nurtured young lady of fashion, interested in clothes and in all the gaieties of the London season.

Sir Ernest loved his only child with a profound and despairing love. Always within him was the fear that she, like her mother, might be carrying within her the seeds of death, and so he watched over her fiercely, lovingly, and unremittingly. In later years a true cameraderie was to spring up between them. He was to sign his letters to her 'your old pal' and would be touchingly gratified by her confidences, but that was later, and in the meantime her health and happiness were the chief concern of his busy life.

Cassel was proud of his daughter, and though it is possible that the problem of a suitable husband for her was often in his mind, he loved her too deeply to try to influence her in the choice of a companion. Besides, he was well aware of Maud's strong will, but he knew, too, that the solid common sense she had inherited from him, together with her own integrity, would guide her heart when the time came. Certainly Miss Cassel did not lack for suitors. Apart from her own appealing personality and looks, her father's immense fortune made her one of the most eligible heiresses of the day.

One after the other, personable and titled bachelors sought to attract and to hold Maud's interest, and though she was patient and sympathetic, and not averse from mild flirtations, she remained detached and heartfree, until she met Wilfrid Ashley. From that moment her mind was made up. He was the man she would marry.

William Wilfrid Ashley, a grandson of the great social reformer, the seventh Earl of Shaftesbury, united in his handsome person all the breeding and distinction of one born of a long line of distinguished ancestors. Indeed, he could trace his descent direct from Edward IV and Henry VII, and if the blood of the wistful Indian princess Pocohontas which ran in his veins did not stir in him, it was to blaze again later on in his eldest daughter.

Tall, handsome Major Ashley, the *beau ideal* of London

society, was thirty-three years old when he fell in love with
Maudie Cassel. He had nine years in the Grenadier Guards
and a battalion command in the Boer War. He was heir to
a fine estate in England and to another in Ireland. Cassel
considered Maudie's choice with a speculative eye. There
was, superficially, little in common between the self-made,
brilliant financier and the English soldier, but Cassel realized
that Ashley could give his daughter happiness and roots, and,
above all, he desired that she have her being in the country
of his adoption. Ashley had integrity and loyalty. He was a
patrician and his standards were high. He was an officer
and a gentleman. If many of his ancestors had been rakes,
gallants, and eccentrics, their behaviourism had been of their
time and all had served their country well. Ashley was the
perfect product of his era. Harrow, Magdalen, and Sandhurst
had moulded him. His world was a narrow one, but it was
the only world he knew or cared to know, and anything beyond
it, any factor which threatened to disturb the traditional pattern by which he lived—and in which he hoped to die—roused
his vehement disapproval.

Spurred by the example of his famous kinsman, Lord
Shaftesbury, Wilfrid Ashley had every intention of entering
the political arena. He was a natural orator, and though
he was to have a solid political career, he was not sufficiently
flexible in his outlook to attain great status in his party. From
his father, whom he admired, he had absorbed many precepts
which were to shape his future.

His father, Anthony Evelyn Melbourne Ashley, born in 1836,
was the son of the Earl of Shaftesbury and Lady Emily
Cowper. His grandmother, Countess Cowper, a sister of
Lord Melbourne, Queen Victoria's first Prime Minister, married
Lord Palmerston after the death of Lord Cowper, and Lord
Melbourne, Evelyn Ashley's godfather, gave him his name, while
Lord Palmerston introduced him to the mysteries of political life.

After Harrow he went to Cambridge, but he left the University before the usual three years of residence to become private
secretary to Lord Palmerston. After Lord Palmerston's death,
Evelyn Ashley was called to the Bar. Joining the Oxford
Circuit, he practised until 1874, when he entered Parliament
as Liberal Member for Poole. He also, during this period,

held the office of a Treasurer of County Courts. He was a pioneer of the movement for allowing prisoners to give evidence on their behalf, and twice he brought forward a Bill in the House of Commons to give effect to his views. Though many years elapsed before this came into being, much credit is due to him who led the way. In 1880 he became, under Chamberlain as President, Parliamentary Secretary to the Board of Trade. In 1882 he became Under-Secretary of State for the Colonies, a position he occupied until Gladstone went out of power in 1885.

In 1886, Evelyn Ashley married Sybella, daughter of Sir Walter Farquhar, by whom he had one son. She died in the same year, and in 1891 he married again. On the death of his uncle, without issue, Ashley succeeded to the family estates in Hampshire and Ireland.

Maud Cassel was marrying into a family whose motto was 'Love and Serve' and to whom the administration of their estates and the welfare of their tenants were matters of paramount importance. To the Ashleys, and to Wilfrid Ashley in particular, it was unthinkable that the world and society in which they lived might ever change. If Ernest Cassel was a visionary and visualized a different tempo of life, and the evolution of the working classes, he kept his ideas to himself, quietly endowing centres to further the education of individuals who might, like himself, spring from humble beginnings to become figures of national importance.

In the meantime, he approved his daughter's choice and, concealing the sadness which beset him whenever he thought of Maudie's leaving him, he made certain that her marriage settlement would provide handsomely for her children, and grandchildren, and it was with his blessing that his beloved Maud entered into marriage with Wilfrid Ashley.

Maud Cassel was doing more than marry the man she loved. She was marrying into a tradition and a way of life which would be part of the birthright of her children. She had much to offer Ashley. Great riches, a loving nature, humour, and a fierce enjoyment of a life which was to be so very brief.

The marriage of Maud Cassel to Wilfrid Ashley took place early in January 1901. King Edward VII attended the ceremony, once again giving proof of his friendship for Sir Ernest

Cassel. The young couple set out on their honeymoon, and Cassel returned to his empty house and to his work.

It had been her father's hope that Maud should sink her roots in the good English soil, and this she might have done, had she had time to sink any roots at all. As it was, her husband's estate, Broadlands, never became her home, nor could any earthly dwelling claim her interest, for already, though she did not know it, she was detaching herself from all that might absorb her and prevent her from enjoying the precious fragments of life and time left to her. But being with Ashley at Broadlands gave her, perhaps for the first time, a clue to his real nature. Here she saw him in his own setting, welded to a tradition and a way of life which she had not time nor energy to adopt. More clearly than he, for she came as a stranger, she saw what Broadlands meant to Wilfrid Ashley and unconsciously it irked her that he should be claimed instantly and insistently by the past and by his ancestors. Broadlands, to Wilfrid Ashley, was a living entity, a continuity with his line. To Maud it was a monument to the dead, and she preferred the living.

In this ancient house history had strolled amid the paths laid out by Capability Brown. Always its portals had welcomed the great; King James I had scrawled his signature in the visitor's book, and within its walls had beaten the pulse of the political and social life of England, and to some extent of Europe, in the last sixteen years of the eighteenth and the first sixty-five of the nineteenth centuries.

The estate of Broadlands was originally part of the Abbey of Romsey, an ancient nunnery founded by the daughter of the Saxon King Edward the Elder, who was its first abbess in 907. In 1539 the Abbey and the entire estate were surrendered to King Henry VIII. The portion known as 'Brodelandes' was separated from the Abbey and sold to John Foster, Steward of the Abbey. The Manor and all the fishing in the water around it were then let, and later sold, by Foster to Sir Francis Fleminge, whose elder son, William, married one of Foster's daughters. Their only daughter married Edward St. Barbe of Ashington, Devonshire. They had several sons, but it was the youngest, Henry, who succeeded his grandfather at Broadlands in 1606.

The third Lord Palmerston and Emily, Countess Cowper (later Palmerston's wife) painted in 1803. Both pictures are in the Broadlands collection and were painted by Sir Thomas Lawrence

Broadlands, the seat of Lord Palmerston, now the country residence of the Earl and Countess Mountbatten of Burma

Princess Pocahontas, ancestress of Edwina. Painted in 1616 (*Hulton Picture Library*)

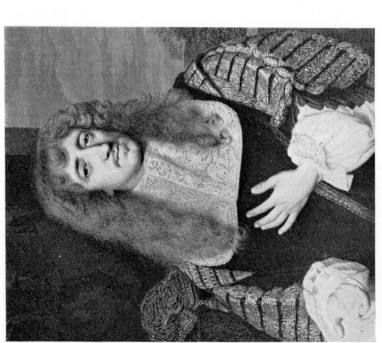

Anthony Ashley Cooper, First Earl of Shaftesbury, 1621–83. Engraved by W. Hall from a miniature by Samuel Cooper (*Hulton Picture Library*)

In 1661 John St. Barbe inherited Broadlands, in which he lived for sixty-two years, making considerable alterations to the house and estate. John, the last of the St. Barbes, died in 1723, leaving the estate to a cousin with instructions that it was to be sold to pay the mortgages with which he had burdened the estate by his speculations in the South Sea Bubble.

In 1736 the first Viscount Palmerston purchased the estate for the sum of £26,500. The house was then still the original one, in the form of an H, with casement windows.[1] It was in a bad state of repair, for it had not been inhabited for many years, and the farmer tenant placed in the farmhouse by St. Barbe's cousin, had done little to keep the house in order. Palmerston, having purchased the estate, announced that he would make it into a 'suitable house for a gentleman to live in', and set an army of builders to work. They pulled down part of the old house, built a brew-house, altered the stables and coach-houses, removed the farmyard from the back of the house, and altered the river-front.

The first Lord Palmerston was formerly Henry Temple, descended from the Temples of Stowe, who were Earls of Buckingham. He came of a family who produced many public men, for Peter Temple of Stowe was an ancestor of Sir William Temple, the seventeenth-century diplomat. Peter's youngest son William was secretary to Sir Philip Sidney, and Provost of Trinity College, Dublin. His lawyer son took the Parliamentary side, and published an account of the Irish Rebellion of 1641 and was Master of the Rolls until his death. His elder brother, William, was the correspondent and afterwards husband of Dorothy Osborne.[2] The younger son, John, was Speaker of the Irish House of Commons and, having the Whig principles of his family, was prescribed as such by the Irish Parliament which supported James II. In 1669 the Battle of the Boyne restored him to lands and office, and he was Attorney-General until 1695, when he retired to East Sheen, where he later died.

He was succeeded in his Irish lands, and Surrey home, by his son Henry, who had sat as a boy in the English House of

[1] For alterations see *The Journeys of Celia Fiennes* published by the Cresset Press, pp. 54/7.
[2] Daughter of Sir Peter Osborne, Governor of Jersey under Charles I.

C

Commons.   As a supporter of Sir Robert Walpole, he had
been given the Irish title of Viscount Palmerston in 1723.   He
first married Anne Houblon, niece of Sir John Houblon, founder and first Governor of the Bank of England.   They had
one son, Henry, and two daughters, who died unmarried.
Henry married Jane Barnard, a daughter of John Barnard,
Lord Mayor of London.   Their son, Henry, was born in
1739.   His father died in 1740, and at the age of eighteen, at
the death of his grandfather, he became the second Lord
Palmerston.

Now Broadlands was to enter into the period of its splendour,
for the second Lord Palmerston, though far less well known
than his grandfather and famous son, was to devote his life
to the beautifying of his estate.   Like all the youths of his age
he did the 'grand tour', which was to introduce him to Italy
and to Gavin Hamilton, painter and art adviser, who was to
help Palmerston found his collection of pictures and sculpture.
Though he had vast plans for the enlarging of the park, it was
not until after his second marriage to Mary Mee of Dublin
that he was able to employ Henry Holland as his adviser and
Lancelot (Capability) Brown to lay out the gardens and park,
in conjunction with Robert Adams.

Henry Palmerston was curious about life and people.   He
enjoyed the company of writers, artists, actors, and poets.   He
himself wrote grandiloquent, if poor, poetry.   He was a
generous patron of the arts.   Garrick, Sheridan, and Reynolds
were among his friends, and as he had the entree to all the
great English houses, his social life was full and varied.   He
dabbled in science, was an inveterate traveller, and used Broadlands as the background for receptions and entertainments
which attracted celebrities from all parts of Europe.   Sir
William Hamilton was a frequent guest at Broadlands, and
Sir William, when Ambassador at Naples, was able to give him
much useful assistance in the dispatching of his statuary from
Italy to England.   The unfortunate Princess de Lamballe was
to spend one peaceful golden day at Broadlands before returning to France and to her death.

Though Palmerston was not a politician, foreign affairs
fascinated him, and certain letters in his vast correspondence
incline one to believe that he was sometimes sent *en mission* to

European trouble spots. The Journal of his visit to Paris in 1791 [1] gives a detailed account of life under the Jacobins, and makes surprising reading when one considers that this English aristocrat was not only able to attend the meetings of the Commune, and to wander about Paris unmolested, but was also able to lead a full social life, with visits to theatres and art dealers, where he made a number of expensive purchases for Broadlands.

Once Lord Palmerston had begun embellishing Broadlands, he knew no rest, for always there was one more masterpiece he must possess, one more piece of ancient statuary to set in the hall, and even mounting debts and financial reverses did not deter him from an occupation which had become an obsession. But the result was very splendid. Henry Holland had designed the dining-room ceiling and the saloon walls; the ceiling in the drawing-room was designed in the elaborate Adams manner with additional embellishments by Angelica Kauffman, whom Palmerston had met in Rome. A visit to the Wedgwood factory, and subsequent visits of Wedgwood himself to Broadlands, produced the exquisite decoration of the book room, in which were housed Palmerston's collection of French plays. Console tables were ordered from Hervé, special commodes, chairs, and marble-topped tables—the marble imported from Italy at vast expense added greater distinction to the beautiful rooms. He had indeed created a residence fit for a gentleman. He was to enjoy this perfection until his sixty-third year, when, quite suddenly, he died, and his son, Harry, then completing his education at Edinburgh, became the third Lord Palmerston. He was then seventeen years old.

Broadlands was to be Harry's haven of refuge during all the years of his stormy and brilliant career. From 1805, when his mother died, until 1839, when he brought his bride home, Broadlands was without a chatelaine. Palmerston, who could have married any of the lovely girls who languished for him, preferred to remain a bachelor. His official excuse was pressure of work; a career which gave him no respite. Unofficially, he had given his heart to little Lady Cowper, married to a good dull Earl and an excellent mother to several babies. Palmerston's name was often linked with that of reigning

[1] The Broadlands Archives.

beauties, but his liaisons never lasted. Under Lady Cowper's bright, accusing stare, he made excuses, dented hearts, risked torrents of tears, and returned, laden with gifts for the Cowper children, to the side of his beloved. She, all maternal love and decorum, was faithful to her husband and loved her 'Cupid', as she called him, with as great a passion as that of Lady Bessborough for Leveson-Gower.

Emily Cowper was the daughter of Lady Melbourne, a remarkably intelligent and unscrupulous woman whose twin ambitions, to be a famous hostess and to marry her children into a *milieu* from which she was excluded, were, in the course of time, to be fully realized. Born Elizabeth Milbanke, only daughter of Sir Ralph Milbanke, fifth baronet of Halnaby in the county of York, her extreme good looks and poise attracted many suitors, only one of whom, however, had a sufficiently large fortune to give Miss Milbanke the latitude she desired. This was Sir Peniston Lamb, whom she married, despite the fact that she found it difficult to reconcile herself to marrying a man whose origins had been extremely humble. The fact that the founder of the family, the first Peniston Lamb, had been astute enough to provide handsomely for his descendants did much to mitigate her chagrin at the lack of an impressive family tree, and when, shortly after her marriage, Peniston Lamb was made an Irish peer, with the title of Lord Melbourne of Kilmore, Lady Melbourne launched herself, *con brio*, into the dazzling social round of the day. She met snubs and rebuffs with coolness and good temper. She knew how to bide her time, and she knew, too, how to make influential men fall in love with her, and how, once romance was over, to keep their friendship. She entertained on a lavish scale; Lord Melbourne had bought her a house in Piccadilly, London, and a country estate, Brocket Hall, near Hatfield. Six children were born to the Melbournes: four sons—Peniston, William, Frederick, and George—and two daughters—Emily and Harriet. Peniston was his father's favourite, Lady Melbourne had a particular weakness for William, while rosy Emily was beloved by all. Lady Melbourne had ambitious plans for the future of her children, and one of the first calculated moves in her social progress was to win the friendship of the young Duchess of Devonshire. Her trenchant mind and worldliness appealed strongly to the graceful, warm-hearted Georgina, who flung open the doors which had so long been closed against Lady Melbourne. Nor was Lady Bessborough proof against Lady Melbourne's icy intelligence and acumen, and she, like her sister, encouraged the growing friendship between her children and those of the Melbournes. Married to Frederick, third Earl of Bessborough, she had three sons and one daughter, Caroline. When Caroline was twelve years old she paid a visit to Brocket Hall. Here she met William Lamb, who 'liked her much'. So much that from then onwards he decided that of all the girls of Devonshire House, Caro was the one he would marry. Lady Melbourne was early aware of her son's feelings for Caro. But she had misgivings. Caro was an unusual child, and became an unusual young woman. She looked like a boy. Her head was small, her mouth exquisite, her fair hair was cut short and curled about her head. Her eyes were dark and her voice was low and husky. She was wild, undisciplined, romantic, and eccentric. The Bessboroughs did not care for William Lamb, who had no prospects and was indolence personified. The death of his elder brother, Peniston, made it possible for William to ask for Caro's hand. Caro declared that she wanted to marry William, and in May 1805 her engagement to William Lamb was announced. In the meantime, Lady Melbourne had the satisfaction of stage-managing another and more satisfactory romance, that of the pink-and-white Em with Peter Leopold, fifth Earl Cowper. Lady Melbourne considered Lord Cowper an excellent *parti* for her daughter. Young, handsome, immensely wealthy, a Prince of the Holy Roman Empire, and a Whig, he was the ideal son-in-law, and as his country seat, Panshanger, was near to Brocket, she felt that her daughter would not be too far removed from her beneficial maternal influence and advice. All her life Lady Melbourne was to dominate her pretty Dresden-china shepherdess of a daughter.

The two young women, Caroline and Em, were to begin married life at the same time. The one was to bring misery and unhappiness to her husband and family, the other was to lead a happy, untroubled existence and to end her days with the love of her life. The Melbournes were devoted to one another, and Caro's behaviour to Em's dear William did nothing to stimulate friendship between the sisters-in-law. Em, drawn into the perpetual squabbles between William and Caro, sided with her mother against the troublesome wild young thing, and after her desperate love affair with Byron strongly advised William to leave her. Neither mother nor daughter could understand the ties that bound him to Caro, and finally becoming impatient of the 'whole squalid mess', Em refused to have anything to do with her sister-in-law. But she continued always to take the warmest interest in the welfare of William, Frederick, and George. All were to have distinguished careers. William, second Viscount Melbourne, was Queen Victoria's first Prime Minister, Frederick became a distinguished diplomatist and peer under the title of Lord Beauvale, George, the youngest son, was in Parliament for some time and assisted his brother at the Home Office during some important years.

Immediately after her marriage, Em Cowper 'took her place in the brilliant galaxy of beautiful and accomplished women of rank, who continued to form the chief ornament of the British Court during the successive years'. Em was a leader of society, one of the first patronesses of the exclusive Almack's, and numbered among her friends the wittiest men and the prettiest women of her time. In spite of her absorbing social life, however, she had five babies: Emily, nicknamed Minny, Frances Elizabeth, George Augustus Frederick (afterwards sixth Earl Cowper), William, and George Spencer. From the time she was born, Minny was the pampered darling of the family. She was an exceedingly pretty child, with curly dark hair, long lashes, and eyes of a deep and unusual shade of blue. She was wilful, tiresome, and spoilt, but she had character and heart, and her mother could find no fault in her.

In 1839 Minny Cowper was considered to be one of the prettiest debutantes of many decades, eligible young men paid careful court to her, while Em, who had much of the tough worldliness of her mother, Lady Melbourne, advised caution, told Minny to bide her time and to remember that wealth was more durable than love. Minny was seemingly an obedient daughter, and the prospects of the young men were discussed at length by mother and daughter. But there was one suitor

whom she discussed with nobody. This was Lord Ashley,
the eldest son of Lord Shaftesbury, who was 'all energy,
earnestness, and tenderness'.   He was, too, remarkably handsome, but Minny, mischievous and somewhat impatient of
Ashley's deep sincerity and burning principles, refused to make
up her mind to marry him.   Ashley was so different from the
other young men who admired her, and he was interested in
such odd things. Lunatics, for instance. He was a member
of a committee to inquire into the treatment of lunatics, and
having visited numerous asylums and seen evidence of terrible
ill-treatment, he brought in a Bill to amend the law in one
particular. All his life, in fact, he continued, as one of the
Commissioners in Lunacy, to interest himself in the subject,
and before his death he was responsible for securing a complete
reform of the Lunacy Acts, and had effected untold improvements in the condition of unfortunates who had formerly been
treated with such severity and cruelty.

Ashley was obstinate and intelligent enough to know that
if he could obtain Em's help, his chances of winning Minny's
heart would be greatly increased. She, being mature, realized
that though Ashley might appear to be a crank, an eccentric
even, he would make her daughter a devoted husband, and
her pleading of his cause did much to influence Minny.

The marriage took place on June 10th, 1830. The Cowpers
liked Ashley, and he was soon integrated into their warm
family circle, and until the death of Lord Cowper the young
couple spent all their holidays at Panshanger.

Ashley was the eldest son of the sixth earl, and of Anne,
fourth daughter of the third Duke of Marlborough. Her
dimpled little face enchants the group painted by Reynolds in
which she appears depicted in the act of frightening a grey-
hound with a mask.

The lineage of the Ashley Coopers was ancient. Coopers
had long lived in the manor house of Rockbourne, Hampshire.
Some little distance away, at St. Giles House, Dorset, was a
country gentleman of some considerable standing, Sir Anthony
Ashley, who had served as war secretary under Queen Elizabeth, and whose keen observations on campaign in Holland
had led to the introduction of cabbages into Great Britain.
The daughter of the Knight of St. Giles had one daughter.

The Baronet of Rockbourne fell in love with her and married her. Their son, born in 1621, on inheriting the properties of both families, assumed the name of Anthony Ashley-Cooper, and after the Restoration was raised to the peerage by Charles II, as Baron Ashley. He was to become the most eminent and enigmatic politician of his time. 'His subtlety and readiness of resource fitted him especially for a foremost place, under the existing conditions of political life. The leaders, with scarcely an exception, led lives of mystery and intrigue; in Shaftesbury's case the springs of his action can even now be only guessed at.'

At the age of nineteen he represented Tewkesbury in Parliament, but losing his seat at the time of the General Election which brought in the Long Parliament, he sided with the King on the outbreak of the Civil War. Soon afterwards, however, he became so zealous an agent on the popular side, that he took Wareham for the Parliament, and subjected the surrounding country. He sat in the Legislature as a servant of the Commonwealth during Cromwell's regime; but after the death of the Lord Protector, he bent all his energies on helping the Restoration. In 1672 he was created Earl of Shaftesbury and Lord High Chancellor, but after a year was dismissed from office for opposing the Duke of York, who became James II, was sent to the Tower and later released. His most famous achievement was the passage of the Habeas Corpus Act. Pepys mentions him as 'being a man of great business, and yet of pleasure and drolling too' . . . Dryden, having flayed Shaftesbury in 'Absalom and Achitophel', had second thoughts, and in a later edition wrote:

'In Israel's courts ne'er sat an Abathdin with more discerning eyes, or hands more clean, unbribed, unbought, the wretched to redress, swift of dispatch, and easy of access.'

Shaftesbury was always a wealthy man, having plantations in Barbadoes and a quarter share in a ship, the *Rose*, engaged in the Guinea Trade. He was one of the nine to whom Charles I had given a grant of Carolina in 1663, renewed in 1665, and it was at his request that his friend, and later secretary, John Locke, drew up in 1669 a constitution for it, which, though aristocratic in form, demanded absolute toleration.

The Ashley and Cooper rivers on whose junction Charleston was built commemorate the name of this extraordinary man.

Shaftesbury was thrice married, but had only two sons by his second wife, a daughter of the Earl of Exeter. The elder died in youth and the second boy succeeded to the title in 1683. Though John Locke was his tutor, he in no way distinguished himself, and it was left to the aged philosopher to supervise the education of the third Earl. This he did with such effect and with such co-operation from his pupil, that Shaftesbury was described by Voltaire as 'the boldest English philosopher'. Ill-health having turned him from politics to literature, he became famous as the author of *Characteristics* and in the *Inquiry concerning Virtue* the phrase 'Moral Sense', which occurs in the treatise, became famous in the Scottish school of philosophy of which Hutcheson, a disciple of Shaftesbury's, was the founder. He influenced in various ways all the chief ethical writers of the century and his influence on the Continent was remarkable.

The fourth and fifth Earls left little trace of their passage on earth. The fifth Earl left no son, and was succeeded by his brother, Cropley, who afterwards became sixth Earl of Shaftesbury, and father of Anthony, husband of Minny and son-in-law of Lady Cowper.

She, having married off her pretty daughter, now immersed herself again in her active and gay life. There was never a busier woman than Em, for not only did she keep a close watch on the activities of her brothers, and particularly William's disastrous marriage to Caro, but she had also to keep abreast of Palmerston's career, to snatch him from the wiles of scheming women, to keep her husband in his usual good humour, and to give the benefit of her maternal advice to Minny, who became immediately and fretfully pregnant.

With the death of George IV and the advent of the young Queen Victoria, William Melbourne came into his own. Young Ashley, pursuing his idealistic career, moulded his Minny into the shape and form of an admirable wife and mother. One after the other their children were born and Em was surrounded with a bevy of rosy cherubs. The death of her husband in 1837 brought her life to a sudden stop. Though she had never loved him, she had made him a devoted wife and he had loved her. His death was a great grief to her, and for two years she mourned him sincerely, dedicating herself entirely to her family, who found her sustained interest a little wearing.

In 1839, however, William, Lord Melbourne, had the delicate task of announcing to Her Majesty, Queen Victoria, that his sister, aged fifty, was contemplating matrimony; that she was about to marry Lord Palmerston. Victoria was puzzled, not understanding how two people, to her shining youth in their dotage, could, on the brink of the grave, think of love and romance. Tactfully, William reassured her. Palmerston needed a companion and a hostess. Em could be of wonderful assistance to him in what remained of his career.

Victoria saw the justice of this and made no further comment. Em's children did comment, and harshly. They could see no reason for this autumnal union and said so. But Em was undeterred by their criticism, and on December 16th, 1839, at St. George's, Hanover Square, Em was married to her beloved Palmerston and the most brilliant chapter of her life opened before her.

Palmerston brought his bride home to Broadlands, and the old house, roused from its long sleep, woke again to the sound of children's voices. For wherever Em was, some of her grandchildren, nieces, and nephews were sure to be. Minny, constantly confined, was only too pleased to leave one or the other of her children with her mother, and Palmerston was greatly attached to Em's brood.

The union of Em to Lord Palmerston was of the greatest importance to Ashley, for it led to an intimate friendship between the elder statesman and the young philanthropist. Each man influenced the other for good; Ashley, from association with wit and wordliness, was saved from becoming a crank, while Palmerston adopted many of Ashley's humanitarian views. Ashley, like Tolstoy, was the prophet of love, and, regardless of criticism and obstruction, he continued to fight the cause of the weak and the oppressed. He had entered Parliament as Lord Ashley, the member for Woodstock, the pocket borough of the Marlborough family, and gave a general support to the governments of Liverpool and Canning. He was returned for Dorchester in 1830 and 1831, and

sat for Dorsetshire from 1833 to 1846. His first speech was an
earnest pleading in favour of a proposed grant to the family
of Mr. Canning, after his sudden death.

In 1828, under the Duke of Wellington, he obtained the
post of a commissioner of the Board of Control, and in 1834
Sir Robert Peel made him a Lord of the Admiralty. If he
had chosen a political career, his rank, connexions, and abilities
might have placed the highest offices of the State within his
grasp, but he was held in thrall by another object of pursuit—
the promotion of philanthropic reform, and in the ardour of
his enthusiasm for this line of action, he thought it advisable
to maintain an independent position to politics.

Having done much to mitigate the condition of lunatics in
confinement, he next turned his attention to reforming the
law relating to the employment of workers in mills and factories. A deep impression had been produced in him when
he visited hospitals in Lancashire, where he found many
workers who had been crippled and mutilated under the conditions of their work. They presented every variety of distorted form, 'just like a crooked alphabet'. At many times
in Ashley's life he got the Factory Acts amended. New industries were brought within their scope. He always maintained
that he would never rest till the protection of the law should
be extended to the whole mass of workers. During this
struggle collieries and mines engaged his attention. Here too
the evils brought to light, especially with respect to women
and children, were appalling. Children, sometimes not over
four or five years of age, were found toiling in the dark, in
some cases as long as eighteen hours a day, dragged from bed
at four in the morning. Often they were attached by a chain
and girdle to trucks which they had to drag on all fours through
the workings to the shaft. An Act was passed in 1842, under
Ashley's directive, abolishing abuses and excluding women and
boys under thirteen, from employment underground.

The treatment of 'climbing boys'—as the apprentices of
chimney-sweepers were called—was another of the abuses
which Ashley set himself to remedy. He obtained an Act for
the protection of the apprentices. His interest was intensified
in two movements: the education of the neglected poor, and
the improvement of the dwellings of the people. He was also

the chairman of a sanitary commission for the Crimea, in regard to which Miss Nightingale wrote that 'it saved the British Army'.

Throughout his long life Ashley, later Lord Shaftesbury, strove to implement the family motto 'Love and Serve'. His labours included the Climbing Boys Act, the Factory and Ten Hours Act, Mines and Collieries Regulation Acts, the establishment of Ragged Schools, training-ships and refuges for boys and girls, the protection of lunatics, the abolition of slavery, the promotion of the City Mission and the Bible Society, and also, unsparing efforts for the protection of maltreated and tortured dumb animals.

Much is owing to Lord Shaftesbury for his work in softening the bitter spirit between rich and poor in nineteenth-century England, and the people whom he strove to help were grateful for his efforts, and he had friends in all walks of life, particularly among the costers, whose gratitude for his efforts was expressed by the gift of a donkey.[1]

On the death of his father in 1851, Ashley succeeded to the earldom. Minny had given him ten children, the eldest of whom, Anthony, 'Accy', was born at St. Giles. He was the first heir to be born at St. Giles since about 1600, when the first Lord Shaftesbury was born there. After Anthony came Francis, Maurice, Evelyn, Lionel, and Cecil, and there were four daughters, Constance, Mary, Victoria, and Fanny.

Lady Shaftesbury worried more about Evelyn than about her other children. He was, she felt, a trifle frivolous, and her letters to him at Harrow, and later at Cambridge, were heavy with warning and wisdom. On one occasion she wrote:

'My dearest Evelyn,
    'I am sorry to say that again your Monthly Character mentions that you are rather giddy and fond of trifling, and want method and perseverance in keeping your good resolutions, try darling to overcome this tendency, and above all, pray fervently to God to help you. . . . I daresay you recollect Lord Cantalupe, a Young and Smart Man, fond of

---

[1] The statue of Eros in Piccadilly is a memorial to the seventh Earl of Shaftesbury. Created by Sir Alfred Gilbert in 1893, it was paid for by subscription.

dress and pleasant, poor fellow he died this morning at one
o'clock, it is a very awful thing. Only ill a few days and
taken (by a brain fever) in the midst of folly and vanity,
without time for anything but regret, if even that. These
things are meant as Warnings.

'God bless you my darling . . .'

Evelyn was Em's favourite grandchild and, perhaps because
he had inherited much of her charm and sparkle, Lord Palmerston took a special interest in him. He went to Harrow and
Cambridge, where he took a degree, but left the University
before the usual three years of residence had expired to become
private secretary to Lord Palmerston, an apprenticeship of
incalculable value to an ambitious young man and one that
was destined to bear important fruit in after years, when he was
to write an admirable *Life of Lord Palmerston*, published in
1879, and still today the standard history of the career of this
Prime Minister.

Lady Palmerston continued to live at Broadlands after the
death of her husband, and when she died the property passed
to her second son, William Cowper, who took the name of
Cowper-Temple. He died in 1888, and next in succession to
Broadlands (Lord Mount Temple having died without issue)
was the Hon. Evelyn Ashley.

Two years before, Evelyn had married Sybella, daughter of
Sir Walter Farquhar, thus adding to the already involved
family tree a further complication and a note of high romance
in the form of Sybella's famous Indian ancestress, the Princess
Pocohontas. Princess Pocohontas, daughter of the Red Indian
King Powhatan, was said to have saved the life of Captain
John Smith, father of the colony which Sir Walter Raleigh
founded in Virginia, by pleading with her parent when Smith
was captured by Indian braves. In 1613 Captain Samuel
Argall, of *Treasurer*, came down the Rappahannock River
and took Pocohontas as hostage for some English prisoners
held by the Indians. She was married in James Town, where
she was instructed in the Christian religion, and 'after she had
made some good progress therein, renounced publicly her
country Idolatry'. She took the name of Rebecca and continued to serve as mediator between the English and the

Indians. After some time she married an English colonist, John Rolfe, whose first wife had died. The value of their union for Anglo-Indian relations was not overlooked, and it was suggested that Rolfe, one of the leading settlers, married her for the good of the plantation. Whatever his original reasons were for marrying '*la belle sauvage*', there is no doubt that he was deeply attached to her and to the child he had by her.

In 1616 Sir Thomas Dale, who was acting as Governor of the Colony, carried Pocohontas, with her husband and child, to England, where she and her native attendants were handsomely received by Rolfe's family, Court, and society, the Queen paying her marked attention. She attended the Twelfth Night Masque of 1617 (Johnson's Christmas) in company with the Queen. During her stay in London Simon de Passe engraved the well-known portrait of her, while another portrait in oils was painted by an Italian artist. Pocohontas, much flattered by all the courtesy and attention she had received, was none the less, quite ready to return to the more temperate climate of Virginia, and she prepared to embark with her husband and infant son Thomas in the *George* which lay off Gravesend. Here she fell ill and, after a brief illness, died. She was just twenty-two years old. Smith reports that 'Shee made not more sorrow for her unexpected death than joy in the beholders to heare and see her make so religious and godly an end'. She was buried in the chancel of the church at Gravesend and in the register of the church—the edifice itself was destroyed by fire in 1727—is an ill-written scrawl which informs the reader that on March 21st, 1617, 'Rebecca Wrothe, wyfe of John Wrothe, gent, a Virginia lady borne, was buryed in ye Chauncell'.

John Rolfe, having buried his wife, left his son in the care of his brother Henry, who lived in London. Thomas married Jane Pybus, and through their son Anthony the blood of the Non. Pareil of Virginia was transmitted to Sybella Charlotte Farquhar, wife of Evelyn Ashley, whose only son, Wilfrid, was to marry Ernest Cassel's daughter Maud.

CHAPTER III

THE LAST ENEMY

On a gusty November day in 1901 after a difficult labour
Maud Ashley gave birth to a daughter. Both Maud's husband
and father had hoped that the first born might be a son, but
Maudie, exhausted and battered, was happy enough to have
her baby whatever its sex. The house was filled with flowers,
Sir Ernest presented his daughter with some magnificent
jewels, King Edward was apprised of the happy event, promised
that he would be the infant's godfather, and the babe, heavily
shawled, was trundled out of sight into the nurseries.

Some little time later the christening took place at Romsey
Abbey. King Edward, true to his promise, was present. He
had wanted the child to be called Edwardina, but a tactful compromise was effected and the baby was christened Edwina Cynthia
Annette. Her other godparents, the Countess of Shaftesbury,
the Hon. Violet Douglas Pennant, and the child's great-aunt,
Mrs. Bobbie, made the usual promises to watch over the child's
religious education, and the christening party took place at Broadlands, where the King toasted his new god-daughter. Once
again Edwina was returned to her nursery, where in the care of a
competent Nannie, and in spite of an amazing number of woollen
garments and lacy swaddling-clothes she prospered exceedingly.

As soon as Maudie's strength returned she once again flung
herself with zest into the life she loved. Her house was open
to writers, artists, and politicians as well as to interesting
foreigners. One of her closest friends was the Italian-born
Vittoria Colonna, Duchess Sermoneta. This friendship, begun
in a superficial manner during the London season in 1906,
ripened and deepened with the years and during the course of
her long life the Duchess never forgot the friend with whom she
had made her home whenever she was in England. In her
memoirs *Things Past* she writes:

> 'She (Maudie) was a delightful companion, with a great
> sense of humour and joie de vivre. She was not as beautiful

47

as her daughter, Lady Mountbatten has become but she had the most exquisite complexion I have ever seen, clear hazel eyes and very pretty hands and feet. She was very popular wherever she went and frankly enjoyed society, though her health was so delicate that she got terribly over-tired. I think she enjoyed a good game of bridge, and now and then some poker as much as anything, and for those days played rather high stakes.' [1]

'Dear Vittoria' became a member of the family and saw much of Sir Ernest Cassel, mainly, one suspects, because of Maudie's friendship for the elegant and intelligent Italian. Vittoria, perhaps more than anyone outside the clan, was admitted to Sir Ernest's intimacy and though she admired him, she was somewhat in awe of him.

'He was not an easy man to get on with and his temper was somewhat alarming. I often wondered what his servants felt when he began to clench his fists at the dining-room table, a sign of some furious comment soon to follow; but they were evidently so accustomed to it that they re-mained quite unperturbed. Even with his only daughter whom he adored there were occasional flare-ups and some-times even I got a snubbing, but on the whole he was the soul of kindness, and I think he was very fond of me. He certainly liked to have us both run in and out of his beautiful home, Brook House.' [2]

From the first, Sir Ernest Cassel took a great interest in Edwina. The sturdy, plump little girl with her blue eyes and silver-gilt curls amused him and there was never a time when he was too busy to entertain her, take her on walks, and have her play in his study. Indeed, from beneath his vast desk, the child, playing with her toys, would contemplate the limbs of many a distinguished caller, including the august limbs of the King, whose friendship with Cassel grew closer with the years.

In 1910, Edward VII paid his last visit to Biarritz, and, as in former years, his intimate friends travelled down to the

[1] *Things Past*, by Vittoria Colonna, Duchess Sermoneta (Hutchinson and Co, 1929).
[2] *ibid.*

Sir Ernest Cassel, grandfather of Edwina, painted by Zorn. Broadlands Collection

Edward VII—Godfather of Edwina painted by Sir Arthur Cope, R.A., in 1907. In the Broadlands Collection

Photographic study of Edwina's mother with Edwina and Mary

Basque coast to be with him. Among them was Sir Ernest Cassel, accompanied by Edwina, whose most cherished play-mate on the sands was a long-haired, rough-coated fox terrier whose collar bore the inscription 'I am Caesar, the King's dog'. Edwina, dressed in white muslin and lace, was photographed with Grandpapa, with Grandpapa and the King, and with the King, young Winston Churchill, and Mrs. George Keppel, who smelled delicious and kept violet cachous in her reticule.

Each year Sir Ernest Cassel entertained the King for several days at Moulton Paddocks, his estate at Newmarket. Superficially all was ordered, plushy, and opulent. Myriads of servants swarmed through the great house, hothouse fruit and flowers scented the rooms. Hams, tongues, galantines, cold grouse, pheasant, partridge, and ptarmigan tempted the jaded palate at breakfast time. Vast meal followed upon vast meal. There were delicacies kept particularly for the King: little ginger biscuits which came from Biarritz, and his favourite cigars. The ladies wore elaborate toilettes with frills sweeping to the ground, their waists were tiny, their hats enormous. They were plastered with lace which foamed in torrents all over the delicately rustling silken gowns.

At Moulton Paddocks racing was the order of the day, and after the races, croquet was played every evening. The King did not like losing, and his partners and opponents were carefully chosen. Vittoria Sermoneta, spending a few days at Moulton Paddocks, was asked to play against the King: '. . . I did my duty nobly, missing the easiest hoops and keeping him, therefore, in the best of tempers.'

Sir Ernest could take pride in his magnificently arranged house-parties, in his distinguished and noble guests, in the bounty which flowed from him, but underlying all this plenty, this ambience of luxury, was a scent of decay, and he, exiled in his soul, felt it, remarking the hectic flush on Maudie's cheeks, her febrile gaiety, and the King's frequent bouts of coughing and his shortness of breath.

The birth of a second daughter, Mary, was a severe shock to Maudie's delicate system and now the devouring fires of illness raged through her unchecked. Sir Ernest, pitting his wealth and the skill of the most famous physicians of the time

D

against the last enemy, carried his daughter from the sharp air of the Swiss mountains to the suns of Egypt. At the Assouan Hotel he engaged three floors to insure her not being disturbed by the slightest noise, and when she became weaker, and longed for her children, he chartered a private steamer to bring her back to England.

Now too King Edward's health was giving cause for great anxiety. He was suffering from bronchitis, and on Friday, May 6th, 1910, it was obvious that the gravity of symptoms had increased. Sir Ernest was to see the King at eleven o'clock that morning, but in view of his fatigue, a message was sent to Brook House, cancelling the visit. Some time later the King insisted on seeing his old friend, who came post haste to the Palace. Sir Ernest later wrote a letter to his daughter telling her what had taken place. . . .

> *Brook House,*
>   *Park Lane,*
>   6/5/10.
> 'Own and dearest,
>   'The fathers were so glad to hear this morning that the night had been good and the breakfast ample. Of the day I have no account as yet and I think it was alright. Sent you a long telegram an hour ago to keep you posted.
>   'At 11 o'clock this morning Davidson called me to the telephone to say that the King was too unwell to receive me. Half an hour later there was a message from Lord Knollys that I should come up to the Palace at once. Laking saw me first and asked me to let the King speak as little as possible. Then I was taken up to the Queen first who enquired most fully *after you*, and also exhorted me to stay a few moments. Then came Princess Victoria with the same enquiry about you. Forgot to mention that on the stairs I met the Prince of Wales who asked me to go into details about your illness and the return journey. I had to be short, but you see from all this that the Royal family take a great interest in your progress.
>   'At last I was asked to go into the King's room, but then evidently the order came out that an Equerry was to bring me and it took some doing to find me. Finally, I was

ushered in and found the King dressed as usual, in his sitting room, rising from his chair to shake hands with me. He looked as if he had suffered great pain, and spoke indistinctly. His kindly smile came out as he congratulated me on having you brought home so much improved in health. He said, "I am very seedy, but I wanted to see you". Tell your daughter how glad I am that she has safely got home and I hope she will be careful and patient so as to recover complete health. He then talked about other matters and I had to ask his leave to go, as I felt it was not good for him to go on speaking. . . .'

The last affectionate handclasp was exchanged between them. Sir Ernest stumbled out into the May sunshine knowing that he would never see his friend again.

The death of King Edward was a bitter blow to Cassel, and after it he retired from society, concentrating solely on Maudie's health, which after a slight improvement again began to decline. New cures were tried and rejected, and Maudie, becoming increasingly weak, longed only for peace and sunshine. For the final months of her life she lived in a bungalow in the grounds of Broadlands, a last desperate attempt to combine an open-air cure with her wish to be near her husband and children. She lay all day long on a chaise-longue, watching the trees and the sky. Sir Ernest visited her constantly, and racking his brains to amuse and please her, brought her an unceasing stream of gifts—jewels, furs, and precious bibelots —but Maudie was too ill then to want anything material. Vittoria Semoneta, who spent much time with her during her last illness, wrote, 'Maudie, with her unfailing sense of humour would show me feebly her father's gifts, murmuring "And all I need now are a few nightgowns".' [1]

The present of a highly valuable pekingese from her father was to try Maudie's nerves, for the dog bored her exceedingly, and according to her own account, disliked her so much that he had to be chained to the bedpost when Sir Ernest came to see how successful his Mr. Fo, the peke, was in amusing his mistress.

Towards the end even the children's brief visits exhausted

[1] *Things Past*, by Sermoneta (Hutchinson).

Maudie, though always she tried to read to them, to tell them stories, and to impress on their minds that she loved them. Edwina was nine when Maud died, and though nothing was changed in her daily routine, there was a great coldness and emptiness. Grief pervaded the adults about her; her grandfather, frozen in his misery, sat for hours in Maud's favourite summer-house. He said, 'The light has gone out of my eyes.' For all of them the sweetness and warmth had gone.

In the nursery there was red-headed Mary, aged five. Mary was all storm and petulance. A Scottish Nannie cared for her. A governess, Miss Laura Deveria, was found for Edwina. She was just, kind, and capable, but she could not replace the child's mother. So, from an early age, Edwina became self-reliant and learned to suppress her emotions. There was something pathetically mature in her efforts to show nothing of her innermost feelings. And, on the surface, her childhood pursued its secure, even course.

There were yearly holidays with Grandpapa; once he took the whole family on a cruise to Norway and Spitzbergen, but generally they stayed with him in his villa on the Riederfurka, above the Aletsch Glacier. The villa was accessible only on foot or on mule-back, so that these visits were always an adventure and the children looked forward with delight to their stay.

After Switzerland, the children began a round of visits; they went first to the Grove, Stanmore; then to stay with Auntie Grannie at Branksome Dene, Bournemouth; then to Moulton Paddocks; on to Hampshire to the Jenkins'—Mrs. Jenkins was the niece of Edwina's grandfather and acted as a sort of mother to her during her early childhood. Furthermore, the Jenkins' daughter, Marjorie, was Edwina's favourite cousin and the girls were inseparable friends—and, later, to the Countess of Shaftesbury, at St. Giles House, Verwood.

Each year there was the longed-for exodus to Classiebawn, Lord Palmerston's estate on the West Coast of Ireland, which now belonged to Edwina's father. Here Edwina and Mary were joined by their Packenham cousins, Dermot and Joan, from Belfast, and here they could run wild, bathing on Beltraw Strand, their private beach, fishing, lazing in the sun, riding, picnicking, and, when the weather was bad, playing charades in the castle.

Classiebawn was a spacious Victorian–baronial mansion, filled to capacity during the six weeks of summer with the Ashley children and their entourage. There was a house-keeper, a galaxy of maids, a butler, a chef, a large kitchen staff, governesses, nannies, and the doctor and qualified nurse who had looked after Maud Ashley. The little girls were not lonely. They had their cousins, and Edwina revelled in an open-air life. She loved animals and her most constant companion was the bailiff's collie watchdog, Rover.

Edwina at the age of twelve was a tall, slim child, whose resemblance to her mother at the same age was striking enough to make her grandfather's heart ache each time he compared Edwina with the youthful portrait of Maudie painted by Zorn. She was quiet, methodical, and hungry for love. Surrounded by attention, there was in her always a subconscious nostalgia for her mother's warmth and gaiety. Her father loved and admired his elder daughter, but he was not the man to give companionship to a little girl, and so Edwina found in her pet birds and animals an outlet for her starved affections. It was at Broadlands that she felt most at home. The old house, the stables, the sunny lawns, trees, and familiar faces of the servants whom she had known always were part of the safe, unchanging pattern of childhood, and here her heart was rooted.

The summer of 1914 found the twelve-year-old Edwina at Broadstairs, where the family had taken a house on the beach. On July 23rd the Austrian ultimatum to Serbia became known and many people turned to Sir Ernest Cassel for his opinion as to the imminence of war. It was known that he was in close and constant touch with the leading French, German, American, and English financial magnates. He, of all people, would be 'in the know'. Sir Ernest was unperturbed. He planned his summer holiday in Switzerland as usual, and on the night before he left he was at Brook House playing bridge with his niece, Mrs. Jenkins, and the First Lord of the Admiralty, Winston Churchill. All appeared gay and optimistic.

Colonel Ashley, though less well informed than his father-in-law, was not as sanguine as to future events, and his daughters were sent immediately from Broadstairs to London, and from thence to stay with Auntie Grannie, who was ill from worry at the continued absence of her brother. It was not until Sir Ernest's servants were mobilized that he decided to return to London. According to his old friend, Sir Felix Semon, who had been his guest in Switzerland and who accompanied him on the return journey, it took them twenty hours to get from the French frontier to Paris and seventeen hours to get from Paris to Folkestone; and not even Sir Ernest's influence and millions could get them seats on the various trains. The war was to bring great sorrow to two loyal English patriots, Sir Ernest Cassel and Admiral Prince Louis of Battenberg. Both were to suffer the attentions of contemptible spy-hunters whose actions wrecked the public life of one man and the career of the other. And both, had they known it, were to find burning champions in their son and granddaughter, who would later, and together, epitomize English patriotism and courage in a second world war.

In 1915 an action was brought against Sir Ernest Cassel and Sir Edgar Speyer to show by what authority they claimed to be Privy Councillors, as they were not natural-born British subjects. The decision was that the appointments were valid, but this did nothing to mitigate the bitterness engendered by the action brought against a man of whom Lady Oxford said, 'No one was ever more loyal and generous to the country of his adoption'.

.   .   .

In the meantime a small drama, which was nonetheless to affect Edwina's future, was being played out at Broadlands. Edwina was one day summoned by her father, and on her return announced to her cousin, Marjorie Jenkins, with whom she was sharing a room, that her father was going to marry again. Marjorie, full of compassion for the motherless Edwina, remarked, somewhat tactlessly, 'How awful for you!' 'Not at all,' said Edwina, 'I rather like her.'

The new Mrs. Ashley was elegant and an excellent hostess. As with the second Lord Palmerston, the care and beautifying of Broadlands became an obsession with her, and, since she was a single-minded woman, there was little time and even less inclination to cherish her young step-daughters. She did her duty by them, but she did not greatly care for children, and only much later in life did she come to realize how much more of

herself she might have given Maudie's small girls. Miss
Deveria had left, and a new governess, chosen by Molly
Ashley, was chosen to look after the little girls. Mary, more
pliable than Edwina, scraped through this difficult period
without incurring her stepmother's wrath, but Edwina, silently
rebellious, fretted and planned to escape. She made no
demands, but even her presence at Broadlands, where Mrs.
Ashley was 'doing her bit' by entertaining army officers, was
irksome, and so she was sent off to school at Eastbourne. It
was a good school, but the classrooms were dark and dingy,
and the atmosphere was oppressive. She suffered from chil-
blains and hated having to drink Ovaltine topped with wrinkled
skin. She rose in the bleak, chill morning to practise endless
scales. Her passion was geography. The flat maps in her
Atlas took on colour and meaning, and she vowed that when
she grew up she would explore the world. Her companions
chanted parrot fashion, 'India, China, Scotland, Wales, all
tied up with monkeys' tails'; to Edwina the childish tune had
meaning. India was big and mysterious and there were
Maharajahs and elephants with howdahs and tiger hunts, and
from India one might slip into Tibet. She read *Kim* and was
enthralled. The school prided itself on being 'modern', and
a course of lectures on current events was inaugurated. These
lectures, known as 'currents', did little to enliven the general
dreariness of the lives of the scholars. The aura of riches
which surrounded Edwina by virtue of her grandfather's wealth
encompassed her even here, and though Colonel Ashley was
far from well off and Sir Ernest Cassel had very strict ideas
about allowing young persons to have too much pocket-
money, Edwina was expected by her school-mates to fill the
offertory plate with gold pieces. When asked why she gave
so little, she replied, 'If I give too much They might think I
was showing off, and if I give too little They might think I was
mean.' They, the invisible and omnipotent critics who would
shadow her all her life, were already gathering in the wings.

Mary had prevailed upon her stepmother to send her to a
fashionable establishment, where she was petted and happy.
Edwina, conscious that her role of 'little mother' to Mary
was now at an end, begged to be removed from her school.
Finally it was decided to send her to an entirely new type of

school. It was the first Domestic Science College in the country and Maudie Ashley's friends were appalled at the idea of
her daughter being made to work like a 'skivvy'. As it happened, this experience was to prove of the greatest value in
Edwina's future life. The school was housed in an old country
mansion and was staffed and run entirely by the pupils.
There was not a single servant in the whole establishment and
the young ladies learnt domestic science the hard way. They
cleaned, cooked, and waited on one another. Edwina, besides acquiring useful knowledge on the practical side of running a house, gained a profound knowledge and sympathy
for the life and work of the staff. Most of the pupils came from
middle-class homes; their aim in attending this college was
to enable them to acquire sufficient tuition to go out into the
world to take up posts in schools which taught domestic science
and other branches of work for women. Edwina worked as
hard as her companions. No exceptions were made for the
granddaughter of Sir Ernest Cassel, and often she tumbled
into bed sick with fatigue, her hands cracked and chapped,
her knees aching from scrubbing floors.

Mary had been sent to a select finishing school, but Edwina,
on leaving her Domestic Science College, asked to be allowed
to go to Italy. She went, escorted by a governess who acted
as chaperone, and dutifully she visited galleries and museums,
was invited to sedate tea-parties, and though closely guarded
by a chaperone, enjoyed the admiring glances of the Italians,
who so obviously found the blonde young English girl attractive. This, thought Edwina, was a peep through the portals
of adult life, and the notion of returning to the schoolroom
was deeply depressing.

Her stepmother's welcome did little to melt the chill from
her heart. Though it was obvious that she could no longer
be relegated to the schoolroom, she was deemed too young to
attend adult parties and dances, and so she hovered miserably
on the fringe of a life in which she had no part. It was not
in Edwina's nature to complain, but Sir Ernest Cassel, whose
perception where his granddaughter was concerned amounted
to an almost feminine sensitivity, was well aware that she was
unhappy, and, with his customary bluntness, he suggested to
her father that he would like Edwina to live with him and act

as his hostess. Colonel Ashley knew the implications which lay behind this offer, and he knew too that the lonely old millionaire had definite plans for the future of Edwina. The choice, he said, should be hers, and when she was told, Edwina had no hesitation in accepting to leave Broadlands and to go and live with her grandfather at Brook House.

Sir Ernest Cassel had purchased Brook House, Park Lane, from Lord Tweedmouth. It was his ambition to make it into a dream palace. According to the lyrical descriptions of the Press of the time, he succeeded in making it 'the most wonderful house in London'. It was certainly unique. The architect, Thomas Henry Wyatt, while neglecting the façade, lavished a fortune on the structural alterations and decoration. Some eight hundred tons of Tuscany marble were brought from the quarries at Sarravezza for the main hall and staircase, and a year was spent in quarrying it. Corinthian pillars, twenty feet high, rose like petrified jets of water in the air. The floors and walls were of marble, with mahogany in the balustrades and wrought metal to enhance the general effect. Rare blue marble was imported from Canada to add to the magnificence of the whole, and the architect, visualizing the possibilities of a *coup d'oeil* all marble and glittering lights as a setting for social functions at night, added an effect of rising galleries culminating in a vast skylight dome. The dining-room, with its thirty-foot arched ceiling and lighted by Roman lamps of antique bronze, could seat a hundred guests. Even the kitchen had marble walls, and the final gesture of Eastern splendour was the installation of a set of Turkish baths.

Torn with regret at leaving her beloved Broadlands, Edwina, with her small schoolgirl treasures, her lonely heart, and her ebullient youth, moved into the marble mausoleum, which, apart from an army of servants, was occupied only by her grandfather and herself.

Sir Ernest had promised Colonel Ashley that Edwina would not be spoilt or indulged. Nor was she. Her allowance was £300 a year, which, after the pound-a-week pocket money she received at home, seemed unlimited riches. She was not allowed to go to parties without a chaperone, and her wardrobe was of the simplest. There was no question of make-up, which, in any case, she did not need, having inherited her mother's fine, clear skin. Her eyes, her best feature, were widely spaced and of an intense, almost Mediterranean blue. Candidly and curiously they surveyed her new world. There was much in this new existence to arouse her curiosity and misgivings. For she was fundamentally shy, and though Sir Ernest loved her devotedly, he had little knowledge of the social needs of a sketchily educated young girl of seventeen. Being Sir Ernest's hostess would have tried the nerves of a mature woman of the world, for he entertained continually, numbering among his guests royalty, statesmen, politicians, financiers, musicians, and scientists. Not only did Edwina have to plan the meals, the wines, decide the floral decorations, arrange the seating plans, but she was also required to converse intelligently with the guests, to remember their favourite dishes, and to impress them with an erudition she did not possess. In fact, she touched their hearts, and some of her mother's friends, watching her diligently interpreting her grandfather's demands, wished that she might have a more normal and less austere existence. Sir Ernest was anxious that Edwina should administer her small finances methodically. He expected her to pay her own laundry bills and travelling expenses. He himself practised many small economies. He kept an eye on the food brought into the dining-room and saw that none of it was wasted. On one occasion there were partridges for dinner, and after the meal, one was left over. Next day Cassel sent for the butler and asked what had become of the partridge. The butler, knowing his employer's idiosyncrasies, was able to produce the bird. Edwina, young as she was, was a match for her grandfather, and when her eyes became diamond cold and her mouth obstinate, he rejoiced inwardly at having an adversary worthy of his steel. He had for so long encountered such meekness and obedience in his family that it was refreshing to find that his eldest granddaughter, like her mother, had a mind and a will of her own.

But the period of probation and seclusion was not long, and by 1920 Sir Ernest felt that Edwina was ready to make her début. For the first time the Press became aware of the granddaughter of Sir Ernest Cassel, and from now on Edwina's name was to appear prefaced with monotonous regularity by the words 'the richest heiress in England'. Her coming-out

ball, given at Brook House, caused match-making mammas to
polish their tiaras and lecture their sons on the advantages of
making a favourable impression on the young heiress.   This
ball, at which Edwina wore a dress of pale gold, was the signal
for an avalanche of invitations, and the mantelpiece of her
sitting-room was piled high with bits of pasteboard asking her
to house-parties, dinners, concerts, and balls.   Sir Ernest,
delighted at the excellent impression Edwina had made on
society, himself scrutinized all invitations before she was
allowed to accept them.   Edwina, caught up in a whirl of
amusements such as she had never known, danced, rode, and
flirted with her many admirers—and always in the presence
of a chaperone.   Sir Ernest was taking no chances with his
ewe lamb, and indeed he hoped that it would be many years
before she decided to marry.   She, however, had no concern
on this score.   She was interested only in savouring her new
life and comparative freedom.   In the winter of 1920 Sir
Ernest became seriously ill, and as soon as he was well enough
he went to the Riviera to convalesce.   Edwina accompanied
him on what was to be their last journey together, and she was
always happy to remember that despite tempting invitations
she had devoted most of her time to him, entertaining his old
friends and seeing much of Sir Frederick Treves, surgeon to
King Edward VII, who was then writing his book of memoirs,
On the Corniche Road.

It was at a ball given by Mrs. Cornelius Vanderbilt at
Claridges' Hotel that Edwina first met young Lieutenant
Mountbatten, who was already something of a hero to the
débutantes of the year.   He was handsome, well connected,
and—most interesting of all—was said to have a broken heart;
for after a whirlwind romance lasting a fortnight he had become
engaged to one of the season's prettiest débutantes, Audrey
James.   He had left her to accompany his cousin, the Prince
of Wales, as A.D.C. on a long cruise to Australia and New
Zealand, and during that time she had become the wife of a
cotton millionaire.

Edwina was happily unaware of this broken romance.   She
knew only that this was the best-looking young man she had
ever seen, and as she danced round the ballroom in his arms
she was wondering what impression she was making on him,

and whether he, like herself, felt the significance of this first meeting. Dickie, in fact, was thinking that this pretty girl danced extraordinarily well, and that never before had he seen eyes so blue, so widely spaced, and so candid. Edwina returned to Brook House that night in a mood of intense excitement. She longed to talk to someone about the handsome lieutenant in whose casual grasp she had felt so violent an emotion sweep through her that the rest of the evening, during which he had not danced with her again, had been flat and dreary; but since she had no confidante and was a reasonable young woman, she decided to put him out of her mind, got into bed, and lay thinking about him until the sun touched the tops of the trees in Hyde Park.

Their next meeting was at Cowes during Regatta week, when she was staying with Sir Godfrey and Lady Baring. The young people met with mutual pleasure, and, since they were members of the same set, were inevitably invited to the same parties. Lord Louis' gaiety was infectious and irresistible, his good looks, in a galaxy of handsome young men, were overwhelming, and Edwina knew now that his broken heart had only been slightly damaged and was now completely repaired.

On a cruise to France in the Vanderbilt schooner, *Atalanta*, Edwina and Dickie fell irrevocably and hopelessly in love, and throughout the endless sunlit days of sailing, and nights of putting in at French ports where they dined and danced, they made plans for the future. Edwina was nineteen and Dickie was a year and a half older. In Edwina, Dickie—subconsciously perhaps—recognized his *alter ego*. This, he felt, was no affected young lady of fashion. Here was a friend, a companion, who in trousers and jersey could crew a yacht and sit, as he liked to sit, for hours in silence, listening to the song of the sea. This girl, like himself, had endless vitality; her warmth and glow attracted all about her. Life with her would never be dull, the world lay at her feet, and in her, he knew, there was strength and humour.

If Edwina had been born with a golden spoon in her mouth, Dickie Mountbatten's cradle could have been liberally decorated with royal armorial bearings. A great-grandson of Queen Victoria, he could claim kinship with most of the crowned heads of Europe. His was a background of colour and violence, of romance in high places, morganatic marriages, tears, suffering, and noble courage. The Battenberg line, from which he sprang, had its beginnings in the Russia of Czar Nicolas I, brother of the Czar Alexander. In 1841 his son married the seventeen-year-old Princess Marie of Hesse, daughter of the Grand Duke Louis II. When the time came for the little Princess to leave her family she begged that her eighteen-year-old brother Prince Alexander might accompany her to her new country. This wish was granted, and the young Prince decided to make his life near his sister in Russia. He entered the service of the Russian Army and was appointed a Colonel in the Household Cavalry. Prince Alexander was handsome and fearless and was in great favour at Court, when he wrecked his career by eloping with one of the Empress' Maids of Honour. Of excellent family, but not of royal birth, his wife, Countess Julia Theresa von Hauke, was the daughter of a Russian general. Infuriated by this gesture of independence, the Czar ordered that Prince Alexander be cashiered. Deprived of his command rank, the young couple took refuge in Geneva, where their first child, a daughter, was born.

Touched by this romance, the Empress of Austria, one of Prince Alexander's relatives, saw to it that he was able to continue his fine military career under her flag. Four sons were born to him—Louis, Alexander, Henry, and Francis Joseph—and in 1862 Prince Alexander decided to return to his native Hesse, now ruled over by his brother, Grand Duke Louis III of Hesse.

Some years before his sister Marie's husband had become Czar Alexander II, and yielding to his wife's entreaties, he decided to restore to Alexander his rank and rights in Russia. There was one fact, however, which disturbed Prince Alexander. His children, by reason of his morganatic marriage, were, by the rules of the Hesse dynasty, prohibited from bearing any royal title. This ban was neatly circumvented by the Grand Duke, who bestowed upon his sister-in-law the extinct title of Princess of Battenberg. Her heirs and their descendants became Princes and Princesses of the House of Battenberg. Thus Prince Alexander's honour was satisfied, and his wife and children, if they did not share all royal prerogatives, were, nonetheless, Serene Highnesses.

Through his British cousins, among whom was Princess Alice, Queen Victoria's second daughter, and Prince Alfred, Duke of Edinburgh, Queen Victoria's son, Prince Alexander's eldest son, Louis, had one desire in life, and that was to go to sea in the British Navy. Neither Prince Alexander nor his wife could understand this development in their son's character, but since the boy was evidently in earnest, arrangements were made for Louis to go to England, where he was prepared for examination. In 1868 he became a British subject and passing his examination with no difficulty, Prince Louis of Battenberg became a cadet in H.M. Queen Victoria's Navy.

Closely linked with the English royal family, capable, obstinate, and in love with his career, the cadet became an outstanding officer. His marriage to his cousin's daughter, Princess Victoria, favourite granddaughter of Queen Victoria, strengthened the links which bound him to the English throne, and made him one of the pieces of the intricate pattern of European royalty. His wife, Victoria, was one of four lovely sisters, Elizabeth, wife of the Grand Duke Serge; Alix, wife of Czar Nicholas II, and Irene, wife of Prince Henry of Prussia, brother of the Kaiser.

Queen Victoria was delighted with the match. She liked the good-looking Louis, who had chosen to become one of her loyal subjects, though indeed neither she nor her son, Edward VII, had an inkling of what it meant to Prince Louis to be British and to serve in the British Navy. He was dedicated to his chosen career and to the country of his adoption, and although his close connexions with the Royal Family may have smoothed his passage at times, there is little doubt that even in those days he had to work all the harder because of his royal connexions to establish himself as a really competent naval officer in his own right.

Prince Louis and Princess Victoria were a devoted couple. Theirs was an ideal union and the children born of their marriage were tenderly loved. There were four children—George, Alice, Louise, and then, in 1900 Louis Francis Albert Victor Nicholas made his appearance. He was born at Frogmore House in the grounds of Windsor Castle, where the aged Queen could still keep an eye on her favourite granddaughter. His behaviour at his christening did not create an altogether

favourable impression on Queen Victoria, for, with a gesture
of gay bravado, the first of many, he knocked her spectacles
off her nose.

Nicknamed 'Dickie' by his family, the young Louis spent
his childhood with his mother, 'following the Flag', as did other
naval families—at Malta, at Gibraltar, and in England.
When his father, Prince Louis, was at sea, on cruises, or on
long leave, the family lived at their seat Heilinberg Castle in
Hesse. At other times they visited their many relations all
over the Continent, staying often with Prince Louis' first
cousin and Princess Louis's sister, who were Czar and Czarina
of Russia. When nearly ten Dickie was sent to preparatory
school—Lockers Park—and after three years there, he entered
the Royal Naval College, Osborne, as a cadet.

In the meantime Prince Louis had made a brilliant success
of his career in the Royal Navy, where he was held in universal
esteem. He had established a reputation as an exceedingly
skilful tactician—'he was never defeated in manœuvres until
1912—and was, in the opinion of many, the greatest naval
officer of his day'.[1] In 1911 he had returned to the Admiralty
as Second Sea Lord, the year in which Winston Churchill had
become First Lord of the Admiralty, and the following year he
selected Prince Louis as First Sea Lord.

In July 1914 a test mobilization of the naval reserves was
carried out and the ships were due to disperse after carrying
out exercises in the English Channel. By the third week in
July relations between Great Britain and Germany had become
strained, and during the critical week-end July 25th–27th
Winston Churchill was absent from the Admiralty owing to
the illness of his wife. During this week-end the decision had
to be taken as to whether the Fleet should be dispersed and the
reserve ships demobilized, in accordance with the plans already
made. This decision therefore rested with the First Sea Lord
—with Prince Louis. The Commander-in-Chief of the Home
Fleets at Portland was instructed that no ship was to leave that
anchorage without further orders. This provision of the First
Sea Lord insured that when war became inevitable the Navy
was in a state of readiness.

[1] Vol. 2, p. 49. *Fear God: Dread Naught*, The Fisher Letters, edited by
Arthur J. Marden.

But within a few months this act of prescience with its far-reaching effects was forgotten in the hysteria engendered by the 'yellow Press', which started a regular campaign of unpleasant insinuations about the Navy being under the command of a man of German origins. The *Globe*, announcing the death of Prince Maurice of Battenberg, killed fighting valiantly in the retreat from Mons, together with a glowing tribute to the valour of the Royal Family, in the same issue denounced his uncle Prince Louis of Battenberg for his German birth and demanded his resignation.

On October 29th, 1914, in a letter to Mr. Churchill, Prince Louis resigned his appointment.

'Dear Mr. Churchill,
     'I have lately been driven to the painful conclusion that at this juncture, my birth and parentage have the effect of impairing in some respects my usefulness on the Board of the Admiralty. In these circumstances I feel it to be my duty, as a loyal subject of His Majesty, to resign the office of First Sea Lord, hoping therefore to facilitate the task of the administration of the great Service to which I have devoted my life, and to ease the burden laid on H.M. Ministers,
                    'I am,
                         'Yours very truly,
                              'Louis Battenberg, Admiral.'

Prince Louis lived to see the complete triumph of the naval weapon which he had helped to forge. With the coming of peace he was promoted to Admiral of the Fleet and made a Knight Grand Cross of the Bath. In 1917 the King decided that the Royal Family should give up their German names and adopt British ones. Thus the Royal House of Saxe-Coburg became the House of Windsor; Queen Mary's family, the Tecks, changed their name to Cambridge. The Battenbergs adopted the name of Mountbatten. Prince Louis, as head of the Battenberg family, became the first Marquess of Milford Haven; his nephew, Prince Alexander of Battenberg, became the first Marquess of Carisbrooke. Prince George of Battenberg became the Earl of Medina, and the young Prince Louis, then aged seventeen, became Lord Louis Mountbatten.

In 1916 Dickie became a midshipman, serving under Admiral Beatty, first in H.M.S. *Lion* and then in H.M.S. *Queen Elizabeth*. He also served in submarine *K.6*, and ended the war, being barely eighteen years old, as second in command of one of the Portsmouth Escort Flotilla.

He developed more slowly than his distinguished father and his brilliant brother George. The records show that he was well down in the Order of Merit on passing into Osborne, but he came out top in the final examination passing out to sea. From then on he appears to have done consistently well, and this in spite of the obvious temptation to try to 'wangle' extra leave to keep up with the social life in London. He could not possibly have risen to the ranks and position he subsequently held if he had not worked hard as a full-time naval officer all his life.

Lord Louis spent the first year of peace at Christ's College, Cambridge, where he made many lasting friendships. When finally he entered the circle to which his birth, looks, and background gave him the entree, he found it both pleasant and stimulating. The future was rosily indeterminate. His slight means, for his family were far from wealthy, somewhat interfered with his expensive tastes, but under the debonair social mask was a sailor determined to succeed in his chosen career.

A chance discussion with his cousin, David, Prince of Wales, brought about his first voyage as A.D.C. on a tour to the West Indies, Australia, and New Zealand. It was on this tour that Wallis Warfield—Wallis Spencer as she then was—first saw the Prince of Wales. The battleship *Renown* called at San Diego to refuel, and the local authorities, delighted at an opportunity of welcoming the heir to the throne, immediately arranged an impromptu ball at Coronado. Among the guests were Wallis Spencer and her husband, and though they were presented to the Prince, there is no record of any meeting of twin souls. 'The young glamorous Prince, accompanied by the magnificent young Mountbatten, went his way, and young Mrs. Spencer continued her rather drab and penniless existence.' [1]

So competently had Lord Louis acquitted himself of his

[1] *She Might have been Queen*, by Geoffrey Bocca.

E

duties as A.D.C. on this trip, that the Prince had invited him to accompany him on his Indian tour planned for the following year.

In the meantime Lord Louis had met Edwina Ashley. The fact that she might one day be one of the richest heiresses in the world did not in any way influence this romance, for both Dickie and Edwina were at this stage totally unaware of the disposition of Sir Ernest's fortune. She knew that he might leave her well provided for, but since she knew nothing of his business affairs and had, all her life, virtually no money of her own, the question of finance had no bearing whatsoever on the love affair. In fact, as Edwina was later to regret, she did not tell her grandfather of her growing interest in Dickie, feeling that there was time enough to take him into her confidence when matters had progressed a little further. Both Edwina and Lord Louis were young and attractive enough to marry for love.

One of Edwina's most helpful supporters throughout this period was Mrs. 'Ronnie' Greville, an old friend of King Edward VII and of Sir Ernest Cassel. A brilliant hostess, her house-parties were famous, and as she liked young people, it was natural that Edwina and Dickie should often be invited to Polesden Lacy. There was no lack of diversions for her guests: there were excellent tennis courts, a private golf course, and for young lovers there was a colonnaded terrace and charming gardens and a park studded with oaks and beeches.

Here, in this idyllic setting, what had been a violent mutual attraction developed into a serious affair. Edwina and Dickie, discovering love for the first time, now discovered one another, and were, by turns, charmed and irritated to observe vast differences in each other's characters. Lord Louis was an extrovert, passionately convinced that his views and judgement in all things were correct. Edwina was an introvert and she kept her views and judgements to herself. Dickie was inclined to be dictatorial; Edwina, brought up in the belief that man was a superior being, bowed easily to masculine argument and correction. Dickie was brilliant and spontaneous; Edwina was quiet, and her dry humour and flashing wit were as yet undeveloped.

Though Edwina had decided to await an opportune moment to talk to her grandfather about Dickie, he took her to meet his family, who welcomed her warmly. Prince Louis, now become the Marquess of Milford Haven, was, to her, the epitome of the grand seigneur, and her warm and sympathetic heart went out to one who had shared the same ill-merited public eclipse as her grandfather. Lord Louis' father, however, was to have one great satisfaction before his death. He was invited to take the chair at a Navy Club dinner in July 1921. This function, usually ill attended, was packed out with his friends and contemporaries who had gathered together to cheer him, and some little time later the then First Lord of the Admiralty, Lord Lee of Fareham, was happy to tell him that the King had promoted him to the rank of Admiral of the Fleet on the retired list. A signal honour, accorded only once before in its history.

In September of this year Edwina went to Scotland to stay with the Duke and Duchess of Sutherland at Dunrobin. Here she was joined by Dickie on leave from his ship at Invergordon. Lord Louis' father and sister-in-law were preparing to go to Constantinople, where Lord Louis' brother, George, was serving with the Navy. Feeling unwell, Prince Louis decided to postpone their departure. Within a few days he had suddenly died of heart failure. Dickie left at once for London, and was followed four days later by Edwina. It was a gloomy journey, for she knew how deeply attached Lord Louis had been to his father. She arrived at the station to be met by Sir Ernest Cassel's secretary, Miss Underhill. She had come to tell Edwina that her grandfather was dead. He had died that afternoon. A footman bringing him a telegram had found him crumpled over his desk in his study. Brook House, more tomb-like than ever, with its vistas of darkened marble rooms, engulfed Edwina. She and Miss Underhill dined together. Edwina, stupefied by grief and fatigue, found it impossible to realize that her grandfather was dead. The servants moved about like mutes, automatically performing their functions, but they were aware that the pulse of the great house was stilled for ever.

The next day Auntie Grannie came from Bournemouth to arrange for the funeral. Dickie called to see Edwina. Each was plunged into a dark climate of grief. Neither had any reserves of philosophy or experience of death. Like the children they still were, they were bewildered and afraid. Their future plans were now clouded and uncertain, though their own feelings for one another were intensified by their shared distress. Edwina was always to regret that her grandfather had not met Dickie, and they were often to discuss the curious coincidence that the two men, Prince Louis and Sir Ernest, whose declining years had, in many ways, run along parallel lines, should have died within a few days of one another, unaware of the new link that was to unite their respective families.

After the funeral Edwina returned to live with her family at Broadlands. Her stepmother, who had been more than a little envious of Edwina's role as hostess at Brook House, was not particularly sympathetic now that she had come home and made it firmly but charmingly clear to her that there was to be only one chatelaine at Broadlands. Dickie was leaving with the Prince of Wales in October, and though he had begged her to join him in India, where her grandfather's friend, Lord Reading, the Viceroy, had invited her to stay, she had no money of her own, and knew that it would take many months before her grandfather's estate was wound up. It never entered her head to borrow from the trustees; nor probably would they have advanced her any sum for what they would have considered a madcap adventure.

On October 26th, 1921, H.M.S. *Renown* left Portsmouth and against the booming of a salute of twenty-one guns the battle cruiser carrying the Prince of Wales and Dickie slid from Edwina's view. It was the first of many such farewells that Edwina, as a naval wife, would be called upon to experience, and always, as she turned away to resume her life of waiting, the pangs would be as acute.

This time, however, she had a purpose. Hurrying off to Bournemouth, she poured out her financial troubles to her grandfather's sister, Mrs. Cassel or Auntie Grannie, as she was then known. It was not often that the quiet, reserved Edwina pleaded with such urgency for any favour. Auntie Grannie, considerably shaken at the thought of what her strict brother would have said to his granddaughter's gallivanting off to India, was nonetheless touched by the romantic aspect of the

situation. Having obtained Edwina's promise to travel with
a chaperone, she consented to lend the £100 necessary for
the fare. It did not take Edwina long to book her passage,
though the finding of a suitable chaperone offered some
difficulty. Finally, however, she consulted the passenger list
and, discovering a likely cicerone, promptly communicated with
the lady, who said she would be delighted to 'look after'
Edwina.

Colonel Ashley, knowing that Edwina was to stay with the
Viceroy and Vicereine of India, had somewhat grudgingly
given his consent to this voyage, but nothing could damp
Edwina's spirits, and the prospect of the reunion with Dickie
made even the hot second-class inner cabin of the liner bear-
able.

She arrived in Bombay flushed with triumph and excitement. She was in India. Now to get to Dickie. But Dickie
was at Delhi, and many miles separated them. Though
her financial assets were nearly nil—her return fare had
accounted for most of Auntie Grannie's loan—she still had
enough for a ticket to Delhi, and still buoyed up with the hope
of reaching Dickie as soon as possible, she went to the booking-
office at Victoria Terminus and asked for a third-class ticket.
The railway official was shocked and pained, and explained
that it was quite impossible for a European, and a young lady
to boot, to travel third class with a horde of Indians. 'What,'
asked Edwina, 'is wrong with travelling with Indians?' The
booking-clerk, casting his eyes to heaven, emerged from his
office and pointed silently at a long queue of Indian travellers
waiting to entrain. There were men, women, and children—
many children. Piled high about them was their bedding,
household equipment, food, and more children. 'Forty or
fifty of them crowd into one compartment,' said the booking-
clerk, 'the journey takes two days, and the coaches are equipped
with wooden seats.'

Dickie, summoned from his duties, took a somewhat incoherent trunk call from Edwina at the Taj Mahal Hotel,
where she had booked a room. When her situation became
clear to him, he too became slightly incoherent. The idea of
her travelling across India in a third-class carriage had never
entered his head, and sternly enjoining her to book a berth

on the Frontier Mail, he rushed off to make financial arrangements for her journey to Delhi.

.   .   .

'Nineteen twenty-one was an extraordinary year for us.
There was a strange mixture of nationalism and politics and
religion and mysticism and fanaticism.   Behind all this was
agrarian trouble and in the big cities, a rising working-class
movement.'

Thus wrote Jawaharlal Nehru.   Mother India was indeed
stirring convulsively, but as yet her cries had reached only the
ears of the initiated, for the star of the British Raj was still
high and it was thought that anything that might offend the
ears and eyes of the heir of the King Emperor would be kept
from him.   But Congress, inflamed by Gandhi, had imposed
a boycott of all the functions in connexion with his visit, and
wherever he was taken he was met with *hartals* and deserted
streets.   It was obvious that from the Indian point of view the
Royal visit was not an unqualified success.   This, however,
did not in any way affect the purely social side of the Prince's
sojourn.   It was still the India of the Maharajahs, still the
land of harems, jewels, tiger hunts, and marble palaces.   The
British could and did offer a round of garden-parties, receptions,
durbars, military parades, polo, and cocktail parties.   Dickie,
a scrupulously attentive A.D.C., was endlessly busy, and
Edwina, under the benevolent eye of the Viceroy and Vicereine, flung herself headlong into all the gaiety.   There was
no time to reflect on the political situation, and the names of
Gandhi and of the young Nehru were merely the names of
two unruly personages, an old and a young agitator who were
making things 'difficult' for poor Lord Reading.   To Edwina,
India was exciting and strange, but it was only the painted
backdrop of her romance.   It did not affect her in any way,
and no mysterious voices told her that twenty-five years later
she and Dickie would, for a brief while, become the chief
protagonists in the drama which was to bring down the curtain
on the British Raj.   At that time they were merely two young
people in love, and their appreciation of India and its problems
was subordinate to the ecstasy of their few hours together away
from the crowd.   The Prince of Wales, always a loyal and

understanding friend, gave his A.D.C. the key to the private bungalow which Lady Reading had had specially built and decorated for the Royal visit. The key is still in Dickie's possession.

In this hothouse atmosphere of palms, exotic flowers, oriental spices, and tropical nights, Miss Edwina Ashley was blossoming and, somewhat to Dickie's alarm, she was so much in demand that he began to wonder just how much claim he had on her. Also the Prince was shortly to leave India and so, to make matters quite clear to Edwina and to her admirers, Dickie proposed, after obtaining King George V's permission and blessing. Their engagement was announced from Viceregal Lodge, and there was considerable jubilation, for Edwina and Dickie were popular, both with their contemporaries and with the older people, who thought them 'a charming couple'. The next day the Prince's A.D.C. fondly embraced his new fiancée and hastened off to accompany H.R.H. on the remainder of his tour. Edwina, feeling suddenly homesick, took a passage in a cargo-boat and sailed, unchaperoned, for England.

CHAPTER IV

JEUNESSE DORÉE

GOSSIP GAVE way to certainty when *The Times* and the *Yorkshire Post* announced the engagement of Lord Louis Mountbatten, son of the late Marquess of Milford Haven, to Miss Edwina Cynthia Annette Ashley, daughter of Colonel Wilfrid W. Ashley. Auntie Grannie was vastly relieved that Edwina had brought her rash adventure to a conventional conclusion, and the genteel lady reporters, adjusting their pince-nez and cosily wallowing in the governess-nannie complex which shaped their writings, prepared to enjoy themselves. The engagement of the season turned their bones to treacle and their paragraphs to slush. Housewives all over England pored over the descriptions of the trousseau that was being made for Edwina.

'Every woman [trilled one lyrical journalist] will envy the sweetly pretty fairy-like garments now being created for Miss Ashley. Ninon, triple ninon, crepe de chine and the new washing satin are being used in these ravishing confections. White ninon is still modish but the fashion for coloured underlinen is becoming stronger. Ochre, pale pink, mauve and yellow are all represented in this *trousseau de luxe*. Every garment has its yoke and insets of lace, and *all* the lace is real. The nightgowns are daringly sleeveless and straight. As to monograms, Miss Ashley has chosen a tiny diamond shaped frame that surrounds the intertwined initials "E.M.".'

From now until the wedding hardly a day would pass without some paragraph referring to Edwina's trousseau. Under the heading of 'Daring Innovation' a writer over the signature of 'Lady Marcia' wrote:

'Part at least of the lucky young heiress' trousseau comes from India. During her recent visit to Lord and Lady Reading, she picked up some bits of material with golden

borders and the embroideries that Orientals take such pleasure in producing.   These will be made into original tea-
gowns . . .'

What the envious readers of these effusions did not know
was that Miss Ashley, for the first time in her life, had been
given permission to buy what she wanted, and remembering
certain patched and ragged combinations she had been forced
to wear at one period of her childhood, she now concentrated
on filling her cupboards with the softest and sheerest lingerie
she could find.   It was with a sense of unreality that she found
that she could gratify her every material wish, and her first
coming-home present for Dickie was an immense and shiny
automobile which she drove herself, parking it with some
difficulty during her shopping forays in the West End.

The date of the wedding was set for July 18th.   Two days
before Dickie's return, Edwina marched into the Vicar-
General's office in Creed Lane.   Cleaning operations were in
full swing and a tousled charlady was dabbing the floor with a
mop, while the registrar, in a bare and carpetless office, was busily
writing.   Without lifting his head, he heard Edwina announce
that she was going to be married in St. Margaret's, Westminster, and what must she do to obtain a licence?   The
Registrar waved her to a rickety wooden chair, while the char,
breathing heavily, continued to slosh water about the floor.

'Your name?'

'Edwina Cynthia Annette Ashley.'

'Your age?'

'Twenty.'

'In that case you will require your parents' consent.'

'Here it is.'

'And who is it you wish to marry?'

'Lord Louis Mountbatten.'

The startled official leapt from his desk, rushed from the
office, and returning with a piece of frayed carpet, endeavoured
to place it under Edwina's chair and, mumbling something
about the respect due to one who was about to marry into the
Royal Family, he issued the licence forthwith.

At long last H.M.S. *Renown* brought Dickie home, and the
moment his duties were over he hurried to see Edwina, who

was staying with cousin Marjorie, now Lady Brecknock. Journalists loitering around the house in Belgrave Place for a glimpse of the couple reported excitedly that they had whirled off in the new car. They had, in fact, driven to Claridges', where Edwina, in one of her simplest trousseau dresses, was given dinner by Dickie.

From now until the wedding the young pair were endlessly trailed by photographers, whose pictures hardly did justice to Edwina's glowing good looks. She was photographed racing at Newmarket wearing a bright red dress under a blue coat, with red revers; in a white gown at a ball given by the Duke and Duchess of Devonshire for their daughter Lady Rachel Cavendish; playing golf in a shapeless jumper suit; and peering from under a cloche hat on her way to a luncheon as Buckingham Palace. This last was something of an ordeal for her, for the first time she faced a battery of inquiring eyes intent on scrutinizing Dickie's fiancée. Chatting lightly with Queen Alexandra, Princess Victoria, the Infante Alphonso, and Princess Mary, Edwina began to have some idea of what her future life was to be, but the Prince of Wales' good-natured grin reassured her. Pomp and ceremony had not, it seemed, damped his good spirits or his enjoyment of life. Queen Alexandra talked to her at length about her grandfather, and once again Edwina felt a pang of regret. He would have been very happy to see how her adult life was shaping.

She took Dickie down to Broadlands to meet her family. Suddenly everything had fallen into perspective. She was, for the moment, beyond reach of any petty irritations. She now had a life of her own, and in some mysterious way her relationship with her father had resumed its tender and affectionate quality.

Edwina now said farewell to the ghost of the unhappy child she had once been and mentally regained possession of the Broadlands she loved. It would be many years before she and Dickie would live there permanently, but always the house, the river, and the ancient trees would be a symbol of peace and serenity.

.   .   .

Wedding presents began to pour into Brook House. Arrangements had to be made to guard them, for many of them were extremely valuable. Queen Alexandra sent Edwina a diamond pendant with the royal cipher in diamonds; her father gave her a diamond bandeau, rings, and diamond ear-drops; Auntie Grannie sent a diamond ring and a diamond tiara. The Marchioness of Milford Haven sent precious stones and a diamond necklace. Nor did Sir Ernest Cassel's friends forget his granddaughter. The Aga Khan presented her with a diamond-and-platinum brooch, while the Maharajah of Jaipur, who had been Cassel's guest for the coronation of King Edward VII, offered a superb horse, which however, Edwina, to her great regret was not allowed to accept. Other gifts, which occupied a page in *The Times*, included leather cushions, blotters, photograph frames, spectacle cases— Edwina's short-sightedness was well known—water-colours, china ornaments, paper-knives, book-markers, Roumanian embroidery, bell-pushes, walking-sticks, fruit-dishes, inkpots, lamps, and twenty-four umbrellas.

Dickie fared equally well, though many of his wedding presents were of a more practical nature. The Warrant Officers of H.M.S. *Repulse* sent him a ship's telescope, a copper hot-water jug, and an aneroid barometer. The Prince of Wales presented his cousin with a silver figure of Atlas support-ing a silver globe of the world. On the globe, traced in fine enamel, were the routes of the *Renown* on her Indian and Australian tours.

By the time July 18th approached Edwina was a nervous wreck. What with fittings and parties, and wrangling with Dickie, who longed to make use of his genius for organization by directing all operations, she began to long for the wedding to be over. Public interest, now that it was known that the Prince of Wales was to be best man and that the Royal Family would attend the wedding, had reached fever pitch, and the lady reporters, many of whom had never seen Edwina, variously described her as being 'petite, dark, and vivacious' or 'truly English with blonde curls and a patrician cast of feature'.

By breakfast time on July 18th, 600 people, the vast majority of them women, had gathered in the square in front of St. Margaret's. It was pouring with rain, but, undeterred, the ladies sat on their camp-stools under their umbrellas. Provi-sions were unpacked from baskets and street vendors of favours and illuminated programmes did a brisk trade. By luncheon time it was impossible to move on the pavements and the police were having difficulty in keeping the roads clear.

Just before two o'clock a faint cheer went up as the seven bridesmaids arrived. These were the Greek princesses, Margarita, Theodora, Cecile, and Sophie, nieces of the bridegroom,[1] Mary Ashley, sister of the bride, Joan Packenham, and Lady Mary Ashley Cooper, cousins of the bride. All wore 'pale delphinium crepe romaine, with wide sleeves, and a bateau neckline'. These sack-like garments were vaguely girdled by 'narrow folds of cyclamen mauve, jade, blue, and mauve grosgrain'; Dutch bonnets of silver net with ear-pieces of silver lace completed these devastating ensembles. The colour scheme of the blue-and-silver wedding was completed by the sheaves of delphiniums clutched by the nervous bridesmaids. The decorations of the church had been entrusted by Edwina to a Captain Hope, a blind officer who had made a great success of his flower-shop in Piccadilly.

The first faint cheer grew to a roar as King George V, Queen Mary, and Queen Alexandra entered the church. The Duke of York, Prince Henry, and Prince George were present, and Princess Mary with her husband, Viscount Lascelles. The church was packed with royalty, foreign ambassadors, relations, and friends. Edwina, as pale as her tulle veil, felt her knees giving way under her gown of frosted silver as, leaning on her father's arm, she walked up the aisle. The Prince of Wales and Dickie were waiting for her. Canon Carnegie of St. Margaret's alone conducted the ceremony. Lord Louis, it was noticed, held Edwina's left hand with his right, and several times during the service smiled down at her. The responses of bride and groom rang out loud and clear. The Prince of Wales produced the ring: a modern very narrow circle of gold, thought the dowagers, looking down at their heavy, old-fashioned wedding bands. The organ pealed triumphantly. Lord and Lady Louis Mountbatten, united in the sight of God and man, were about to begin their lives together.

Outside, in the rain, the crowds were making jocular remarks to the bluejackets who were waiting to pull the bridal carriage from the church. Finally their patience was rewarded, and

[1] Sisters of the Duke of Edinburgh.

bride and groom, followed by the distinguished gathering, streamed out into the grey afternoon. There were cheers and greetings and shouted good wishes. This was a wedding that would long be remembered by the crowds, for Edwina and Dickie, with their youth and good looks, had captured popular imagination, and forever afterwards there would be a soft spot in their hearts for the bronzed sailor and his wife.

The scent of flowers was overpowering in Brook House, where the reception was held. The hall was decorated by gigantic delphiniums; bronze and white lilies filled the refresh-ment-rooms, and great vases of Malmaisons, Sir Ernest Cas-sel's favourite flower, were a homage to his memory. Edwina and Dickie received their guests at the entrance to two recep-tion-rooms, where a narrow dividing room had been made into an avenue of orange trees, the cone-shaped greenery bearing the blossoms and ripe fruit at the same time. By the time the young couple had shaken hands with some 500 guests—800 had been invited—their longing to escape was unbearable, and in due course, when royalty had departed, Edwina fled to change into her going-away clothes; a coraline-coloured crepe romaine worn under a coat of ruched crepe romaine with a full round collar.

The Press had made many inquiries as to where the honey-moon was to be spent, but Edwina had countered their ques-tions by giving them a vague itinerary. In fact, she herself was not quite sure where Dickie intended taking her. They were to motor through the Continent to Spain, but before setting out they were to spend a few days at Broadlands.

The weather had cleared a little as the Rolls Royce driven by Lord Louis purred off in the direction of Hampshire. Removing her hat, the bride stared anxiously at her husband's taut profile. Both were so exhausted that, apart from a few remarks about the reception, they drove in silence. Stopping on the way to buy petrol, Dickie spied an acquaintance. Be-fore embarking on a brief conversation, he nervously intro-duced Edwina—'My fiancée, Miss Ashley', and in vain did Lady Louis hang her hand decorated with the new wedding ring out of the window. Dickie said goodbye and, ignoring Edwina's reproachful eye, drove blithely on.

Dickie had indeed drawn up a complete and detailed

itinerary of their projected honeymoon tour. Edwina, at this stage, was decidedly romantic, and would have preferred to wander from town to town, stopping in picturesque places as the spirit moved them. Dickie, eager to please her, gave in, and on their first night out of Paris they drove airily towards the south without having reserved accommodation anywhere. By nightfall, travel-stained and tired, they tried to book a room in an hotel. There were no rooms to be had in the whole town, and finally a good-natured hotelier, taking pity on their plight, gave them a hot and airless attic furnished by a small and lumpy double bed. So narrow was this bed that first Dickie fell out and when he had climbed back, speechless with rage, Edwina tumbled out. Finally Dickie could bear it no longer, and until the grimy panes of the attic window were streaked with the morning light he lectured her on method and organization.

The remainder of the honeymoon was spent in touring the Continent and in visiting Dickie's relatives. Amusing incidents marked their passage. Edwina, whose sole piece of jewellery until her marriage had been a pearl necklet, had insisted on taking all her magnificent wedding presents with her. News of this rich loot had spread to the underworld, and on one occasion a thief gained access to their bedroom, but was frightened off by Dickie's vigorous scrabblings under the pillow which concealed his revolver. In Germany, then in the midst of financial chaos, they had to load the car with suitcases full of marks to pay their bills. At Santander they stayed with the King and Queen of Spain.

They returned to London in September to prepare for a trip to the United States. Dickie had six months' leave of absence from his ship, H.M.S. *Repulse*, and Edwina had always longed to see the New World which Sir Ernest Cassel had known so well and where he had many friends. After a visit to the Duke and Duchess of Sutherland at Dunrobin in Scotland, the young Mountbattens embarked in the *Majestic*. Edwina was ingenuous enough to be charmed by a passenger list which included such celebrities as the Dolly Sisters and Fanny Brice. Both Edwina and Dickie were quite unaware that they themselves were listed as celebrities and they took part wholeheartedly in all the ship's entertainments.

When the ship docked, journalists swarmed aboard and proceeded to overwhelm the young couple with a barrage of questions. Edwina, in a plain dark blue serge dress, wearing a long string of pearls, sat on a sofa and smoked endless cigarettes. Dickie refused to be drawn into a political discussion. The journalists, forgetting that Dickie was not an elder statesman and in view of his recent tour with the Prince of Wales, asked him about conditions in India, about labour affairs, and about the crisis in the Near East. To which Dickie's only comment was, 'It's not the Navy's business to talk, you know.' Some enterprising pressman asked Edwina what she thought about divorce and the conduct of the modern woman in general. The young bride indicated that she believed in being an old-fashioned wife.

On the night of their arrival they dined with Jerome Kern and his wife, and went with them to the New Amsterdam, where they saw the Ziegfeld Follies. The next day they were taken to a baseball game. The star player, Babe Ruth, was introduced to the distinguished visitors. The Press reported that the Mountbattens ate ice-cream cones, cheered mightily, and that Edwina watched the game through a tortoiseshell lorgnette. A caption under a photograph showing Dickie chatting with Babe Ruth said: 'King of Swat hobnobs with Royalty at World Series.'

After a round of dinners, theatres, and bouts of shopping in Fifth Avenue, the Mountbattens as guests of Colonel Robert M. Thompson, set off on a transcontinental tour. At Niagara Falls the President of the Niagara Falls Power Company entertained them.

On their arrival at Chicago their private car was met by a bevy of pressmen who waited for Dickie to emerge from the train, which he finally did, splendidly attired in a blue striped shirt and collar, a purple tie, and checked suit. Amiably, he offered his open cigarette case to the 'boys', who dived upon it, for their ambition was to gain possession of the 'monogrammed pills' as souvenirs.

Excerpts from supposed interviews with Lord Louis in Chicago make it obvious that 'the boys' had cast him in the role of a P. G. Wodehouse character. 'My word,' he is reported to have said on one occasion, 'what a beautiful London fog you have here. Was this arranged to make us feel at home? American ingenuity, what?' ''Pon my soul,' Edwina is supposed to have exclaimed, when asked what she thought of the American flapper, 'I'll see to it that my husband doesn't meet any.' 'Rippings' and 'toppings' were said to mark most of Dickie's conversations to the Press, and their joy was complete when, incorrectly quoting Dickie as its innovator, they were able to introduce to America the favourite fad games of the English nobility, 'Decameron' and 'Beaver'. The former, it seemed, was played by any number of players, who, having picked out a woman with a mole on her face, shouted out 'Yoo Hoo, Decameron'. This counted fifteen points. The first to gain sixty points was the winner of the game. 'Beaver' was similar, except that beards, not moles, made winning points.

At Beverley Hills the Mountbattens stayed with Douglas Fairbanks and Mary Pickford at 'Pickfair'. Here they met Charlie Chaplin and other celebrities of the celluloid world, and it was at this time that Dickie began collecting a film library; one of the first reels being a private film featuring himself, Edwina, and Charlie Chaplin in the leading roles.

For the first time in her life, Edwina was really enjoying herself. The American way of life intrigued and interested her, and instead of allowing her visit to be regulated by the exclusive circle who ruled American society, she and Dickie mingled in democratic fashion with anyone who interested them; and while the mass took them to its heart, voting them 'lovable children, and regular guys', the Four Hundred took violent exception to their doings, feeling somehow that they had been snubbed. Fashionable society was sadly disappointed in Lord and Lady Mountbatten. It had been planned to lead them from one fashionable drawing-room to another and to dazzle them with glimpses of the luxury in which America's leaders of wealth and fashion live. Instead, the Mountbattens had politely but firmly made it clear that they had no intention of being set apart, to be entertained only in the homes of the élite, and to get their ideas of American life from riding up and down Fifth Avenue. They preferred the Broadway cabarets, and when they were tired of Jazz they went out West, met Indians and cowboys, rode mules through

Wilfrid Ashley (Lord Mount Temple), Edwina's father. By Lady Granby

"Auntie Grannie": Mrs. Minna Cassel, 1917

King Edward VII with a group of friends at Biarritz in 1907. Among his guests were Winston Churchill, Sir Ernest Cassel, Mrs. Wilfrid Ashley, Edwina and Mrs. George Keppel

(*Left*) Edwina at the age of eighteen

(*Below*) Edwina and Dickie at the time of their engagement

the Grand Canyon, shot at a deer or two, and caught a few fish. The smart set deplored Edwina's habit of chatting to cab-drivers, negro waiters, and shop assistants, but any attempt on their part to point out the error of her ways was met with a chilling glance. She was perfectly aware of what she was doing, and if a certain section of society criticized her activities, she nonetheless made it her business to see her grandfather's old friends, to subscribe generously to the American Red Cross, and to visit institutions such as 'The Dug Out', the vocational shop for disabled veterans of World War I.

This first visit to America was the first strand in the pattern of the life she was to lead for many years. The gaudier hues —scarlets and purples—would stand out, glaringly obscuring the plainer textures of the daily round, and her would-be hostesses would not forget, then or ever, that she had not needed or wanted their advice. The Mountbattens returned to England having made many new friends, and with a feeling for Negro spirituals, Jazz, and the knowledge that their voyage had been one of discovery in every sense of the word.

F

CHAPTER V

FOLLOWING THE FLAG

O N RETURNING to England, Dickie and Edwina went down to Broadlands to stay with Colonel Ashley. Edwina, once more under the spell of the green and lovely countryside, rested and tried to sort out her impressions of her American visit. Cuttings and word-of-mouth reports had preceded her homecoming, and she was astonished, and not a little dismayed, to discover that her doings in the States had made news, not always of a pleasant nature. Then, as later, many of her innocent and well-meant forays into the lives and ordinary pleasures of simple people had been misinterpreted. Puzzled, and somewhat hurt, Edwina put the cuttings away. It never struck her that her zest for life and experience and her direct approach to it might be a handicap in the life she was now expected to lead. Her link with the Royal Family and her own background ordained that it should be a circumscribed and formal life, worked out to a routine pattern which left no room for the reactions of an original and restless nature.

Now, too, she was faced with a problem which would take her many years to solve. Dickie had been appointed to the battleship *Revenge*, the flagship of the 1st Battle Squadron in the Mediterranean, and it was apparent to her that while she was as important to Dickie as he was to her, his career as a naval officer was going to take him from her as surely as any rival. Dickie loved the sea and his career, and nothing was going to deflect him from pursuing it as ardently as his father had done before him. She knew enough of her husband to realize that no compromise could be effected between what Dickie deemed his duty and her own desire to travel and express herself, and because she loved him, she put aside her own longings and devoted herself to becoming a naval wife. This, on the face of it, was no difficult task. A very large income could smooth out many of the material difficulties which made the life of the average naval wife a continual struggle, but it could not change the inflexible routine of the Navy, or the fact that, like all other young naval wives, she had to endure the loneliness of endless waiting and of being present at all times in ports which had little to offer in the way of entertainment and amusement. Her early married life, then, was lived on two separate and distinct planes: waiting for Dickie, and being on infrequent occasions with Dickie in London.

This was an era which produced the background for *Decline and Fall*; *The Beautiful and the Damned*, and *The Green Hat*. This was a time of speed, of bath-tub gin, Flaming Youth, post-cubism, and matinée idols modelled in the images of Noel Coward and Gertrude Lawrence. The swelling curves and whipped-cream hair of the Edwardian beauty gave way to the flat, 'little-boy' figure, whose short skirts displayed slim, adolescent legs and whose sleek, bobbed hair was hidden by a cloche hat.

Edwina, with her boyish figure and the beautiful clean modelling of her head, wore triumphantly the new uniform, and she, together with the Spanish Duchess de Penaranda and Mrs. Reginald Fellowes, became the symbols of *chic* in a coterie which was nervous, brittle, and constantly in search of stimulation.

Thus the Mountbattens, young, wealthy, and gay, were vulnerable targets for the moralists. Few of those who viewed with reproving eyes the reports of parties, visits to night-clubs, and spectacular entertainments, gave a thought of what might conceivably lie behind the fireworks of youth. The critics never imagined that Lady Mountbatten, seen one night assiduously 'doing the new drop-heel step of the foxtrot' at the Embassy Club, spent five out of seven days in a room at the Grand Hotel at Plymouth waiting for Dickie, or that her first married home was a modest house which she had taken outside Dorchester, so that Dickie could get easily to Weymouth. 'They', that hidden band who had haunted her schooldays, were now once again ensconced in the wings of her new life, and as dizzy paragraph after dizzy paragraph underlined the activities of the fashionable Lady Louis Mountbatten, the invisible chorus chortled with glee. Edwina was 'seen' wearing a nasturtium-coloured georgette gown embroidered in paillettes; she was 'noticed' supping with the Prince of Wales and his party. On this occasion she wore an 'Egyptian mummy dress with a sable stole', and it was observed that the guests at the Royal table pelted one another with coloured cotton-wool balls issued to the guests. She was 'glimpsed' driving her grey Rolls Royce with her black retriever Simon sitting bolt upright by her side, and on the reopening of Brook House it was reported that 'all the Royal princes as well as Lady Elizabeth Bowes-Lyon were present at the very small dance given by Lord and Lady Mountbatten'. The fifty guests danced to Paul Whiteman's band, and the tunes of the period, 'Chicago', 'Dancing Honeymoon', and 'Are You Playing Fair' echoed in the great room, whose walls heretofore had resounded only with select pieces of chamber music played by Sir Ernest Cassel's classical orchestras.

But even then there was a more serious side to her activities, and much of her time was occupied in attending social functions given in aid of deserving charities. She was expecting her first child, and for this reason, perhaps, anything to do with children touched her. She attended a dance in aid of the Infants' Hospital, Westminster, and was happy to loan the vast salons of Brook House for a matinée concert in aid of 'Our Babies'. She was, in fact, fitting well into her role of fashionable young society matron. For the first time, too, she began to realize the ramifications of her grandfather's investments and since, unlike him, she was not equipped with a mathematical brain, her trustees had difficulty in explaining the complications of stocks and shares, endowments, policies, and the long-term policy with which the financier had hoped to secure the future of his descendants. Edwina did not then have any notion of the value of money translated into terms of ordinary life. She knew that it was an important commodity —everyone told her so—and, being possessed of so much wealth, she unconsciously joined the group of select human beings destined to live all their lives in a fishtank. But, unlike those who were content to swim about in the narrow confines of their glass prison, she was to make many strenuous efforts to fling herself into the moving streams. And just as a tropical fish endowed with a similar desire might be labelled eccentric, so would her efforts to escape be watched with malice, and never with pity.

In February 1924, while Dickie's ship lay in Funchal Bay, Madeira, Edwina's first daughter was born. She was named Patricia Edwina Victoria after her godparents, the Prince of Wales, Lady Patricia Ramsay, and the Dowager Marchioness of Milford Haven, born Princess Victoria of Hesse and of the Rhine. Some months later Dickie finished his turn of sea-duty and began the long Signal course for officers at Portsmouth.

Since Dickie was going to be ashore for some time, it was obvious that they must have a home near Portsmouth. Accordingly Edwina went house-hunting, and soon found what she wanted. Adsdean was a large and comfortable house, built of grey stone and covered with Virginia creeper. Standing in the midst of an agreeable park, it was some twenty miles from Portsmouth, which meant that Dickie could easily drive in and out to his course. It was the Mountbattens' first home together, and while Dickie concentrated on the planning of a small golf course, a paddock, and a riding-school, and the construction of a special pit for polo practice, Edwina gave herself wholeheartedly to decorating the house according to the taste of the moment. Cream and pink were then her favourite colours, and the bedroom had pink silk curtains and was furnished with French walnut and gilt pieces. The boudoir was gay with cream walls and pink-upholstered furniture, and the dining-room walls were covered in brown canvas, as a suitable background for oil-paintings, while the curtains were of saffron brocade.

Eighteen servants ran Adsdean. Heading the staff was Frank Randall, the butler. The Austrian chef, formerly Sir Ernest Cassel's cook, who had known Edwina since babyhood, ruled the kitchens. It was not habitual for young married couples to make a special study of conditions suitable for staff to live in, but both Edwina and Dickie attached considerable importance to the welfare of their servants, and had built for them a staff recreation-room which was equipped with a radio, billiard table, darts-board, and table tennis. They also had permission to make use of the golf course. Edwina gave her servants every consideration, but she also expected, and received, superlative service. Also they were expected to share her passion for exotic animals, and whenever she returned from a voyage into the blue, bringing with her a souvenir in the shape of a lion cub, wallaby, ant-eater, or lemur, the staff were required to nurse, care for, and feed these quaint guests. Today Charles Smith, who has been in Edwina's service since 1930, can gravely relate the life and often peculiar death of some of these pets.   On one occasion, when Edwina was trying to remember the sequence of her animals and the fate that befell them, the following dialogue took place:

'What did we have after darling Sabie, Charles?'

'Coco and Boso, Milady.'

'Ah yes, two miniature kangaroos from the Austral Islands.'

'And then, Milady, there was the bush-baby who broke his leg in a destroyer, but he recovered satisfactorily.'

'So he did.   Which was the one which fell into the lavatory?'

'A most unsavoury beast, Milady.   Snozzle, the ant-eater.'

CHAPTER VI

THE GREEN-HAT ERA

THE YEAR 1924 saw the opening of the British Empire Exhibition, which was inaugurated by King George V on April 23rd. This city of pavilions, each of them designed in similar style to the particular Empire country whose activities were displayed within, had an especial fascination for the glittering cohorts of society, particularly since the Prince of Wales had made a visit to the Amusement Park. H.R.H., accompanied by Dickie and Edwina, had toured the Australian Pavilion, and then, to the immense delight of the crowds, had visited the Amusement Park, where they wholeheartedly enjoyed the 'Whip' and a journey on the Giant Switchback. The spectacle of their sunny-haired Prince clinging grimly to his seat as he was hurtled up and down the giddy heights of the switchback endeared him even more to their hearts. 'Now he is really enjoying himself,' they said approvingly, as he whizzed dizzily past them in the 'Whip'.

It was not long before Edwina and Dickie were back at Wembley, this time accompanied by Douglas Fairbanks and Mary Pickford, who had come over to England to attend the christening of the Mountbattens' small daughter. Mary, having just completed a film, *Dorothy Vernon of Haddon Hall*, had expressed a desire to visit the real Haddon Hall. This was arranged for her, and Mary was heard to murmur that she feared she had taken some liberties with the Hall in her picture. That evening Doug and Mary dined with Edwina and Dickie at Brook House, and on the next day the Fairbanks attended the christening of Miss Patricia Mountbatten. The 'World's Sweetheart' was next seen with Dickie and Edwina at *The Midnight Follies*. On this occasion Mary was in palest pink from top to toe, her famous golden curls emerging from a froth of palest pink georgette and her stockings and shoes dyed to match her gown. So great was the vogue of Doug and Mary, and of the Kinema which they represented, that London

society, headed by Dickie and Edwina, inaugurated entertainment in private houses.   Among the first films to be thus pre-
viewed was *The Thief of Bagdad*, which was shown at Brook
House to an audience composed of some sixty guests, among
them the Prince of Wales, Prince Henry, and Prince George.

Edwina, with the same ardent concentration she brought to
whatever engaged her attention, was coruscating in a sky of
social meteors.   Her life at this period was a continual round
of parties and dances, many of them in aid of charity functions.
She was on the committee of 'The Heart of the Empire Costume
Ball' arranged in aid of the Combined Docklands Settlements,
a ball at which Lady Diana Duff Cooper, fresh from her
triumph in *The Miracle*, invested the figure of Britannia with
spectacular beauty.   Edwina danced the schottische at a
dinner given for the Queen of Spain at the Spanish Embassy;
she attended a magnificent State Ball at Buckingham Palace
in honour of the King and Queen of Roumania, she ran her
house efficiently and well, and sometimes, between undressing
after one function and dressing for another, she sat at her
dressing-table staring curiously at the fashionable lady who
stared coolly back at her.

The summer of that year was highlighted by one of the
annual voyages which were to become a feature of Edwina's
life.   The Prince of Wales was to visit the United States and,
much to his satisfaction, his friends Edwina and Dickie, with
their brother and sister-in-law the Marquis and Marchioness
of Milford Haven, took passage in the same ship.   The
Berengaria was the former German liner *Imperator*.   The suite
reserved for H.R.H. was that designed for the Kaiser, a suite
which he never saw, as the ship made its maiden voyage from
Bremen to New York in the summer of 1914 and remained in
New York Harbour for the duration of the war.

When it became known that the Prince of Wales was to
travel in the *Berengaria*, the steamship line was besieged by
eager travellers, and when finally she sailed she carried more
débutantes and young girls among her 700 saloon passengers
than any other great liner has done before or since.   Cotton
and oil kings and merchant princes with young daughters
found themselves cutting short their European tour and being

hustled home aboard the *Berengaria*. A contented passenger
was a tycoon of the advertising world who had paid £1,000
for a suite adjoining that of the Prince of Wales and the
Mountbattens. Among the other passengers were Lady Diana
Duff Cooper, returning to America to play again in *The
Miracle*; Vera Rubia, a well-known actress; Clara Novello
Davies, mother of Ivor Novello; and the owner of the famous
race-horse, Epinard.

The Prince of Wales spent the evening with the Mountbattens before crossing to the *Berengaria* in a steam launch,
where he embarked with the least possible ostentation. The
next day, sailing day, Edwina and Dickie gave a farewell party
at which were two of her best friends, cousin Marjorie and
Paula Gellibrand, then married to the Marquis de Casa Maury.

Anguished young ladies, vying for a sight of H.R.H., reported that he spent most of his time playing Mah Jong with
the Mountbattens, though he was to be seen entering into
shipboard life on several occasions: once when he organized
a British tug-o'-war team for the ship's sports, and at the fancy-
dress ball, when he appeared as a Limehouse apache wearing
a sweater inside out and a cap at a jaunty angle. He and his
partner, a girl dressed as a lad, secured the booby prize. Night
after night a battery of eyes was glued to the entrance of the
ballroom while three Jazz experts engaged to supplement the
ship's orchestra jazzed up popular tunes such as 'June Night',
'Seal it with a Kiss', and 'Believe Me'.

The London to which the Mountbattens returned, much
invigorated by their sojourn in America, was gayer and
'brighter' than ever. Everyone was being madly original and
amusing, and freak parties had supplanted the Treasure Hunts
of the previous year. Mrs. James Corrigan gave a party which,
in its lavishness, almost excelled that given many years before
by Boni de Castellane in Paris. It was an 'Arabian Nights'
cabaret dinner and dance at her house in Grosvenor Square.
The staircase was converted into the semblance of a garden,
with trellis-work, hanging bunches of grapes, orange trees,
and was lighted by Oriental lamps hanging on tripods. A
special pavilion was erected in the garden, decked with Persian
tapestries, while tiny Chinese lanterns set in red roses on the
tables supplied the illuminations. Dinner was served by

waiters in Oriental costume and red turbans, while the star of
the evening was the Maharajah of Kapurthala, who appeared
in magnificent brocaded robes, with a staggering array of
jewellery decking his person.

Another party which made social history was the 'Night-
time Day Party'. The idea itself was simple enough. The
guests stayed in bed all day and slept, rising about nine o'clock
at night. They then breakfasted and began the 'day'. At
1 a.m., in the chill hours of the morning, luncheon was served,
and the 'day' was filled in with moonlight tennis and golf,
while some of the guests chose to paint nightscapes by the light
of electric torches. A feature of the game was the heavy fine
imposed on any guest saying 'What a lovely night' instead of
'What a marvellous morning'. The fine of five dollars was
given to charity.

It was at this time that a new member of the Ashley family
made an appearance on the social scene. Mary, Edwina's
younger sister, left her finishing school in France, and under the
aegis of Edwina was groomed for her début in London. The
creamy-skinned, red-haired Mary was presented at the same
time as the ebullient Barbara Cartland, whose first novel, *Jig
Saw*, described as 'Mayfair with the lid off', had created almost
as great a furore as Fanny Burney's *Evelina*. Mary was splendidly launched by a ball given for her at Brook House. The
guests of honour were the Duke and Duchess of York, and Prince
Henry and the Princesses Margarita and Theodora of Greece
attended. Roses alone were used for the decorations, and in
the other rooms were large bowls of lupins. Edwina had
inherited her grandfather's love of flowers, and wherever she
had her being her rooms were filled with the malmaisons
beloved of Sir Ernest.

Mary's beauty was, perhaps, more vivid than that of her
sister, and soon she too was the centre of a group of admirers
of her own age. With Mary successfully launched, Dickie
working with ardent concentration at his course, and her
daughter living a well-disciplined nursery existence, Edwina
was conscious of an inexplicable restlessness in herself. The
social round continued with unabated frenzy, there were more
original parties, new nightclubs opened, but somehow these
distractions had lost their savour, and in avid reading Edwina

searched for an explanation of the staleness of her spirit. For the first time she began to realize the lacunae in her education. It became her ambition to travel and to see the world, and so at the end of a brilliant season she slipped off quietly into the blue. Alone and with a meagre baggage she travelled through Russia to China and finally to San Francisco.

It was a strange experience, strange and stimulating. Suddenly the known background had become kaleidoscopic, and the pattern, shaken by the jolting of trains and rickety carts and cars, changed with a changing landscape. Here the anonymous traveller, unable to communicate by the spoken word, might find friendship in unknown faces. A spiritual exile by virtue of that rich and restless strain of alien blood, she travelled in search of an imaginary haven. She sought it in the snows of Russia, in the palm-studded beaches of the South Seas. In an album is a photographic record of a unique voyage undertaken in a fifty-ton sailing-schooner. Edwina had teamed up with a couple who were doing some kind of survey work for Scandinavian countries, and the three of them signed on as members of the crew of the *Gisbourne*, a fifty-ton, sixty-year-old sailing-schooner which traded in copra. The Polynesian captain spoke only a little broken French, the crew was Polynesian. In the middle of the hurricane season the ancient schooner, which carried no radio or doctor, sailed from Tahiti, where the manes of Gauguin, who had blazed trails of the spirit in other golden voyages, waved them farewell. For four months the small vessel, lost to the world, plied its course among the islands, trading prints, beads, clocks, and trinkets in exchange for copra.

Edwina trimmed sails, scrubbed down decks, stood her trick at the wheel, and took her turn at lookout. The voyage ended at Rapa, the southernmost island in the South Pacific. Edwina returned to London brimming with energy, and her superabundance of vitality found a temporary outlet during the General Strike of May 1926, when she worked as a volunteer switchboard operator on one of the National dailies. The paper, stripped of almost everyone outside the editorial staff, was run by E. W. Robertson, while Bonar Law's youngest daughter helped out, and Edwina and one of her friends manned the office telephone switchboards.

In 1927 Lord Louis was appointed Assistant Fleet Wireless Officer to the Commander-in-Chief Mediterranean, Admiral Sir Roger Keyes. The fleet was based at Malta, and once again Edwina followed the flag. For nearly ten years Malta was to be the headquarters of the Mountbattens, and this island was in that time to become very dear to them. Dickie had known it well as a child, and, like all naval officers, he had a very sincere regard and affection for the Maltese.

At first view it is difficult to understand how a woman used to London and the seasonal routine of the international set can have settled down so successfully to life in Malta, which, though gay, was circumscribed by the mere fact of its geographical position. But one of Edwina's greatest gifts was the ability to adapt herself to whatever tempo or mode of life she was called. Also, Malta had much to offer to those who are attracted by the outdoor life and by the historical significance of an island which for centuries has been washed by the waves of history. Lying 60 miles south of Sicily and 180 miles north of the mainland of Africa, Malta has been an important stage in the archaeological and historical development of civilization. In A.D. 60 St. Paul was wrecked on the coast of Malta, and in 1530 the Emperor Charles V conferred on the Knights Hospitallers—the Order of the Hospital of St. John of Jerusalem— the island of Malta. From their new home the Hospitallers, henceforward to be known as the Knights of Malta, carried on their legendary prowesses until their military history ended with the capture of Malta by Napoleon in 1798. From that time onwards the Knights of Malta devoted their energies to works of charity.

Here, in this island dedicated to the spirit of the Knights, enshrined in the great church of St. John, in the former palace of the Grandmasters, in the library with its priceless archives of the Order and Incunabula and in the auberges or hostelries of the different divisions of the Order spread among the old streets, Edwina was to absorb, unconsciously perhaps, the message of the Knights and their Order. 'Pro utilitate hominum', which, when the time was ripe, would come to the surface and drive her to accomplish the mission to which she would subsequently dedicate so much of her life.

But steel must be tempered, and the time was not yet

for the Knights to claim their twentieth-century champion.
Edwina was still bound by the shackles of her background and
environment, and her main object at this moment in her life
was to create a comfortable home for her husband and child,
to take her part as a naval officer's wife in the Fleet, and to
surmount any invisible barriers which might have been raised
in the minds of those who had only read of her lavish life as
depicted in print in England. The possession of great wealth
creates considerable problems both for those who possess it and
for those who are less fortunate. The former, never having
been conditioned to consider financial stresses or limitations,
have no yardstick to measure the all-absorbing and ever-
present problem of the mechanics of living, while those always
tormented by the strictures imposed by a meagre bank balance
are prone to judge as ostentatious any manifestations of luxury
which, in fact, are relatively reasonable. It would take many
years for Edwina to become conscious of the resentment built
up against her by the mere fact of her possessions, and possibly
even now certain facets of ordinary living still escape her, but
the fundamental issue is not one that can be gauged by cal-
culating on how she would have adapted herself if she had been
stripped of her money, or if her life would have taken the same
course. The fact is that she broke through this almost em-
barrassing cocoon of wealth to follow, haltingly at first, in the
footsteps of Elizabeth Fry and of Florence Nightingale.

The Mountbattens' first home in Malta was the 'Casa
Medina', a tall, sun-filled villa over Sliema Harbour. Edwina,
instead of trying to shut out the sunshine, invited it into the
large rooms and filtered it through curtains of primrose-yellow
linen. The highly polished furniture gleamed darkly, reflect-
ing great bowls of strident, multi-coloured zinnias. Soon the
Casa Medina bore the unmistakable imprint of Edwina's personality. There were about her, as always, books, flowers,
and animals. The Mountbattens lived quietly and without
ostentation. Dickie worked relentlessly, and in his leisure
hours organized a superb polo team composed of naval officers.
Known as the 'Bluejackets', they made polo history by beating
regiments with teams of two or three times their total handicap.
Any spare hours were occupied in producing a series of notes
for signal lectures and a manual of wireless telegraphy, both

of which have since become standard instructional works.
Healthy, dynamic, and ceaselessly alert, he was brimming
over with ideas and enthusiasm. Edwina, while filled with
admiration for this vitality, wondered sometimes whether her
own drive and initiative were not being wasted in the particular
fields in which they were applied. But since it seemed that
her role as naval wife and hostess had been mapped out for
her, she was too well disciplined to rebel, and in any case there
appeared to be no other outlet for her energies. So she continued to entertain with grace and simplicity, all the while
analysing those about her, and though, at this stage, her reactions were more subjective than objective, she was gaining an
ever-widening knowledge of psychology, and all the time she
was reading voraciously thick and heavy tomes, whose contents
on subjects as widely diverse as philosophy and archaeology
would have much surprised her more frivolous friends.

Her sister's marriage marked another milestone. Mary,
like Edwina, was married at St. Margaret's, Westminster.
Afterwards a reception was held for her at Brook House by
Edwina and Dickie. Always Edwina had cherished, and felt
responsible for, her highly strung 'little' sister, and it was with
clouded eyes that she watched the tall girl in her gown of shining
silvery tissue walk up the aisle. There was no doubt that Mary
was radiantly happy. She was young, beautiful, and she was
marrying the man she loved. Yet, as Mary came out into the
sunshine on the arm of her husband, Edwina was suddenly
afraid for her. The young couple departed on their honeymoon, and Edwina, prolonging her visit to London, entered
with zest into the life she had temporarily abandoned. Towards the middle of the year there is a record of her one and
only appearance as a model. This was at a Theatrical Garden
Party given in the grounds of the Royal Hospital, Chelsea.
While a galaxy of theatrical stars—among them Tallulah
Bankhead, Vi Lorraine, Gladys Cooper, Phyllis Dare, and
Owen Nares—dispensed ices, cocktails, and fruit drinks,
Edwina, Lady Plunket, and Lady George Cholmondeley, led
by the Countess of Carlisle, paraded the latest fashions. A few
days later she was escorting her small daughter, Patricia, to a
children's party at Buckingham Palace. The party was given
by Queen Mary to celebrate her sixtieth birthday.

In January 1929 Edwina was expecting her second child. This did not deter her from continuing her travels, and towards the end of this year she and Dickie arrived in Egypt, crowded at this period with wealthy sun-followers. The season was in full swing, and artistes of the calibre of Loie Fuller and of the classical dancers Clothilde and Alexandre Sahkaroff were drawing full houses at the Kursaal Theatre. Edwina, passionately interested in Lord Carnarvon's discoveries, risked the ancient curse attached to those who trod the soil of Tutankhamen's tomb at Luxor, and she spent much time visiting and exploring the various digs.

The baby was not due until the end of April, and Edwina saw no reason to curtail her activities. When Dickie's ship put in at Gibraltar, she was waiting to rush off with him for a weekend in Morocco. Bad weather prevented them from returning in the packet steamer and Dickie had to charter an open launch to get back in time. Seemingly unmoved, Edwina spent a night bouncing on the crest of the waves, and the next day she set out alone by car for Barcelona, where Dickie was due to rejoin her. As soon as she saw him she announced calmly that, in her opinion, a young Mountbatten was due to arrive at any moment. In a brief space Dickie had organized a specialist—the fact that he was an ear-and-throat man did not lessen his willingness to help—he had rung the Queen of Spain (she was away from Madrid), and had spoken with King Alphonso, who promised instant assistance. Immediately, he telephoned the Governor of Barcelona, and very soon the hotel was cordoned by a guard complete with brass band, and to the sound of the clash of cymbals, Pamela Carmen Louise Mountbatten entered the world. She was later christened in the Chapel Royal, and numbered among her godparents King Alphonso XIII of Spain, the wife of the Duke of Penaranda, Queen Louise of Sweden, and the Duke of Kent.

Not all Edwina's trips were carefully planned; some were arranged on the spur of the moment. Such a one was the visit to Hollywood with Marjorie Brecknock, which was decided one gala night at the Café de Paris. The cousins stayed first with Doug and Mary at Pickfair and then went on to spend a week-end with Randolph Hearst at his ranch, San Simeon. Their hostess, Marion Davies, struck them as being one of the

most brilliant women they had ever met, and though they were
fascinated by the charm of W. R., they were quite often reduced to irrepressible giggles by life at San Simeon. W. R.,
regardless of guests, and surrounded by newspaper men,
carried on his work in a vast hall. Gramophones blared,
visitors chattered, and in the imposing bedrooms an array of
bells unattached to wires summoned nobody. The estate was
littered with packing-cases containing Italian fountains, Tudor
rooms, and Scottish castles. On one occasion W. R., wanting
to give his guests a treat, took them to visit an English manor-
house which was being reconstructed brick by brick. Unfortunately, the packing-cases containing the front door had
been lost in transit, and W. R., in a rage, pounded back to his
'office' to send furious cables—his favourite means of communication—winging across the world. Before returning,
Edwina and Marjorie watched Charlie Chaplin making a film.
He gagged so much on the set that the entire film had to be
re-shot, which seemed to them a reasonable explanation for
the length of time that it took him to make one of his masterpieces. Knowing Dickie's interest in the progress of the revolutionary 'talkies', Edwina watched a 'talking film' being made
and was able later to quote chapter and verse to her husband.

Her return to England was marked by the addition of a
new member to the family circle. This was nine-year-old
Philip, Dickie's nephew. The blond Prince, son of Prince
Andrew of Greece and of Princess Alice, Dickie's sister, had
already, in spite of his tender years, had an uneasy childhood.
Born in 1921, on his father's estates in the island of Corfu, off
the coast of Albania, he was only a year old when his father
was arrested on the orders of the revolutionary group that
seized power after the failure of the Greek Army, in which he
had led a corps, during the campaign against the Turks in
Asia Minor. He was tried and sentenced to disgrace and
permanent exile.

The baby Prince with his family was brought to England
aboard a British destroyer. Soon afterwards Prince Andrew,
with his wife and children, moved to Paris. Princess Andrew,
in an effort to help the Greek exiles, opened a Hellas shop in
the Faubourg St. Honoré, where she exhibited and sold paintings, lace, and embroidery made by her protégées. Prince

Wedding group including the Prince of Wales, Lord Louis' best man, the four sisters of Prince Philip, Edwina's sister Mary and their two cousins, Lady Mary Ashley Cooper and Joan Packenham

Edwina with Sabi her lion cub

Edwina with Pamela, 1930

Philip's first school was a French one, but his mother, loving and remembering the Country in which she had been brought up, influenced his father to allow him to be educated in England. His uncle, the second Marquess of Milford Haven, became his guardian, and Prince Philip came to Britain, where he was welcomed by both his uncles and their families. He was sent to Cheam School, near Newbury, Berkshire, and soon adapted himself to the life of a British schoolboy. Dickie took great pride in this nephew, who was to take the place of the son he would never have. During the holidays the placid and feminine Mountbatten nursery was much enlivened by the appearance of young Master Philip, who, always a tease, imposed his will on Patricia, who soon became his willing slave and imitator. Having a boy among them was good for the little girls, and they soon became as proud of his achievements as were their parents, boasting of his exploits to their small friends, among whom were their future Queen and her sister.

.   .   .

But the limited confines of the nursery could not long hold Edwina. Almost as if anticipating her future, self-imposed discipline, she now wanted to see more of the world. Her idea of travel, unlike that of Dickie, who liked comfort when it was possible, was to travel light, to mingle with ordinary people, to talk with them, learn their problems, and live like them. She was impatient of red tape, of orthodox tours arranged only to show places and people to their best advantage. She wanted always to 'get behind the scenes'. She sailed for the West Indies, returning via New York.

Now the idea of going to Persia claimed her, and with her sister-in-law, as tireless and intrepid as herself, they set off on an archaeological tour. Their belongings were few, their knowledge was limited, but their enthusiasm was boundless, and the land that had known the dreams and plans of Lawrence knew these curious travellers. At Damascus, where women veiled in black and orange eyed them curiously, they explored the *Suq's*, unaware of the keen eyes observing them, and conscious only of the glittering colour, rich embroideries, and the ringing of camel-bells. This was the Damascus whose seven rivers shone under the silken tent of the sky; it was the Damascus in which St. Paul had lingered, and it was a political

G

hot-bed. Untroubled by the interest aroused in them, Edwina and her companion bought an aged automobile, which, rattling and shuddering, brought them safely over some 600 miles of open desert to Bagdad. Here they dined with the British Minister to Persia, who did his best to dissuade them from continuing their hazardous journey. Politely but firmly disregarding all advice, the two women pushed on towards Teheran. The route lay over a mountain range through wild and hostile country which few unescorted women had ever attempted to traverse. At last, when their bones ached with weariness, they reached Teheran. Here there was much to see.

In the grottoes of Tak-i-Bostan they admired angels with Coptic faces and, as the sky deepened into azure dusk, they were enveloped in the inimitable blue which is the colour of Persia, and is reflected in the sky, the water, the water-jars, and often in the clothes of the women. The British Ambassador invited the travellers to dine and reiterated the Minister's warnings, illustrating his words with lurid thumbnail sketches of what their fate would be should they fall into the hands of the Kurds. Unshaken by these dire prophecies, Edwina climbed into the ancient car, and with a valedictory toot on the squeaky horn, they were off again, on their way to Ispahan and Shiraz. Lovely as a Persian miniature was Shiraz, its dark cypresses limned against the far, snow-capped mountains, and sweet oranges glowing against their waxy leaves.

One of Edwina's main reasons for coming to Shiraz was to take part in the excavations at Persepolis, the buried city brought to light by Professor Herzfeld. The learned archaeologist did not, in a general way, welcome sightseers, and was known to be stern indeed with photographers, but since it was at his express invitation that Edwina had come to Persepolis, it was his pleasure to give her the freedom of 'his' city, and immediately she was absorbed in the beauty of Persepolis.

With Herzfeld as a cicerone she stood before the carvings on the cliff at Nash-i-Rustan, and twenty centuries were abolished as he explained that the Elamite, Achemenian, and Sasasian civilizations were represented in the rock carvings. The Achemenid kings, long dead, made of their tombs memorials, and forced the living to admire their works; and everywhere the great masses of stone, coloured grey and cream and admirably wrought, compelled the eye.   Under the moon the columns, stairs, and platform, balanced with brilliant engineering skill on massive blocks, formed a vast and crushing whole, and the cicadas jabbing the air with their cry transmitted in some indefinable way a message of continuity: the cities of the plain buried by the plain lived again.

Each journey was an enrichment, yet with each return the urge to wander again became stronger, and some time in 1934 Edwina began to contemplate another voyage, this time to South America.   In the meantime, she and Dickie, though sentimentally attached to Brook House, found that the maintenance and taxation on this vast and little-used establishment made serious inroads on their finances, and after much deliberation they decided that it should be sold, pulled down, and a modern block of flats erected in its stead.   In due course the architect's plans were submitted and approved, and the grandeur that had been Brook House tumbled in great cataracts of masonry.

CHAPTER VII

BRISE MARINE

ON MONDAY, January 22nd, 1934, Edwina and cousin Marjorie caught the train from Paris to Lisbon, where they installed themselves at the Avenida Palace Hotel. They spent the next morning sightseeing and then went out to Estoril. Here they ambled about in the sun until they realized that their ship sailed at 3.30 and that unless they hurried they would not be aboard when it sailed. On the return journey a burst tyre delayed them even more, and when they finally sighted the *Highland Chieftain* it was to see all her officers standing at the top of the gangway. The Captain received their excuses with frozen politeness and, having asked if any more luggage was coming aboard, remarked quietly that it was time they were getting along to South America.

The first port of call was Las Palmas, which held little charm that day, as the harmattan was blowing sand from the Sahara into the eyes of the passengers who had come ashore. Cousin Marjorie, who recorded the trip, was laid low with a cold, but recovered sufficiently to accompany Edwina to the Captain's quarters. Here, having quaffed his special brew of 'planter's punch', she was obliged to retire in a dazed condition. Many cups of black coffee restored her in time to present the prizes for the games tournaments later in the evening.

After calling at Pernambuco they reached Rio in the early hours of the morning and having risen with the sun were rewarded by the sight of Rio harbour, with its background of fantastically shaped mountains and small hills covered with tropical vegetation. In a short while the travellers were installed in the Copacabana Hotel, where they dispatched various letters of introduction, some of which were to bring them curious acquaintances. Determined to bathe at once, they gave the porter the shock of his life by appearing in bathing-dress and cloaks in the foyer. It transpired that any guest 'eccentrically' clad in any form of undress must be spirited in the lift down to the basement, where, after a walk of several 'miles', he emerged behind the concierge's desk, two yards from the main entrance. Edwina and Marjorie obeyed these rules, and spent a pleasant morning bathing off an island whose owners were away.

In the afternoon one of their letters of introduction bore fruit in the person of a young woman who invited them to see the countryside with her.

'She took us for a drive in her car, an experience which is likely to remain for ever fresh in our memories as one of the most terrifying of our lives. The sight of a bend in the road, preferably coming down the mountain, had a most remarkable effect on her, as it apparently necessitated her pressing hard down on the accelerator, taking both hands off the wheel, removing her glasses and cleaning them, and finally jamming on her brakes which were not at all efficient.'

Invitations now poured in from every quarter and Edwina and Marjorie were kept constantly on the move. After visiting friends in country estates 'We all went up to a lovely little lake in the forest. Trees covered with orchids and moss, exquisite reflections, waterfalls, etc' they returned to Rio and found themselves swept up in the Carnival:

'The most fantastic sight imaginable, the entire population going completely mad for three days. They have tiny syphons of ether with which they squirt everyone and everything and the fumes of which apparently keep their spirits up as they never stop singing and dancing and jumping about and the streets are packed with people in fancy dress, either prancing about or sitting all over motor-cars covered in a mass of streamers, confetti, etc.'

Their next destination was Buenos Aires, which they reached after a bumpy journey by air. Here they collected Rosa, an Argentine maid, who was sternly determined to do things her way, and since neither Edwina nor Marjorie could understand one word she said, she managed to impose her will on them. Here, too, there were many invitations, and Marjorie, by now somewhat exhausted by Edwina's vitality, records a visit to a

working-people's club 'built entirely out of money from un-
claimed prizes in the weekly lotteries. There are some 20,000
members, who pay five pesos a month, for which they are
provided with everything the heart can desire, riding school,
swimming bath, net-ball fields, and a club house which is even
supplied with a special passage in which young ladies and
gentlemen can sit together undisturbed, the nurseries being
rather appropriately at the end of the passage.'

They were driven out to an *estancia* belonging to a family 'in
whom the herd instinct seemed to be very strongly developed,
all the various members of the family having built themselves
houses close together on the same estate, French chateaux,
colonial houses and various other styles hobnobbing together
in the most friendly fashion. We were then received by the
Patriarch and several other members of the family, the genea-
logical tree of which I found it quite impossible to unravel.
Needless to say, by the end of tea Edwina and the Patriarch
were as one and he was reciting Shakespeare to her.'

The highlight of the journey was their trip across the
Andes.

'Our luggage, consisting of a brown canvas bag, a blue
leather cushion, and containing a spare pair of jodhpurs
each and lots of woollies and other odds and ends, was finally
taken ashore, as well as our sleeping bags. Next our food
was packed, consisting of a large piece of raw meat and lots
of bread. We had proudly refused to take a tent, which
was lucky, as the pack-horses were already overloaded.
Finally, everything was ready, and we mounted our steeds,
nobly attired in borrowed "chaps", hundreds of woollies
and leather coats with large knives stuck through our belts.
What clothes we could not get on our bodies or force into
our bags were tied or hung all over our saddles, as also were
handbags, cameras, etc., the nett result being a close resemblance to a party of travelling tinkers.'

Their guide was a Mr. K—— 'whose only fault appeared to
be a complete lack of interest in the fact that we were trying
to follow him.' They climbed steadily the whole morning,
and at about one o'clock emerged from the forest and came out
on to a completely bare, rather volcanic part of the mountain,

quite near the snow-line. They were allowed to stop for a hurried lunch, and then plodded steadily on. Soon they were caught in drenching rain, which did not let up all afternoon and all night. At about five o'clock, in the streaming rain, their eyes lit on a small white object which, as they approached, proved to be a tent belonging to the police, but which, fortunately for the travellers, was unoccupied by its owners. It was small and disreputable, with leaks everywhere, but to the drenched and frozen Edwina and Marjorie it looked a haven of refuge. It was too wet to light a fire and in the hustle of the departure alcoholic refreshment had been overlooked. The tent measured 8 feet by 6 feet, and once the packhorses had been relieved of their burden and the guide and his dog had installed themselves there was little room to move about. However, Edwina and Marjorie curled themselves up in their sleeping-bags and despite mutterings about bandits from Mr. K—— they slept soundly. The next morning they were off to an early start. It was still too wet to try and light a fire: 'We breakfasted off some bread and butter, and at about 8 a.m., the pack horses being loaded, K—— set off at high speed, regardless of the fact that we were not yet mounted and that the packhorses had either not observed, or ignored, his departure.' They rode throughout the morning through bamboo forests, descending through them and through miles of deep, squelchy mud almost up to the horses' bellies: 'Altogether the riding was pretty rough, as there were some very nasty roots of trees, rocks and fallen trees, and some pretty steep places, and this mud over everything.'

The journey ended at Puyehue, where they found a magnificent-looking hotel. Having demanded two bedrooms with bathrooms, they were told that there were no bathrooms, and that if they wanted baths they would have to go to the hot sulphur baths which were outside in the garden. Undismayed, they tramped off in the dark, carrying their spare jodhpurs and sponge bags, and after some five minutes' walk reached a long, tumble-down shed, where, by the light of guttering candles, an attendant prepared their baths.

On the following day they bade a tender farewell to their guide and crossed Lake Puyehue in an ancient Chris Craft with a defective clutch. Their next stop was Santiago, from whence they flew to Antofagasta: 'Rather a sad town, having once been extremely prosperous, but now practically bankrupt owing to the invention of synthetic nitrate, and with no prospect of ever returning to prosperity.'

In the train on the way to La Paz in Bolivia they awoke to the unpleasant sensation of 'mountain sickness':

'The train having climbed from sea level to 14,000 feet during the night, our heads felt as though they would burst, and we felt sick and faint and short of breath. Edwina bravely got up and dressed and consequently collapsed periodically. . . . The scenery, however, was quite magnificent and the Bolivian national costume very picturesque and colourful, the women wearing very full coloured skirts and different coloured ponchos and sweet little pork-pie hats made of felt or white straw, and firmly anchored to their heads. The llamas and the little mud villages also helped to add local colour. The first view of La Paz, about an hour before one arrives and from approximately 1,000 feet above, is wonderful. You see the town in the valley below, surrounded by marvellous coloured mountains of very curious formation with the snow-capped Ilimani (the mountain worshipped by the Indians) as a background and the thing you particularly notice is the bright, bright green of the grass.'

At La Paz they went to an hotel with the resounding name of Hotel de Paris. Though it was clean and comfortable, it was entirely devoid of hot water. The next morning Marjorie and Edwina were awakened by the sound of rifle-fire:

'We immediately concluded that a revolution had started. However, the waiter informed us that it was only manœuvres, only to reinform us a few minutes later that it really was a revolution after all and that, by great good fortune the centre of fighting was a little lower down the street which passed our windows and was plainly visible from the balconies. My efforts at photographing the scene were very badly received by the soldiery below who eventually levelled their rifles at us and caused us to retire hastily. A detachment then appeared to demand my film, but having fortunately foreseen this eventuality, the camera was by then loaded with a dud film, which I had much pleasure in presenting to them. After this we thought it was safe to reappear on the balcony, minus camera, but while we were explaining this to one of the soldiers who appeared to resent our presence, another one had a pot shot at us, so after that we gave up watching, except for an occasional serpentine sortie to the balcony. The entire hotel being barricaded up it was impossible to get out and we had to lunch at home.'

The 'revolution' ended early in the afternoon. There were twelve killed. The affray had been supported by the cadets of the Military College, incited by two officers, supposed to be from the Chaco, where Bolivia was waging a fierce and unsatisfactory war against Paraguay.

Having bought many vicuna rugs Edwina and Marjorie moved on to Cuzco to visit the Inca remains:

'With considerable trouble we got inside the Monastery of San Domingo, women not being allowed in, and here we were escorted round by a very nice monk. Part of the Monastery is built on top of the old Inca Temple of the Sun, one of the finest bits of Inca masonry left.'

For the next few days the travellers visited other villages and other Inca ruins, the most interesting of which were the ruins of Macchu Pichu, though Marjorie, after some hard climbing, remarked thoughtfully that she very much deplored the Incas' passion for emulating the habits of the mountain goat and placing all their buildings on the highest and most inaccessible peaks.

Mid-April found the indefatigable couple at Yucatan in Mexico, where they made a comprehensive tour of the Mayan Chichen Itza ruins. In the Temple of Warriors they encountered two ladies, one of whom Marjorie recognized as being Katherine Hepburn. The return journey was made via Cuba and Havana, where they had 'an exquisite lunch mainly off Morro crab'. When they reached Miami, Edwina, always interested in statistics, reckoned that they had covered 5,771 miles in the air up the west coast of South America, across Central America from Merida to Miami, and about 1,500 miles down the east coast from Rio to Buenos Aires, making a total of 7,271 miles in all. This was virtually the end of the trip, for they spent a few days in New York and then went by ship to Naples. Here Edwina disembarked to join Dickie at Malta, and Marjorie sadly recorded a last note in her diary: 'We said goodbye, having spent practically four months together and enjoyed every moment of it. I have never enjoyed a trip more and for variety of entertainment, surroundings and people, it will take a lot of beating.'

CHAPTER VIII

PENT HOUSE IN PARK LANE

Edwina's return to Malta coincided with the Abyssinian crisis when the island, anticipating the Sanctions which never came, was turned into a fortress. Everyone was mobilized, and listeners in Malta were intrigued to hear the voice of a new woman announcer broadcasting the news relays from Britain. In due course it was discovered that the new announcer was Edwina. The Navy, which at that time was responsible for the long- and short-wave broadcasting from Malta, had asked Edwina whether she would take over from a naval officer who was urgently required for special duties. This venture lasted four months, during which time Edwina worked conscientiously and well, and when finally she was released, she missed the discipline and sense of fulfilment which having a job gave her.

Once again she returned to her normal life. Besides her many social activities she was busy planning the details of their future London home in the block of flats in Park Lane, now in the course of construction. She was seen at Cannes, which that year had gathered together a coterie of visitors who might have emerged from the pages of *The Green Hat*. Indeed, the Armenian writer Michael Arlen was there, with his wife, observing Lord Portarlington in his brand-new Rolls Royce panelled in wood; Mrs. Simon Marks in dashing white linen trousers, and Maxine Elliott, that perfect hostess, entertaining her friends at the Chateau de l'Horizon near Juan les Pins.

Dickie was doing extremely well. He had turned his 'V and W' class destroyer H.M.S. *Wishart* into the most efficient ship in the Mediterranean Fleet. When Dickie arrived in Singapore in her, he was met by Edwina, who was on the first leg of the journey which would later take her from the Far East to Australia and Sydney. Her travelling companion was an endearing young female honey-bear named Rastus, which she presented to Dickie's ship. By the time *Wishart* had returned to Malta, Edwina was there to greet Dickie. She arrived triumphant, if exhausted, after a flight, as one of the first passengers, in one of the first commercial planes to fly from Sydney to London.

In 1936 Dickie was given a staff appointment in the Naval Air Division of the Admiralty in London. With a feeling of sincere regret at leaving Malta, which for so long had been their headquarters, the Mountbattens saw to the transfer of their possessions. Their farewell party is still remembered. In all the years they had lived there, their entertaining had been on a moderate scale, befitting Dickie's junior rank, but on this occasion they did things in the grand manner. Three hundred guests invited to the Polo Club danced to the music of two alternate bands. There were cabaret turns and a surprise finale, with Fred Astaire and Ginger Rogers dancing on a cinema screen at one end of the ballroom. The ball was the close of a chapter of warmth, work, and friendliness in the lives of the Mountbattens, and much would happen to them before they returned again to live on the ancient island.

.   .   .

On the site of what had once been Brook House now rose a tall block of flats topped by England's first penthouse. Eighty feet above Park Lane, the west windows overlooked a view of unparalleled magnificence, while from the dining-room the spires of two churches were the only landmarks visible above the trees of Hyde Park and Kensington Gardens. The rent of this thirty-room apartment was £4,200 a year.

Dickie and Edwina had always been impressed with the American type of penthouse and they had wanted a 'streamlined' apartment which would be vast without being cumbersome. Much thought and care had been given to the arrangement of the two floors which they were to occupy. The five reception-rooms had been designed with soundproof partitions which, when they were rolled into the main walls, formed a ballroom or a cinema capable of seating 150 people.

The upper floor was reserved for two master suites with guest-rooms and bathrooms. On the lower floor were the nursery wing, complete with kitchen, the servants' quarters, long gallery, and reception-rooms. Each of these rooms was decorated to set off the superb furniture, pictures, and bibelots

Edwina had inherited from her grandfather. The interior decoration had been carried out by Mrs. Joshua Cosden, who ably interpreted Edwina's very definite ideas on colour and decoration. Here, as in every home in which the Mountbattens lived, was the clash and mingling of their vivid personalities. Edwina's bedroom and sitting-room were cool and feminine and reflected her pleasure in lovely objects, and here, as always, were flowers and books and photographs of the children and Dickie. Dickie's quarters had the austerity of a cruiser's cabin, though curtains and covers were in the orange shade he liked. Here, too, were many photographs of Edwina, the children, his family, friends, ships and polo ponies, and small souvenirs collected through the years. Few of these had any intrinsic value, but all had some sentimental appeal to their owner, and in these rooms too, as in all those occupied by Dickie, were a variety of gadgets, some of which worked smoothly, and many of which reserved sharp surprises for their inventor.

Other tenants occupied this luxury block, among them Gordon Selfridge. From his back windows he could virtually overlook the famous departmental store he had founded. But the Mountbatten penthouse was as secluded as a town house. A private lift separated it from the other flats in the building. This lift ascended from a private entrance in Brook Street. No one could open the doors to leave the lift at the end of its swift journey unless, from ground level, he had previously telephoned the butler. Once the call had been received he walked to a particular spot in the reception hall and there, actuated by his weight, was a floor-switch which allowed the lift doors to open. The family, of course, had special keys which admitted them and their servants more informally to the penthouse.

As was to be expected, distorted descriptions of the fabulous Mountbatten penthouse were legion and there was great surmise and angling for invitations. A ride in the spectacular lift—four seconds from ground level to seventh floor—became a popular occupation, and even Queen Mary's interest was aroused in this new-fangled contraption. Dickie greeted Her Majesty at the Brook Street entrance, and explaining that the lift was as safe as a rocking-chair, escorted her into it. Before

he had time to press the button to take them skywards, the
lift rocketed up to the eighth floor, the lift doors flashed apart,
and an open-mouthed workman, busy on last-minute adjust-
ments, stared horror-stricken at the unmistakable toque and
well-known features of the stately Queen.   Closing his eyes,
he pressed another button and the lift shot promptly down to
the ground floor.   Not the least whit disturbed, Her Majesty
remarked that she hoped the next ascent would result in longed-
for tea.

The penthouse symbolized all that the Mountbattens seemed
to stand for at this stage in their lives: a glittering film set in
which to entertain, a millionaire's fantasy filled with gadgets
devised to make living easier and faster.   Their wealth, voyages, motor-boats, yacht, and luxury automobiles were a part
of the glamorous if not authentic legend which made grey-
beards nod sage heads and murmur of the follies of youth.
But it was felt that these diversions were incidental and that
inevitably the wiser counsels of maturity would prevail.   In
so thinking, they underestimated the intelligence of two people
whose mental growth and development had been so rapid that
already it had passed the stage of finding in conventional
friends and the social circle to which they had been born sufficient stimulus for their pulsating curiosity and interest in
humanity.   Superficially they continued as they had begun.
They were part of what *The Times* had called 'an exotic society',
for its leader, the Prince of Wales, had gathered about him an
entourage which was largely American or Anglo-American.
The Mountbattens continued to entertain the Fort Belvedere
set and to be entertained by the Prince of Wales, and their
parties were attended by men and women from the worlds of
music, art, and letters, and, more singular still, by politicians
who at first must have been slightly bemused at finding themselves welcome in a Tory household.   Contact and discussion
with people of different political thought and background, but
with acute and trained minds, shattered the gates of the ivory
tower in which Edwina had lived for so long.   The words 'the
people', which until then had had a very restricted meaning,
now took on a human significance for her which would finally
guide her to try to identify herself with them and their problems.   But the first efforts towards this comprehension were

fumbling and expressed by parties which were intended to foster the new spirit of democracy in the penthouse. Beer replaced champagne, kippers and fried sausages supplanted
caviare and smoked salmon. Royalty sat on the floor while
new-found friends from the East who distrusted the intensity
of such a *volte face* squatted, their faces inscrutable amid the
wreathing cigarette smoke.

The penthouse was a beautiful toy, but Edwina did not much
believe in it, or in herself while she inhabited it, and one night,
when the last load of guests had departed, leaving behind them
the debris of a successful party, she fled in search of the atlas
which always, all her life, has lain on her bedside table, and,
opening it, she found she was looking at the pear-shaped bulge
of Africa. And somewhere in her mind was the memory of
her soldier father's description of the immensities of the veld,
and of camp-fires and of stars that burned bright and large in
the African sky.

CHAPTER IX

LAND IN THE SUN

AN ALBUM filled with photographs records this African journey. Records it in subdued black and white that cannot do justice to the colour which flames in this sun-drenched continent. Here all was immensity under a sky of intense and luminous blue.

In the Highlands of Kenya, Edwina was welcomed by old friends who had made this new land their home. With them she went on safari, getting up long before dawn, and driving into the still and dangerous night. And with the rising of the sun she looked on a world that seemed newborn, primeval, and unreal. As the sun rose she watched the game performing the opening of the ballet of their day; across the honey-coloured plain streamed the zebra, and, dancing in their wake, the tiny reedbuck, duiker, and dik-dik, and then, heraldic, across the skyline, the impala, their horns spiralling into the still air.

Here all was new, and the scent of the morning was potent and exhilarating. There was endless motoring along non-existent roads, an encounter with a python which slithered across the path of the car, and an unforgettable journey across a river with the African ferrymen solemnly chanting. There was red dust and more red dust. There was an interlude with a family who numbered among their pets a kindergarten of young chimpanzees, all of whom partook affably of tea and sandwiches neatly laid on a table built for their own convenience.

Edwina longed to own a chimpanzee or a baby elephant or even an Okapi, a specimen of which rare animal she photographed soon after its capture. The Belgian Congo, with its unique volcanic mountains and vast lakes, fascinated Edwina and her companions, who next travelled through the dense Ituri forests, being plunged into almost perpetual darkness. Here and there they came upon clearings inhabited by pygmies who lived in bamboo huts. Their chief encounters were with monkeys, gorillas, and chimpanzees. In the course of their wanderings they met another intrepid traveller, the writer Rosita Forbes, with whom they camped one night 'sitting on skin rugs and talking unceasingly'.[1]

There was much to remember: the white teeth and gleaming skins of African girls laughing in the sun as they bathed in a river; African markets; a Zulu war-dance with the warriors, shield and assegai upraised, leaping high into the air. Edwina visited Johannesburg and Kimberley, where she saw the famous diamond mines and an impressive array of de Beers diamonds; and in the Sabi Game Reserve she fell in love. The object of her passion was a lion cub, a honey-blonde bundle of fur and muscle. Sabi was given to her, and from then on he never left her side. In a short time he became a seasoned traveller, sitting happily in truck or car and taking a keen interest in the landscape. As long as Edwina remained in the wilds, her cub was no problem, but the moment she returned to civilization and her first port of call after acquiring Sabi was Cape Town, she found that few people shared her enthusiasm for living at close quarters with a rapidly growing lion cub. Hoteliers, particularly, were unreasonable, and after meeting with a number of determined refusals to house her with her 'baby' she finally found a hotel proprietor who, moved by her plight, allowed her to stay, providing she occupied an attic room and never left Sabi alone in it. Certain hostesses in Cape Town still remember welcoming a distinguished guest to drinks, a slim, tanned, and beautiful guest accompanied by a decorous and enchanting lion cub.

After the vast and arid veld Edwina found the green-and-purple beauty of the Cape Province refreshing. Here there were vineyards and white gabled homesteads set among ancient oaks planted by the early settlers. But, much as she would have liked to linger, she had one more journey to make, and early one morning she left the Cape for Southern Rhodesia and the Great Zimbabwe.

These impressive ruins are cloaked in mystery. When was Zimbabwe built? and by whom? For several generations these ruins have been the subject of intense and passionate

---

[1] *Appointment in the Sun*, by Rosita Forbes (Cassell).

controversy among archaeologists, and even today no solution is universally accepted.   It has been suggested that this ancient gold-field was the destination of the Phoenicians sent by King Solomon, according to the Hebrew Chronicles, to bring gold and other products from some distant land.   The Biblical 'Ophir' may have been the modern port of Sofala, while 'Haviliah' is none other than Mashonaland.

Savants affirm that Zimbabwe was built as early as the tenth century B.C.   Some maintain that it was the work of ancient Sabaeans from Arabia Felix, and support this claim by pointing out that counterparts can be found in ancient Arabic for the conical towers, soapstone birds, and chevron pattern seen at Zimbabwe.   Others passionately insist that Zimbabwe was built by the Dravidians from India.   Edwina, standing among the remains of a temple fortress, felt suddenly engulfed by the chill wave of an ancient and brooding evil.

.   .   .

Dickie, meeting her at the airport on her return home, viewed her companion with some misgiving.   'How,' he asked, 'are you going to get through life with a lion?'   'I'm sure he'll adapt himself,' replied Edwina, as Sabi climbed gracefully and unconcernedly into the car.   The lion soon made himself at home at Adsdean.   For the first seven months after his arrival he slept on Edwina and Dickie's bed.   After that his weight induced nightmares or insomnia.   He was then relegated to a loose box.   The Sealyhams at first were suspicious of the large cat, but finally accepted his presence, and while they were careful not to get too close to his paws, they showed no fear of him.   Sabi took a keen interest in sport, and when Edwina went round the golf course he padded along behind her.   He particularly enjoyed watching golf and croquet, and when a match was in progress he would lie yawning benevolently at Edwina's feet.   As he grew to maturity, Edwina noticed that her visiting list was becoming shorter.   Old friends who had been used to dropping in now first telephoned to inquire about Sabi's health and growth, and when they heard that he was larger and healthier than ever, they faded away with murmured excuses.   Finally it became obvious that to prevent any accident Sabi must be sent away.   Reluctantly Edwina consented to be parted from her lion, and after pathetic

farewells he was transported to a 'very private' zoo. Edwina
was disconsolate about Sabi, and when she heard that he was
listless and pining, she sent for him at once.

He returned triumphantly to Adsdean, where he remained
until the war, when his feeding—he ate half an ox a week—
became a major problem. He was then sent to a sailors' zoo,
where, unable to stand captivity, he again pined, and Edwina
decided the only solution was to put him to sleep. Of all
Edwina's exotic pets, Sabi was the best loved, and a photograph
of the topaz-eyed, tawny African lion cub stands always on
her dressing-table.

.   .   .

Early in 1939 Edwina started on the last of her long pre-war
voyages into the blue. Her destination was South-East Asia.
Her plan had been to visit the Spice Islands, but finding that
this presented great difficulties at this time, she decided to
make the journey to China by way of the newly opened Burma
Road. In view of her future activities in Burma, this difficult
and dangerous journey was to give her invaluable information.

From Sumatra she flew to Rangoon to make arrangements
for the trip. In a letter she writes:

'We flew up to Rangoon to try and fix it up and found it
all very complicated as it transpired that one had to take
everything with one, beds, bedding, food, petrol, in fact the
complete outfit, and the only feasible way was to go by
lorry. Also, that nothing could be fixed there as the only
available lorries, if any, would be in Lashio in the Northern
Shan States, Lashio being the starting depot for the Arms
Transport up the new road into China. English lorries
under contract to the Chinese Government operate up to the
frontier and the South Western Transport (Chinese) take
them on to Kumming.'

The Burma Road was begun during the 'China Incident',
when Japan had attacked China. At that time Burma had no
railway nearer than 100 miles from China, and no railroad
connected her with Siam or India. In order to reach south-
western China without going via Malaya, a road through
Burma was essential.

Despite a certain amount of derision, the Chinese started on their Herculean task. From Lashio to the frontier is 125 miles, and over the border lay another 770 miles, besides a good deal of rough track north of Yunnan. The terrain was appalling, the weather treacherous, and the rain caused land-slides. Undefeated by the elements, the coolies toiled on and on, scraping the earth away with their bare hands, installing stone gutters and culverts to drain away the pitiless rain. Men, women, and children laboured on, and slowly and surely the arterial road which was to carry China's life-line neared completion.

In December 1938 the road—the most tortuous and perilous mountain highway in the world—was opened to traffic: to light traffic only, for the work continued unceasingly and the surface could not have borne great loads.

Edwina and her companions proceeded by train and car as far as Lashio to arrange for transport. She was told that a light lorry was the only practical conveyance, as a touring car might or might not get through, and in any case a touring car could not carry sufficient petrol and supplies. So she procured a ramshackle lorry together with a 'boy' to cook, interpret, and look after stores. This was necessary, as the driver would be fully occupied in negotiating hairpin bends and in trying to keep the car on the road. A special pass (important if one did not wish to land in gaol) was obtained from the Chinese Government. Supplies were collected in Rangoon. These included lamps (no lights after Lashio), biscuits (no bread was to be had except at Chefung, and then not always), water-filters, toilet-paper, thick coats, blankets, and cigars and cigarettes as gifts in return for hospitality.

With the lorry well supplied with petrol, Edwina and her companions set off on their journey.

'The journey [she wrote afterwards] was fascinating and I wouldn't have missed it for the world. We took seven days; it can be done in less but we took an extra day and went about 90 miles out of our way to see the new American Aeroplane Factory under construction just over the Chinese–Burma border but not on the main road. . . . The Burma Road is a most marvellous feat of engineering and the scenery is magnificent. The surface is very bad on the whole and some bits were appalling, not more than 10 to 15 m.p.h. being possible for hours on end, bottom gear being used for long stretches. The roads were narrow, one way traffic with hairpin turns and sheer drops of 4,000 to 5,000 feet below with no protection of any kind up and down mountain ranges, the road winding as high as about 8,500 feet. The traffic was erratic. One day one might meet with convoys of 30 to 50 lorries, and on the next nothing except mule caravans and road workers.

'The first 300 miles took us twice as long as the second. The life of a lorry on this road is very short—sometimes a few months (we arrived with 3 springs broken out of 4 and the car literally in pieces). But it [the Road] is a magnificent achievement. They must have about 70,000 Chinese coolies, men, women and children, boys and girls, working on a stretch of road about 200 miles in length, small tots of not more than 5 or 6, girls and boys; all the women with their feet bound (all have this in the interior still, and still practice it on babies in defiance of the law which now forbids it. But as it is the tradition they won't abandon it.) They draft men from the various villages for road work, some having to walk 50 miles across country, and their families come with them and work voluntarily. The men get just enough to feed themselves and their families, about 30 cents a day, but all seem quite contented and put heart and soul into the road work.

'The old walled towns one passes through are quite beautiful, both the people and the animals terrified of lorries, as, till this road was built, Yuncan was the most backward province of China with no communication other than mule-tracks, so they were completely cut off from the world. The people are very interesting. I should not think they have changed in their lives or customs for the last 5,000 years. Nothing but the most primitive wooden implements and even on the new road they use stone hand rollers, bamboo baskets for stone-carrying, and everything is done by hand labour. Most of the South-Western Transport bases are old converted temples. So one gets a funny impression with lorries lined up outside the Buddhas. Most beautiful flowers and trees all along the road, scarlet rhododendrons,

azaleas, cherry and wild anchusas and all kinds of flowering
trees like tulip trees and flame trees. At Yunnanfu the
most magnificent camellia trees everywhere. Beautiful
birds too, turquoise blue, kingfisher colour, and all singing
most sweetly.

'Yunnanfu is a seething mass of activity, having been a
small walled town of no importance before the war. Big
aerodromes, ceaseless flying, troops training, lorry drivers
being schooled, anti-aircraft guns around and holes by the
road as shelters. Factories are springing up and the town
is expanding all round. The scenery is superb, at 6,400
feet on a plateau and on an enormous lake surrounded by
mountains.

'We departed from Yunnanfu by the Eurasia Line (half
German, half Chinese concern) operated with very old Jun-
ker machines by German pilots and with all the blinds of
the machine pulled down. After hours of filling in countless
forms, luggage searchings, money inspection and utter chaos,
and military machines doing rather nervous terminal velocity
dives about us, we got off and had a good flight at 15,000
feet, to Hanoi, from whence we proceed to Saigon and where
I hope I will have more news of you all.'

At Saigon there was news, some of it extremely disquieting.
Edwina returned home as rapidly as possible to a Europe mias-
mic with rumours of war. Already the stench from the concentration camps in Germany had permeated abroad, and
though few were inclined to believe the stories of what was
happening behind the walls of Belsen and Dachau, some of the
Jews who had managed to flee from Germany were imploring
assistance, not for themselves, but for those who had remained
in Germany. Edwina was deeply concerned with the plight
of the Jews. She sent donations to various Anglo-Jewish funds,
but this, she felt, was not sufficient. In a letter to her father in
December 1938, she wrote:

'It is such a ghastly nightmare the Jewish question, but
I am glad to say that I have been able to help individuals as
well as sending donations. I have set up one man in London
and have sent one to America last week, but there is so little
one can do, it makes one despair.'

CHAPTER X

'PRO UTILITATE HOMINUM'

Some time before Munich, Edwina had begun her first-aid training. The classes took place in the penthouse in Brook Street. In this splendid décor the bald lectures on reviving the unconscious, dealing with the concussed, and the application of splints and tourniquets, sounded unreal. Some of the ladies of fashion present listened abstractedly, thinking that Edwina's passionate absorption in this new game was a bit overdone. 'Darling Edwina,' they said to one another, 'being so intense about rolling people up in miles of bandages and behaving as if bombs were dropping on our heads.'

The bombs were not yet dropping, but to Edwina had come a moment of unique clarity. The bombs would drop and then, for the first time in her life, she might be needed. She might be of use. Therefore she must prepare herself. She must be ready. She joined the newly formed W.V.S. Without regret she cut her social ties and worked at first aid, nursing, and civil defence. For six months she was an auxiliary nurse at the Westminster Hospital. She scrubbed floors, emptied bedpans, stood in operating theatres watching the skilled hands of surgeons cutting through the living flesh. She learned to dress hideous wounds and to smile reassuringly into the faces of the sick and the dying. She learned to discipline her own emotions and her own fatigue, and from her contact with disease and death was forged her mission. These sufferers were her responsibility, and for them and for people like them she would fight for the remainder of her life. They must be helped and protected and those who nursed them must be equally helped and protected. The shades of Elizabeth Fry and Florence Nightingale walked by her side in the wards at night, and each had some message, some word of warning which she was not yet ready to understand. . . . Once you have felt this compassion you may not fail. . . . If this is your path all else

must be banished. . . . There will be no time in your life
now for leisure. . . . Thus the voices. . . .

Before the war broke out Edwina left the W.V.S. and joined
the St. John Ambulance Brigade.   She had been a member of
the Order of St. John and interested in its wide field of work
since her marriage in 1922.   Thoughtfully she meditated on
some of the objects and purposes of the Order as defined in its
Statutes:

> 'The encouragement and promotion of all works of huma-
> nity and charity for the relief of persons in sickness, distress,
> suffering and danger, without distinction of race, class or
> creed, and the extension of the great principle of the Order,
> embodied in the motto "Pro utilitate hominum".'

'Pro utilitate hominum.' . . . This was to be her inspiration, and suddenly the past studded with glittering milestones
became reduced to another perspective, a landskip painted in
pastel colours under a fading sun.   But the past, too, had been
rich in experience, in fun, in shared laughter to disown completely.   Now the memories would remain untouched, caught
in the mind like flies in amber.   But there could be no return
to that past ever, ever again.   The death of her father earlier
in the year had severed one of the last links with her youth.
He had left her Broadlands, but it would be many years before
the Mountbattens would walk in peace under the ancient
trees.   The house became first a refuge for evacuees bombed
out of Southampton, and was then offered by Edwina as an
annexe to the Royal Southampton Hospital.   When converted
it provided up to eighty beds, with complete operating theatre
and other facilities.[1]

While Dickie, captain in command of a flotilla of destroyers,
patrolled the icy waters of the North Sea, Edwina organized
her new life.   She closed the penthouse, evacuated, with many
others, under the Government's private scheme, her two young
daughters to America, and went to stay with her mother-in-
law, the Dowager Marchioness of Milford Haven, who was
housed in Kensington Palace.   She was now free to give herself

---

[1] Lady Louis was made President of the Royal Southampton Hospital,
She was the first woman to hold that office in the hospital's two centuries of
history, and is now a patron.

entirely to her work. At first the principals of the organization she had joined looked with some suspicion upon this zealous new recruit. In their experience ladies of quality were generally content to be figure-heads, willing patronesses, but were not often anxious to give themselves entirely to voluntary work. It was not long, however, before they discovered that Edwina's enthusiasm was matched by ability of a high order. In 1940 she became a member of the Kensington Nursing Division of the St. John Organization and having passed the necessary examinations, was made an officer in the same unit.

Her rise was rapid. In March she became simultaneously President for London, Hampshire, and the Isle of Wight; by October she was in charge of all St. John personnel assisting in the London A.R.P. Services, where ambulance volunteers were staffing the shelters, the first-aid and medical posts, and the rest centres which had been organized to give temporary refuge to bombed-out families.

The long nightmare had begun. The blitz of 1940 was at first concentrated on London. Some 18,000 bombs were dropped on the metropolis during October and November of 1940 and the civilian population, deafened by the bombs, blinded by the smoke and seared by the flames, saw their homes turned to rubble and their families in hourly danger. Many of these people were used to hardship, to poverty, and to grief, but this was a trial which none of them in their darkest moments could have envisaged. Yet all of them, when the hour came, responded without hesitation to the call upon their courage and patriotism. Daily, in the face of almost insuperable obstacles, they struggled to carry on with calmness, good humour, and selfless devotion, and it was to these men and women of London town that Edwina came to give what help she could.

Night after night she visited the East End, and particularly Stepney, which had been savagely bombed. In Stepney she received her baptism of fire, and more, the answer to the question which for so long had tormented her. The glass walls of the fishtank which all her life had protected her against contact with the world of poverty, filth, and human suffering were shattered into a thousand bits. Stepney had shelters—thirty-four of them tunnels, vaults, basements, crypts of churches, in which during the raids the people of the borough took refuge, and each and every shelter was dank, damp, the walls crawling with vermin, while rats from the sewers scampered across the recumbent forms huddled in their blankets. The Divisional Superintendent, appalled at these conditions, had made urgent and repeated appeals to the M.O.H. for conditions to be improved, but his demands were ignored. Straight and slim in her dark uniform, Edwina moved among the stupefied people. Appalled by the conditions of these shelters, she sought immediately to remedy them. She was told that all official representations had been fruitless. 'Something will be done at once,' she said.

Edwina went straight to the Minister of Health. Almost immediately the benefits of her intervention were felt in the shelters of Stepney. Sanitary arrangements were made, ventilation was increased, the rats disappeared, benches were provided, and at the same time similar improvements were carried out in the shelters of other boroughs.

Edwina's nightly visits to the shelters did much to raise the morale of London's shelter population. Unimpressed and suspicious of those who came among them when no danger threatened, the sight of this great lady calmly walking in from an inferno of heat and dropping bombs gave them a feeling of security, and they loved her for her warmth, her compassion, and her tenderness.

She organized sing-songs. She brought encouraging and unofficial messages from the Queen. She brought distinguished men and women to help her entertain her friends. Old women sat sipping endless cups of hot, strong tea with her; matrons in curl-papers chatted to her of their sons and husbands.

Always she was cheerful, practical, and understanding of their personal problems. Her fearlessness in the face of danger was a perpetual worry to those who knew of her nightly tours through the blazing streets, but never then, nor at any time since, has she given the slightest indication of physical fear, which is not to say that she is not afraid. 'The greatest battles,' she says, 'are those one fights with oneself.'

If the Londoners were cheered by her never-failing interest in their welfare, she in her turn was astonished and delighted by her close contacts with real Londoners. These people did not seek her help because of her wealth or background. They came to her because of her inner strength and because they trusted her to carry out her promises. In that circle in which she had hitherto moved she had had little occasion to be part of the warm, pulsating human swarm and even if, at times, her fastidious upbringing revolted against certain squalid aspects of this communal life, the proud, loyal, and gay spirit which animated these Cockneys went straight to her heart.

Small incidents moved her and illuminated for her other aspects of human courage. There was the nurse who, one morning was late for duty. Nothing was said to her because she looked ill and tired. She did her full period of service for the day, and then only did Edwina learn that the nurse's home had received a direct hit during the night and that she had been buried in the ruins for six hours. She had been dug out just in time to go to her work.

There was the case of the two Cockney girls whom she met on their way to work after a bad raid. Fires were everywhere, the hoses playing on them. As the girls picked their way through the débris, one said to the other, 'You know, dearie, the trouble of all this is that you could so easily sprain your ankle.'

Among the examples of civilian morale which aroused Edwina's admiration was that of an elderly couple. They were over eighty, and their windows had been blown out by bombs. They refused, however, to forgo their weekly ride in the park in a victoria with a coachman at the reins. The only time the old lady was upset was when she was informed, after one of the worst air raids, that her carriage would have to take a different route, since there were so many bomb craters in the street.

On one occasion the bombs were falling fast as Edwina came upon a man stepping outside his front door with his dog. When she cautioned him to go back into his house, he retorted, 'Madam, I always exercise my dog at ten o'clock, and nothing on earth shall stop me.'

During this period of initiation Edwina was learning to organize her brain. Always adaptable, she had never had to cope with the daily emergencies which now beset her, for besides her personal visits, she had much to learn on the administrative side. Her reward came in the autumn of 1941, when she was made Deputy Superintendent-in-Chief of the Nursing Division of the St. John Ambulance Brigade. For the first time, perhaps, she began to understand something of the discipline which had governed Dickie's working life, and her rise, like his, was due as much to untiring effort, concentration, and her ability to choose able lieutenants.

Now, more than ever, she thought of him, viewing him no longer as the gay, amusing, debonair love and companion of her youth, but as a man of action, a sailor relentlessly pursuing a course which might well end in his death. And whereas before, the ease and smoothness of their life together had perhaps blunted the acuity of her feeling for him, and she had been inclined to take him for granted, the constant separations and imminence of danger made her realize how much she owed him. For it was he, vital, turbulent, reckless, and dedicated, who had, in fact, moulded her adult attitudes and reactions, and as the trappings of her former life were cast away, so did her respect, devotion, and love for him increase.

She could sympathize with the wives of the Fleet who waited endlessly for news, for letters, for a sign that all was well with their men, and her darkest hour was when she heard that *Kelly*, commanded by her husband, had been torpedoed in the North Sea. Finally, with other wives, she waited in the north-east coast port into which *Kelly* was brought, having been in tow for nearly four days. And Dickie was on the bridge, haggard, fighting-mad, but safe and well.

After several more encounters with the enemy, in the last of which Lord Louis lost his beloved *Kelly* off Crete, he was flown home and appointed in command of H.M.S. *Illustrious*, at that time undergoing repair at the United States Navy Yard, Norfolk, Virginia.

At this point Edwina was promoted Superintendent-in-Chief of the Brigade, and one of her first duties as a leading member of the Executive of the Joint War Organization committee of the British Red Cross Society and the Order of St. John was to undertake an extensive speaking tour in different parts of the United States. Her mission was to thank the American Red Cross British War Relief and other philanthropic bodies, as well as the American people as a whole, for their generosity in sending five million pounds' worth of medical supplies and

comforts to Britain in her hour of direst need.   As this was the
pre-Pearl Harbour period, the United States was not yet at
war.

Edwina had never spoken in public before, and the idea of
addressing packed audiences was extremely frightening.   She
therefore spent much time writing out a prototype speech which
she intended to read.   Rather diffidently she asked Dickie
whether he would hear her speech.   He listened to it with
interest, and when she had finished took the sheets of paper
from her.   With a grin, he tore them across.   'If you speak
from the heart, you won't need notes,' he said.

She and Dickie flew together to New York, where, after a
brief reunion with their daughters Patricia and Pamela, who
were attending Miss Hewitt's school, they separated, she to
begin her tour, he to take over *Illustrious*.

The glamorous Mountbattens were well known to the
American Press.   Some of them had interviewed Edwina on
former visits, and all of them had access to file copies of pre-war
interviews.   Nothing in the Mountbatten legend had prepared
them for the severely uniformed Englishwoman who bore
around her eyes the marks of fatigue, overwork, and suffering.
'Of medium height,' wrote one reporter, 'slender and blonde,
the woman who was once listed as one of the world's ten best
dressed women, wore the dark uniform of St. John's Ambulance
Brigade.'   'Her only colouring,' wrote another, 'was brilliant
lipstick and nail-polish, and she had only brought two small
bags.'

It was, therefore, on a note of almost grim austerity that
Edwina reached St. Louis, the first official stop on her tour of
the Midwest.

In two months she was to cover some 28,000 miles, and
wherever she appeared, the direct simplicity of her approach
and the sincere gratitude which animated her words endeared
her to her audiences.   Dickie's impromptu coaching had borne
fruit.   She spoke from the heart, and her audiences were
moved.   Her speeches were unadorned, but the men and
women who listened to this unvarnished prose learned how the
British hospital and A.R.P. and voluntary societies functioned,
what had become of the thousands of garments, dressings,
bandages, tons of food, and other comforts sent by them to

Britain, and they understood, as never before, what a solace their gifts and supplies had given to the suffering and bombed-out population of Britain. By the time the tour was over there was little doubt in the minds of those who had listened to Edwina's speeches of Britain's need of supplies and gratitude to those who had sent them.

The daily itinerary afforded Edwina little leisure, for apart from meetings she visited the British War Relief and Red Cross Headquarters in each city she visited. Her schedule in St. Louis required a page and a half of closely written material. As always, she drove herself unsparingly, and as the weeks passed so did her fatigue increase. There were dawns when, on awakening, she wondered where she was; nights when she could not sleep and a great blurr of expectant faces peered at her from the gloom. Yet each morning found her trim and poised, ready for yet another day.

On one or two occasions she passed through cities in which old friends lived, and time was found to drink or dine with them. But, fundamentally, she was impatient of everything that was not directly concerned with her task, and she had little time or patience to waste on purely social activities.

By October, Edwina had terminated her American tour. Her final mission, before returning home, was a tour of Canada, where she made close contacts with the Canadian St. John as well as the Canadian Red Cross. Here, as in the States, she visited the principal cities, speaking to packed audiences. Among these audiences were women who, living far afield having no domestic help, prepared their husband's meal, popped it in the oven, and sallied forth to honour the English visitor. Most of the luncheons followed an identical pattern and took twenty-two minutes flat to consume. Fruit cocktail was followed by individual chicken pot-pies and ended with ice cream à la mode. The royal toast was drunk with fervour and loyalty—in water.

Edwina arrived in Montreal by train after her plane from Winnipeg was grounded in Toronto. Here she attended a dinner given in her honour by the Quebec Provincial Council St. John Ambulance Association at the Mount Royal Hotel. The day was Friday, November 14th, and a special dispensation had to be obtained from the Archbishopric to enable the guests to do justice to a banquet which starred 'Tournedos aux Champignons, Sauce Bearnaise' on its menu. After dinner Edwina read a message from the Queen, and having made a brief speech, repeated it, to the pleasure of the guests, in French. After which, unhurried, smiling, and completely exhausted, she prepared to go off to inspect the St. John Ambulance Brigade, Montreal Corps.

In the meantime, at the invitation of Admiral Stark, United States Chief of Naval Staff, Lord Louis had flown to Pearl Harbour to inspect the naval installations, with the eye of a commanding officer with considerable battle experience. His visit was brought to a precipitate close by a 'most immediate' signal from the Admiralty cancelling his command of *Illustrious* and directing him to return forthwith to London to take up an appointment, the nature of which was secret. Phase two of his meteoric career was now about to begin.

In New York, on the eve of her return to Britain, Edwina was interviewed by the Press. 'In the eighteen cities I visited from coast to coast,' she said, 'I found the audiences at the Red Cross Chapters most responsive. There was no need of any appeal, and I did not think it necessary. I just wanted to thank the people for the help we couldn't have done without.'

CHAPTER XI

CHESTER STREET

Edwina RETURNED to London to find that her husband had been appointed as Chief of Combined Operations, a complicated and unorthodox organization fathered by Churchill. Mountbatten was faced with the task of welding this unwieldy machine into a smooth-running composite fighting force. Tact was needed, initiative, energy, vitality, and imagination. The new Chief of Combined Operations had all these qualities and was, as well, able to work harder than anyone on his staff.

The Mountbattens had rented a small house in Chester Street, and though for the first time in some years he was constantly ashore, they did not in fact see much of one another. Lord Louis' day began at 7.30, and though he tried to get home for dinner at eight, he was generally out again by ten o'clock attending various meetings. On the rare occasions when no meeting was called he worked at home. His Sundays were spent inspecting establishments such as the Commando schools situated along the coast or in visiting various experimental stations.

Edwina's heavy responsibilities for St. John as well as joint St. John and Red Cross activities kept her strenuously occupied. The success of her speaking tour in the United States had given her confidence as a public speaker, and she was now less nervous when faced with the ordeal of addressing meetings, which she was called upon to do constantly at this time. In Winchester she made an appeal for funds for the Toc H war work; in Glasgow she visited the Flying Angel Missions to Seamen; she spoke at the opening of a Prisoners of War Week in Holborn. At this luncheon Edwina spoke of her two heroes, Admiral Sir Philip Vian and her husband. In Hull she attended Red Cross 'Penny a Week' Rally Week and took the inspection of the Lady Corps Officers of the Hull Nursing Corps, St. John Ambulance Brigade. Tirelessly she toured the country, launching campaigns, and making appeals and attending, as well, to her major work, which was the organizing and training of welfare nursing teams now being prepared for D-Day.

Her critics of the early days of the war still continued their insidious campaign, 'She really is taking things too seriously. Darling, she's not nearly as amusing as she was, and she *looks* so tired. All that rushing about can't be good for one, and surely she must have time for a facial . . .' There was no time for a facial, or for any other kind of beauty treatment. At the best of times Edwina had had little belief in the jars of unguents which decorated the dressing-tables of most women; now she carried things to extremes. She never looked in the mirror at all, and on the rare occasions when there was a moment to 'put her feet up' she reached for her files and folders. The house in Chester Street was not large, there were four bedrooms and the staff consisted of Mrs. Cable, the cook, Jessie, Edwina's old maid-housemaid who had been with her family since she was a child, and a valet. Any kind of dinner-party, no matter how small, taxed the ingenuity of the servants, so exiguous was the dining-room. This was indeed a far cry from the spaciousness of the penthouse, but certainly neither Dickie nor Edwina wasted any time in regretting the vanished pomps of yesteryear. To them, to Edwina particularly, a desire for achievement had replaced the nebulous longings which for so long had haunted her. The past and the future had ceased to exist. *Now* was the hour.

Day after day the Mountbattens carried on with their appointed tasks, and though they saw little of one another the bond between them was strengthened as never before by the common aim which drove each in turn to continue working, long after common sense should have imposed a veto on their activities. Both were upheld by tremendous reserves of nervous energy whose manifestations left their entourage spent and panting, and, at times, thoroughly irritable at the pace set by the Mountbattens. But the work was done and the desired object achieved, no matter what the cost to themselves.

In 1942 Edwina was promoted Superintendent-in-Chief of St. John Ambulance Brigade. She was now in charge of 50,000 women of St. John Nursing Divisions, and of 10,000 nursing cadets.

I

Her work became ever more exacting. No longer a novice, her standards became increasingly high. Like her husband she had a passion for detail, and refused to be fobbed off with seemingly perfect façades. If during her inspections she suspected that she was being sidetracked, she was quite capable of taking matters into her own hands and quietly disappearing behind the scenes to pursue her own investigations. Like Florence Nightingale, she intended having her own way, particularly when it involved the welfare of the thousands of women for whom she was responsible. Withal she did not allow herself to become too intense about her mission, and her sense of humour saved her from becoming ruthlessly despotic. She had always had the saving grace of being able to laugh at herself.

It was at the fountain of the family circle that she found mental refreshment and relaxation. The house was filled with youth. Patricia was attractive and deservedly popular; Pammie had her own circle of juvenile friends, and from time to time Prince Philip, splendidly bearded, dashed in to tease the girls, to smoke his aunt's cigarettes, and to be pampered by the Chester Street staff, who adored him.

Both Edwina and Lord Louis were present at the première of Noël Coward's film, *In Which We Serve*. Indeed, the story of this film was obviously inspired by the exploits of Lord Louis' destroyer *Kelly*, and for both the Mountbattens this was a film which brought back many memories.

Though the Mountbattens were not, strictly speaking, patrons of the arts, and their salon in earlier years had been eclectic, Edwina was interested in all artistic manifestations and made many enduring friendships with famous writers, artists, poets, playwrights, musicians, and composers. Music was her particular passion. Herself a pianist of no mean stature, she found in music a complete relaxation and liberation. Her tastes were classical: modern music, though it held little charm for her, interested her, and she was progressive enough to explore it through the recordings and concerts of modern pianists. Among her intimate friends in the musical world were Yehudi Menuhin, Malcolm Sargent, and the brilliant Irving Berlin. Thus it was Edwina's pleasure as co-chairman of the British Service Charities Committee to announce after the first night of the United States Army all-soldier show at the Palladium, that Irving Berlin had presented the charity with the British copyright, ownership, and royalties of his song 'My British Buddy'. Irving Berlin introduced the song for the first time on the opening night of the show at the Palladium, to an audience which included Queen Elizabeth (now the Queen Mother), King George VI, and the young Princesses, Elizabeth and Margaret.

Opening a newspaper which contained the 1942 New Year's Honours List, Edwina saw that she had been awarded the C.B.E. for her valuable services to civil defence. For a long time she sat looking at her name and then, suddenly, it dawned on her. Like any soldier or sailor on active service, she had earned her medal.

On February 3rd, escorted by Lord Louis, she went to Buckingham Palace to receive the C.B.E. from the hands of her King. An hour later the Mountbattens were met by a battery of camera-men. Looking at the five rows of medal ribbons on her husband's tunic, Edwina held up the case containing the medal and exclaimed to Dickie, 'For the first time, it's me!' Her medal was a record of personal achievement, something she had done herself not as the granddaughter of a millionaire, not as the wife of a distinguished man, but as Edwina. For the first time she had vindicated herself in her own eyes.

In the autumn of 1943 Lord Louis took up his new appointment, as Supreme Allied Commander South-East Asia, and Edwina had, once more, to face a long separation from her husband. She had little time to brood, however, for events were moving rapidly with the turn of the tide, and she was deeply involved with her work, which had become as intricate as a jigsaw puzzle. Each piece, such as co-operation with U.N.R.R.A. and arrangements for the care of Allied prisoners of war after their liberation from the Germans, had to be carefully dove-tailed.

Moments of respite were rare, but whenever it was possible Edwina rushed down to Broadlands, where occasionally she and her two daughters could enjoy a few days together. Patricia, now a rating in the W.R.N.S., was based on the South Coast and was specializing in signals. Pamela was still at school.   An enthusiastic Girl Guide, she maintained a friendly rivalry in camping lore with Princess Margaret.

The major portion of Broadlands had been skilfully converted into an annex of the Royal South Hants and Southampton Hospital, and the Mountbattens had retained for their own use a suite composed of a small dining-room, four family bed-rooms, and one guest-room.   Since the gardens were now devoted to vegetable-growing there was seldom more than a posy in her bedroom, though a large, white-painted box con-taining ferns, standing at the foot of her bed, refreshed her tired eyes when she was on leave at home.   Dickie's room was closed, but often in his letters he referred anxiously to his treasures, models, paintings, and photographs, all of which Edwina was able to assure him were in perfect condition.   He was greatly interested too in the welfare of his horses, and on inquiring about a favourite mount received a reassuring letter from Pamela, who told him that she frequently exercised the horse in a little trap in which she carried salvage to the local depot.

D-Day had come at last, and Edwina began to wonder when and how she could get to the Continent to obtain first-hand knowledge of conditions in the British hospitals in the opera-tional areas of France.   A personal invitation from General Eisenhower, then Supreme Commander, to come over and do a nine days' tour of Northern France was eagerly accepted. Edwina, representing the Red Cross and St. John, who had responsibilities towards both Servicemen and French civilians arrived on an air-strip near the landing beaches.   Here a staff car and escort of military police on motor-cycles escorted her to the well-found seaside villa, where she had luncheon with Ike and with members of his staff.   The remainder of her tour was less pleasant and certainly less comfortable.   It was her first experience of visiting the wounded on the battle-front, and the first few days of inspecting the canvas hospitals were a nightmare of fatigue.   Her concern for the mutilated and shocked servicemen was very deep.   It was only after she had been in several hospitals that she realized that her presence among the patients had a tonic effect on their morale.   She made it her business then, and on future occasions, to make her calls as individual as time permitted.   This meant a talk with

each and every patient, nurse, and member of the hospital
staff. If ever the 'human touch' was put to good purpose it
was with these bandaged soldiers by whose cots she paused to
chat, to listen, and to make mental notes of anything which
might assist their recovery.

Edwina's tour covered the hospitals around Bayeux, Caen,
and Amiens. She stepped amid the rubble of the battered,
shattered towns, and wherever she went she encountered the
stark spectre of Hunger. After four years of nightmare under
German domination the French people lacked disinfectants,
soap, fuel, transport vehicles, clothing, and food. Many of
the French hospitals, she found, were desperately short of supplies, though they had received some help from the British
Red Cross War Organization. Many who had lost their
homes she saw encamped on the roadside. Wherever she
went she looked and she listened. Later, when she returned
home, she talked. She talked of the magnificent work of the
military nurses, of the spirit and devotion of the French women,
some of whom had hidden as many as eight Allied parachutists
in their cellars, with the Germans literally on their doorstep.
What she did not talk about was the gruelling strain of those
nine days of trying to appear serene and composed when
confronted with such widespread suffering, and of her own
skirmish with death when the plane in which she was being
flown to Nijmegen in Holland was attacked by a German
anti-aircraft battery as they flew 400 feet over the German
lines. One engine was destroyed in this encounter, and flak
seared the face of Edwina's neighbour.

The tour ended in Paris, a Paris which was raw and trembling
after its years of occupation and recent liberation. It was a
cardboard city peopled by frightened ghosts, but, as always,
its beauty, heightened by the absence of motor traffic, was
spectacular, and Edwina had ever been a lover of this city.
Sadly, she walked in the streets, looking into the depleted
shops, whose meagre goods were displayed with consummate
art. The city of luxury was stricken. Nowhere was there
any vestige of the former plenty. The best restaurants offered
spam and suspicious-looking stews. Edwina stayed at the
Ritz, then in the hands of the Army. The bath-water was
cold, and there was no light, and her breakfast consisted of

ersatz coffee and more spam.　After visiting the President of
the French Red Cross and friends for whom she had messages
from England, she made a sentimental journey to the places
she had visited with Dickie.　On her way she walked past
Boucheron's the jewellers.　Five years earlier she had ordered
from them a pair of earrings.　Now that the locusts had passed
she had little hope of ever possessing them.　The manager,
seeing her, bounded out into the street.　'Milady! the earrings!'　A few minutes later the pretty earrings rescued from
a secret hiding-place were safely in her hands.

CHAPTER XII

THE FORGOTTEN ARMY

THE YEARS 1944-5 were particularly challenging ones for the men fighting in South-East Asia. The war in Europe was not yet over and every resource was being concentrated in defeating Hitler. As a consequence S.E.A.C. was, inevitably, low on the priority list for both men and materials, including reinforcements, aircraft, doctors, nurses, and auxiliaries.

It may have been as a result of this latter problem that the Viceroy of India, Lord Wavell, the Commander-in-Chief, General Auchinleck, and Lord Mountbatten invited Edwina to undertake a tour of hospitals and medical units throughout the Indian and S.E.A.C. military areas.

On January 9th, 1945, Edwina, with her secretary, Nancie Lees, arrived at Karachi. After lunching at Government House, where she was staying as the guest of Sir Hugh and Lady Dow, Edwina, in spite of a slight fever occasioned by one of the many injections she had had before leaving London, set out on her work. By now she had perfected the technique of hospital visiting she had developed on her first foreign tour. While she concentrated on talking to the patients, her assistant, in this case Nancie Lees, took constant notes on general matters concerned with the running of the hospital. Less than ever now was there any hint of the lady patroness inspecting a clean and comfortable cottage hospital. Edwina refused to allow convention to stand in the way of the welfare, physical or spiritual, of the patients she was inspecting, and, to the consternation of her escorts, she insisted on shaking hands with the Indian sepoys: apparently a flagrant breach of etiquette. Edwina, however, was in no mood for this kind of social taboo and the glint in her eye reduced the objectors to stricken silence. Nor was she content with being shown round one ward filled with Indian soldiers. She inspected the whole establishment from lavatories to kitchens and storerooms, with Nancie Lees and the commanding officer and his staff following faint but pursuing in her wake. By the end of her visits in Karachi there was much gossip in the English clubs. Reports of Edwina's uncompromising methods and dislike of red tape had percolated, via the *memsahibs*, to the bars.

'Here's to a demmed efficient woman,' said one Anglo-Indian old stager, raising his *stengah* in a toast to Mountbatten's lady.

'Too demmed efficient, if you ask me,' grumbled another.

Indifferent to praise or blame, Edwina continued on her way. The flight from Karachi to Delhi was not without incident. Lord Louis had put his personal aircraft, *Sister Anne*, at his wife's disposal. But, as they took off, Edwina barely had time to take in the amenities of the beautiful plane with its green interior and beds and desks, when she observed an oily patch staining one wing. An oil-pipe had been fractured, and they were obliged to return to Karachi without delay.

By the time Edwina had finished her tour and rejoined Lord Louis at his headquarters at Peredynia, in the uplands of Ceylon, the slim white plane had covered more than 20,000 miles, and Edwina had visited 172 hospitals. During this tour, which took her to the front lines of Burma and up to Chungking, she visited not only hospitals, but also medical centres, convalescent homes, blood-banks, canteens, service clubs, and war work committees. Crisp report upon crisp report followed. Most urgent was the need for nurses and V.A.D.s. The shortage of nurses in India and South-East Asia was acute; most hospitals were understaffed by a half of their authorized nursing strength. There was a lack everywhere of operating-theatre equipment, of beds, linen, and stoves. C.O.s and matrons in many cases had used ingenuity and near genius to obtain what they needed. In one hospital operating theatre lights and reflectors had been improvised out of petrol tins. In stark and simple language Edwina set down what she had seen, what was needed, and what must be done.

Everywhere she went she left a feeling of confidence. The men knew that she would implement her promises. Hearsay did not satisfy her. She had to discover things for herself. Hearing that travelling conditions on troop leave-trains were atrocious, she told Major Bryan Hunter, the officer detailed

to escort her, that she would travel in one of these troop-trains
and find out what conditions were really like. Accompanied
by Major Hunter she boarded a night train at Dimapur, installing herself in a third-class carriage occupied by a number
of British soldiers. The soldiers were jammed on the four
wooden seats with their meagre baggage accommodated on one
of the two luggage-racks overhead. The state of the lavatories
and the lack of any water either for drinking or washing purposes was quite incredible. Major Hunter had had the fore-
thought to bring a cushion. He offered it to Edwina, who
declined it. Through the long night she chatted with the
soldiers, listening intently to their grievances. So much of
their time was spent travelling, they said, that when they
got to the rest camps their leave was practically over. With
such matters was she entertained, and when, at a wayside
halt, they were given thick, sweet tea, she drank it gratefully.
Finally, the soldiers fell into uneasy slumber. Major Hunter
did the same, awakening on one occasion to see the Superintendent-in-Chief of the St. John Ambulance Brigade climbing
gracefully into the luggage-rack, where she spent the remainder
of the night. That journey took eighteen hours.

Always Edwina had travelled light. Now her personal belongings were stowed away in one suitcase. She lived rough
with seeming enjoyment, washing out her stockings and hanging them to dry on the guy-ropes of her tent. Philosophically
she accepted heat and mosquitoes and was equal to every crisis.
At Arakan she and Nancie Lees found that their route lay
across a swiftly rushing river. Without hesitation, but with
considerable trepidation, they went into the dark waters and
swam to the opposite bank.

Edwina had once craved action and a purpose. Now she
had both, and if, at times, physical exhaustion threatened her
energies, 'rest days' enabled her to catch up on her paper
work. Nancie Lees dreaded the rest days almost more than
those when they went hospital visiting. It was common knowledge that Lady Louis woke at some ungodly hour when she
sat for hours writing in her bed, stretcher, or pallet. But, to
the astonishment of her entourage, she never seemed anything
but crisp, fresh, and unhurried. Nothing seemed to shake her
equilibrium. Visiting advance dressing-stations in Burma,

Edwina was transported by amphibian duck down the Irra-
waddy River. They landed at Nyaungu and were escorted
by the divisional commander to a field-ambulance unit to
meet stretcher casualties being brought back from the front
line. As they were returning, the General halted his jeep and
turned to Edwina.

'Mind waiting a little. I've got a couple of battles on the
go near here, and I'd like to see how we're making out.'

At this time both Edwina and Lord Louis were living history,
and he, in particular, was making it. Her memory of this
period must be starred with illustrious names which recall
unforgettable moments. At Kunming there was a luncheon
with General Chennault and the 14th U.S.A.A.F. (the Flying
Tigers).

Unconnected incidents were indelibly etched in Edwina's
memory: arriving at Chunking and being welcomed by the
blare of a brass band performing what later turned out to be
their rendering of 'God Save the King'; the sight of Generalis-
simo Chang Kai-shek's impassive face as he stood on the steps
of 'Hwa Lung Chiao', Dr. Soong's house, to welcome the
distinguished visitors; a banquet given in honour of the
Mountbattens, whose thirty-four courses included every known
variety of Chinese delicacy. As Edwina ate her poached
pigeons' eggs she was thinking of a recent visit to a Chinese
hospital, whose clean, vigorous patients had momentarily
deceived her. But only momentarily, for, evading her escorts,
she had gone in search of the sick men, whom she guessed had
been hidden. She found them lying miserably in a hut.

There was the usual scurry and round of visits and inspections; the Kuomintang Government were determined that
Edwina should make a good report to the Red Cross. Her
visit ended with mutual expressions of goodwill, flowers, medals,
speeches, and some special gifts from Chiang Kai-shek.
Among these was some white silk which Edwina hoped to have
made into underwear when she got home. To her vast annoy-
ance, the Customs officials, ignoring her plea that the silk was
a gift, taxed it heavily, making her silken goodwill memento a
singularly extravagant affair.

The aircraft carried Edwina back to Kunming, where she
spent the night. The next day she took the Burma Road, on

which in 1938 she had made so hazardous a journey. This time she was driving in the opposite direction, but the road was as eerie, deserted, dangerous, and dusty as she remembered it in the past. As the vehicle rattled along she peered at her sun-scorched face and wind-chapped lips in the mirror of her compact, and suddenly she was swept with a kind of vertigo and a sense of panic and unreality. What, she thought, am I doing, driving on this frightening road in South-West Yunnan? Where am I going, and what will be the end of all this horror and death and bloodshed? And she thought then of Broadlands, of the green lawns, the trees, of the gentle English rain, of white lilac and the scent of a spring morning, and, strangely, she was comforted.

After a hectic two days in Calcutta, it was a somewhat jaded Edwina who rejoined Lord Louis at his headquarters at Peredeniya. High in the mountains, near the town of Kandy, the botanical gardens for which Peredeniya was famous formed a magnificent decor for Lord Louis' headquarters; and Edwina was much impressed with the thoroughness with which each detail of office and accommodation had been planned. Temporary buildings had been erected in the vicinity of parks and gardens. Roads had been renamed. A path lined with exotic blooms led from the Public Relations Department to 'Fleet Street', which housed the editorial offices of *S.E.A.C.*, the troops' newspaper. Radiating from the Supreme Commander's building, in which were his office and conference rooms, were the camps which lodged the troops. These dwellings were cool and comfortable.

Lord Louis and his personal staff lived at King's Pavilion in a small jewel of a white palace, originally built to receive Queen Victoria, and later used as a summer residence by the Governor. Set among lawns and trees and carefully tended flower-beds, it was a place of surpassing beauty. When Edwina arrived, she found that Dickie, like herself, was exhausted, and it was with relief that she set off with him for a day or so of rest in his mountain bungalow at Dimbula. During that drive in a jeep, as she sat perched beside her husband, her mind turned to the many strange drives they had made together in the course of their marriage. The password then had been speed, and the final destination unknown. In those days they had

stalked death, now death stalked them. In a few days she
would go back to England and Dickie would stay, and thus it
had ever been, for ever and ever, world without end.

.   .   .

On returning to London, Edwina went straight into action.
She had many promises to keep and she intended to implement
them straight away. Ministries, hearing that she was back,
began to feel uneasy. They knew her tactics, and they knew,
too, that finally she would get her way. Priority number one
was to have nurses sent to S.E.A.C. Leaving the Minister of
Health limp and breathless, she hurried from his office with
a promise of 500 V.A.Ds. But to get these nurses sent to the
East was a question for the Minister of Labour to settle. After
some high-pressure sessions with him, Edwina finally obtained
permission for the transfer. That done, she set out to obtain an
immediate consignment of artificial limbs for the disabled men
in Burma, many of whom had been waiting for two years for
their limbs. Having obtained an assurance that this matter
would receive immediate attention, Edwina dealt with a number of similar questions, brought her reports up to date,
attended endless meetings, and realized suddenly that it was
high time she went to the dentist, and to her hairdresser to
have her hair cut.

CHAPTER XIII

SAGA OF SUFFERING

WITH THE defeat of the enemy in Europe, the St. John and Red Cross Joint War Organization was called upon to cope with the sudden release of tens of thousands of prisoners of war and internees freed by the armies of liberation. Before the final break-through Edwina had toured prisoner-of-war camps and concentration camps as they became accessible, and the experience and knowledge gained during this period qualified her beyond all others for the supreme mission she was shortly to undertake.

The atom bombs which smashed the fighting power of Japan and brought about the complete collapse of her military forces were to have an almost immediate repercussion, even upon Edwina. The situation in South-East Asia was even graver from the point of view of the Allies than ever before during the Burma campaign. Within the limits of her husband's command there was a population of some 130 million people long subjected to intensive Japanese propaganda. To this must be added upwards of three-quarters of a million defeated but armed Japanese, and in camps stretching over an area of some 3,000 miles, many of them in unknown places, 200,000 quietly rotting Allied prisoners of war and internees.

Lord Louis' immediate problems were both military and administrative, but the desperate fate of prisoners of war and internees was obviously of primary concern.

On August 23rd, 1945, Edwina, in response to an 'immediate' message from her husband, arrived at Kandy in Ceylon. Lord Louis' instructions were brief and to the point. 'I want you to go to those boys, wherever they are, and help to get them out as soon as you can. I want you to use your own initiative, but you can appeal to any of my military commanders for help. I can accept nothing less than an all-out effort.' Nor did the Supreme Commander minimize the gravity and danger of her mission. Burma, Siam, and

Indonesia were still in the grip of the defeated enemy, and it was on them that Edwina would largely have to rely for information regarding the location of prisoner-of-war and internment camps.

Accompanied by Captain Elizabeth Ward, a F.A.N.Y. officer of Lord Louis' headquarters staff, and Major Abhey Singh, both of whom were to be attached to her for the rest of her tour, she left Kandy for Simla, where she was to attend a Government of India and Red Cross meeting at Viceregal Lodge under the chairmanship of Lady Wavell.

Edwina and Elizabeth Ward arrived at Ambala. They dined in the R.A.F. Mess and entrained for Simla. Edwina seemed to regard it as quite natural to find herself in a none-too-clean compartment, making up her own bunk. This done, she slipped into a pair of pyjamas, neglected to remove her make-up, and while her companion attempted to compose her limbs on what appeared to be a medieval rack, she sat working on her reports in the dim light afforded them.

It was only later, when Lady Wavell asked how she had enjoyed her journey, that Edwina discovered that the Viceregal train had been waiting to carry her from Ambala to Simla. Much to the surprise of Elizabeth Ward, who was feeling decidedly fatigued after the uncomfortable journey, Edwina, having arrived at nine a.m., had a quick bath, and, spruce and composed, was ready to attend the meeting, which, after a short break for luncheon, went on until five-o'clock that afternoon. This was the first, but certainly not the last time Elizabeth Ward would be surprised at Edwina's vitality, and after ten years—for after this tour Miss Ward became Edwina's private secretary—she is still perpetually astonished by the seemingly inexhaustible reserves of vitality displayed by her remarkable chief.

On Wednesday, August 29th, Edwina flew into the Willingdon airport at Delhi. She spent the afternoon having interviews with Generals Lane, Wilson, and Hance, saw members of the Red Cross, and the next morning flew to Bangalore in the Hindustan. Here she lunched with Major-General Telfer-Smollett, attended a meeting in the General's office on the stores situation, and in the evening had a long talk with General Auchinleck on prisoner-of-war problems. The next day Edwina made an extensive tour of Jalahalee Hospital Centre, and inspected military and Red Cross convalescent homes. By nine-thirty that evening she was back in Kandy.

On Monday, September 3rd, Edwina and her assistants, Mrs. Beatrice Girouard (now her Deputy Superintendent-in-Chief in the St. John Organization), Miss Marjorie Miller, a specially selected St. John nursing officer, Elizabeth Ward, and Major Abhey Singh emplaned in the *Silver Fawn* at S.E.A.C. airstrip for the first leg of their heartbreaking journey.

In Rangoon, Edwina had a foretaste of what was to come. Daily European and Asian prisoners of war were arriving from Siam and Malaya. These were accommodated everywhere, except in the hospitals, which were used for the gravely ill. Everything in the city was completely disrupted and military jeeps were the only method of transportation. Edwina arrived at Mingaladon airfield at eleven-fifty a.m. By the end of that day she had visited every hospital and transit camp in the maimed city. There are men today who remember her walking among the beds, carrying a hurricane lantern—for the lights had long since failed—and one of them, the wag of the ward, said something about 'a streamlined lady with the lamp', and the Scot in the next bed snapped back, 'Aye, she's maybe no Florence Nightingale, but forbye she's doin' a grand job, and we chaps will no forget her.'

At Bangkok, Edwina, to her surprise, found that she was being accorded V.I.P. treatment in the Oriental manner. She was met at the airport by Princess Marayatkanya Diskul, and found that a full programme of social events had been prepared for her. Edwina appreciated the courtesy of her reception, but she was impatient to get to work. However, she and her party were escorted in great pomp to the palace, where, after being officially received by the Regent, they were entertained at a formal luncheon of thirty guests. Afterwards she visited the headquarters of the Allied Prisoners of War Headquarters. But her main objective was Camp Nakom Pathom. Since their imprisonment the men in this camp had greeted the dawn with the hope that one day, God willing, they would be freed. Gaunt, starving, sick, but undaunted, they waited, and then, at eleven-thirty one morning, a jeep guided by the Japanese drove into their camp, and in it was the first white women they had seen for three and a half years. Barely able to drag themselves along, they shambled towards the vehicle in which sat Edwina. They stood there, silent and unbelieving, but when she stood up and delivered her message from Lord Louis, when she told them that their martyrdom was nearly at an end and that their return would be arranged as rapidly as possible, then did they break their silence with full-bodied cheers.

In the next camp she visited, Camp Nakom Nayok, Edwina discovered her cousin, Harold Cassel, Auntie Grannie's nephew, of whom nothing had been heard since he had been reported missing. Harold's hair had turned white, but, like most of the other prisoners of war, his morale was high. Some days after he had seen her he wrote to her:

'Dear Cousin Edwina,
    'I felt I must write and tell you how thrilled and grateful all the prisoners here were for your visit.
    'You will realize what a tremendous moment it was for everyone to see a white woman, a real English woman, again after so many years. The men particularly admired your coming right into a danger zone—there's an armed Japanese division two miles away—and getting so far forward so quickly. Somehow now you've come even the restless ones are certain that everything is being done to get us out quickly. As far as discipline goes your visit was worth two companies of M.P.s. . . .'

On Sunday the 9th, leaving Mrs. Girouard and Mrs. Miller to work in camps in Siam, Edwina proceeded to Singapore, which had just been recaptured. The city was completely disorganized. Edwina stayed in a house which had neither water nor light. At ten-forty-five she arrived at Sime Road Camp, in which 4,384 men, women, and children—civil internees—had lived through almost unendurable misery. Edwina walked round the camp, chatting to almost everybody, and explaining what was being done to hasten their release. After luncheon on board H.M.S. *Sussex*, she went to Changi Gaol. Here were some 12,000 men, including British, Dutch, Australian, and a few Italian naval men.

In Changi Gaol, Edwina met Corporal Denny, who had

Edwina and Dickie outside Buckingham Palace, after the award of her medal

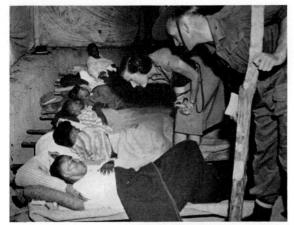

Talking with Gurkha soldiers in a field hospital, 1944

Searching for wounded, Burma Campaign, 1945

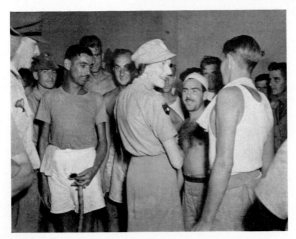

Talking to liberated Prisoners of War

installed a secret radio behind a kitchen sink. This had never been discovered by the Japanese, so the prisoners of war had received almost daily broadcasts of the news throughout their internment. In the workshops she was shown boots and shoes soled with latex, paper made of the same material, filing-cabinets transformed into mugs and spoons, and in another workshop she saw how these same filing-cabinets had been used to make artificial limbs.

In the 47th British General Hospital she heard how the staff had worked day and night to get the wards, which were in a filthy condition, ready for the RAWPI. This same staff had slept on the floor and had fed on jungle rations in order that the RAWPI might be comfortable. There was an acute shortage of water and electric light bulbs and pillows, but the sick RAWPI were all smiling and said it was 'heaven' after the Sime Road Camp from whence they had come. Many of them were desperately ill, some having developed TB from malnutrition. A blood transfusion was in progress in the operating theatre. Most of the staff, many of whom had served three and a half years in the East, had already given their blood.

On Wednesday, September 12th, Lord Louis accepted the surrender of the Japanese Expeditionary Forces, Southern Region, outside the municipal buildings in Singapore. Edwina and her party watched this ceremony from the balcony of the buildings . . .

'You will have read about the Singapore Surrender Ceremony [she wrote], which was quite the most impressive and moving I have ever seen. I took a lot of our Singapore St. John colleagues, British, Chinese and Malayan, many of whom were just coming out of internment camps and many from outside who had been loyal and courageous. Little Chinese nurses and auxiliaries had volunteered to go into the camps disguised, to help nurse the sick, and many of them got caught by the Japanese Gestapo for doing so, and yet they went back again and again.

'At the Ceremony we had thousands of recently liberated prisoners of war from Changi Gaol and other camps from Singapore Island. . . . One of the internees was Dr. Robert

K

MacGregor, Director of Medical Services in Malaya—
before the war the St. John Commissioner. He had done
quite outstandingly good work. I told him that I would
very much welcome the opportunity of meeting any of his
people during the few days I was in Singapore. He welcomed the suggestion but felt that it might be difficult to
get more than a handful of them together, in view of the
fact that they had been scattered for so long and communication and transportation in Singapore were still practically
nil. Word got round, however, and we were amazed,
36 hours later, to find 1,500 St. John men and women
assembled in the grounds of Government House, many of
them in their full uniform which they had hidden during
the occupation, and all of them forming a really smart
parade. Many of them had walked 7 or 8 miles to attend
it, and it was extraordinarily touching and inspiring.' [1]

Each day Edwina visited some of the horror camps—Adam
Park, Tanjong Pagor Camp, River Valley Road, Kranji,
Neeson, Selton, McArthur—and her brief nights of sleep were
made hideous with visions of what she had seen.

From now until the end of her tour some months later
Edwina was to see and hear things which would haunt her
long afterwards. She saw how the lack of vitamins had produced terrible symptoms—raw scrotums, raw tongues and
sores which did not heal—she saw that men had been forced
to live like beasts, eating out of the lids of gaol bedpans and
old hub-caps. . . . She heard about men filled with water
and jumped on by their guards; of men suspended by their
ankles while urine was poured down their nostrils. . . .

While she was in Singapore Edwina got a Council together
representing all the Red Cross and Welfare Organizations
which would be taking part in civil relief work. General
Hone, Chief Civil Officer for Malaya, undertook the Pre-
sidency, and the Bishop of Singapore became Chairman.
She then decided that the moment had come to inspect the
camps in the interior. She visited all the prisoner-of-war
camps and noted briefly in her diary, 'Conditions indescribable'. At midnight on the day of her arrival she attended a

[1] Letter/Report.

conference at Area Headquarters on a plan for the evacuation
of the prisoners of war from Pakenbaroe to Singapore.

Wherever Edwina went she marvelled at the magnificent
morale of the men, some of them sick unto death, and all of
them pathetically grateful for everything that was being done
to help them back to freedom and health. But the overall
picture of illness and lack of supplies and of nursing staff
would have broken the spirit of anyone less optimistic or determined than Edwina.[1]

'I went to a large number of camps in Siam [she wrote],
where the death roll in 1942/1943, during the building of
the railway into Burma, has been appallingly high (17,000
dead), but the men who came through were in amazingly
good spirits, however ill and emaciated they might be. This
applied to every single camp I have seen, and the brave
spirits and real 'guts' have been unbelievable during all
these ghastly years. It certainly has been their spirit and
courage, and refusal to be got down by the Japs, *whatever*
they did to them, that has brought them through. No
praise can be too high for what the doctors, surgeons, and
R.A.M.C. orderlies have done in the camps and the thousands of lives they have saved, even though they had
absolutely no medical supplies, drugs or equipment.'

Elizabeth Ward was privately wondering how long Edwina
was going to stand the pace she had set herself. In her
own notes she recorded some of the few moments of light relief.
A constant diet of tinned baked beans had played havoc
with her digestion, and when faced with yet another plate
of them she murmured something about hating the sight of
them.

'I know,' remarked Edwina, vigorously spooning them
into her mouth, 'but they're supposed to be so *good* for
one.'

On one occasion Elizabeth had been silently astonished
when the fastidious Lady Louis had rushed into an Oriental
bazar and bought an enormous bottle of cheap scent. Later,
when they were camping in some spot where water was
unprocurable, Elizabeth, approaching her chief's tent, was

[1] Letter/Report sent to St. John/Red Cross H.Q.

conscious of the overpowering odour of 'Dream of Delight' and when bidden to enter, found Edwina pouring the entire bottle of noxious scent over her person.

'You see,' said Edwina with satisfaction, 'I had a presentiment that the ghastly stuff would come in handy some time. After all, if it does remove the skin, what's left behind feels much cleaner.'

On September 20th Edwina went to Saigon, where she visited the camps. Conditions here were far better than in Sumatra. On her return to Singapore she gave a small dinner-party at the Great World, a Chinese restaurant, for several prisoners of war, among them Ronald Searle, the artist, who had been interned in Changi Gaol. Here, in spite of severe illness, he had produced *Exile*, a fine magazine, considering the conditions under which it was printed.

The following day the party emplaned for Batavia. At the Hotel des Indes, in which accommodation had been reserved for Edwina and her party, a wing had been set aside to house convalescent ex-internees. The future of the civil internees in the Far East constantly exercised Edwina's mind.

'The civil internees [she wrote] [1] had a particularly hard time and were really pathetic, especially those who had spent $3\frac{1}{2}$ years in internment camps, were already advanced in years and had lived in comparative peace and comfort in the days before the war. They will need great help and sympathy. Many of them are permanently broken in health and many are homeless and are too old to start all over again. The internees in the Netherlands East Indies (a few British women, but the large majority being Dutch) have been treated shamefully. They have been herded into overcrowded camps made of native bamboo huts, with no sanitation, lighting, chairs or any sort of comforts. They were made by the Japs to do coolie labour, sometimes heavier than the men, and a large number of the women died during internment.'

The camps at Semarang were shocking. The internees in one of them had been allowed only $\frac{1}{4}$lb. of rice per day and were living in a space of approximately 1 foot 7 inches by

[1] Letter/Report.

6 feet 6 inches each. There was a fearful plague of flies, which could not be kept off the food.

In Camp Sruswyk there were 1,300 women and children. In the hospital the patients were all suffering from under-nourishment, and many were seriously ill. They had only thirteen litres of milk per day for the whole hospital. In the children's ward babies were dying of starvation, and the older children were desperately ill.

In the Mater Dolorosa Camp Hospital there were 470 patients. Many of them were lying on the floor. Few looked as if they could live much longer. Their heads were shrunken into skulls with blackened and broken teeth.

So it was in every camp. Wherever the Japanese had taken prisoners was death, sickness, and desolation. But by the time Edwina had visited camps and hospitals in Borneo, Labuan, Morotai, and Manila, whence she had gone at General MacArthur's invitation, conditions had begun to improve, and by October 25th she was making an optimistic report:

'Just over five weeks since it started active operations, the organization for the Recovery of Allied Prisoners of War and Internees had cleared all the areas of South East Asia Command for which it was responsible. Prisoners of War and Internees had to be shipped not only to U.K. but to India and Australia and had to be recovered from 230 camps stretched over an area of 3,000 miles . . .

'The physical conditions of the prisoners, especially in the worst camps in Sumatra and N.E.I. necessitated early contacts, and evacuation made even though some risks had to be taken. In Sumatra, for instance, the whole of the evacuation of the prisoners of war was carried out before the Allied troops had landed, or even before our ships had been able to reach the coast. Evacuation, however, by Dakota, and light aircraft from emergency strips and also by river boat to the coasts, was carried out successfully and with small loss of life. Psychologically it was considered important to evacuate them so that they should feel that they were at least moving homewards.' [1]

[1] Letter/Report.

Hong Kong was one of the last ports of call, during which Edwina had flown some 33,000 miles and visited sixteen different countries on her mission of mercy. According to the Acting Captain of the Fleet at Hong Kong, who was also Chairman of the Released Allied Prisoners of War and Internees Committee, Edwina's impending visit was a matter of grave concern to the authorities, for it was well known that the aerodrome suitable for comparatively small planes could well prove a death-trap to a plane requiring every inch of a runway which was bounded by hills.

However, at the appointed hour *Sister Anne* made a perfect landing, and a good many officials present sighed with relief. Hong Kong at that time was a typical example of Japanese occupation, electrical power-stations were not operating, the sewage system had failed and the drinking-water supply was contaminated. The inhabitants were dependent on the Fleet for their food. The civilian prisoners from Camp Stanley were being cared for by the Navy, and though their morale was high, physically they were at low ebb, particularly the adolescents, who had lost all their teeth through beri-beri. Every dental surgeon in the Fleet was making plates and every false tooth available in Australia was flown up to Hong Kong.

On October 11th, Edwina, having returned to Singapore, visited Neesoon Camp. Conditions here were shocking: forty-five men had died in three weeks, and each day there were two or three deaths. The Sime Road Camp was no less gruesome.

A day later Edwina and her staff emplaned for Kandy. But even here there was little rest or respite. Mountains of paper work had to be dealt with, and there were continual meetings on Red Cross and other urgent matters. The one bright spot in this Agenda of Misery was the arrival of Patricia on leave from Delhi. She had joined her father's staff as third officer W.R.N.S., and for a few days the Mountbattens were reunited. After a week-end at Dimbula, Edwina again set out on her travels. This time she flew to Bangalore, where she made an extensive tour of hospitals and convalescent centres at Jalahalie. She was delighted to note that many of the ex-prisoners of war whom she had seen on the verge of death in Sumatra were greatly improved in health, some of them being so far recovered as to be able to attend a B.O.R. dance, where each of them in turn clamoured for a dance with the Guest of Honour, who had become in their eyes a symbol of freedom.

The Mountbattens, due to go to Delhi, took advantage of the invitation of an old friend, the Nawab of Bhopal, and broke their journey there for a night. Their plane was met by the Maharajah of Bhopal and his entourage, and after the Supreme Commander had addressed some 200 of the R.A.F. at the airport he and Edwina were driven out to Chiklod, the country palace of the Maharajah. For a few hours Edwina tried to shut her mind to the many problems which occupied her and to enjoy the outdoor dinner-party which had been arranged in honour of the distinguished guests. A military band played during dinner, and there were bagpipes, their penetrating wail sounding a little unreal in this decor of Oriental splendour. The following morning there was breakfast on the terrace, a quick and refreshing swim in the pool, a brief expedition into the jungle and sightseeing at Bhopal. After which the Mountbattens had luncheon with their hosts at Ahemdabad, their Bhopal palace, and by two-thirty they were flying off to Delhi.

In Delhi Edwina and Patricia were guests of Lord and Lady Wavell at Viceroy's House. The days which followed were filled as usual with meetings and discussions on Tuesday and paper work, and on Wednesday, November 7th, Edwina and her party emplaned for Calcutta, where there was the usual desperate rush to try to cram visits, inspections, private interviews, and paper work into the little time at her disposal.

The following week-end was spent at Jodhpur as guests of the Maharajah of Jaipur. At first view, Jodhpur teases the mind of the European visitor. It has a familiar decor, in that it has something of the background of the Italian Primitives; the colours are umber and ochre under a sky of brilliant blue.

The party was lodged in one of the Palace guest houses, and after luncheon, they were taken round the new palace, whose vast modern kitchen were staffed by 300 servants. Later they attended a polo match in which the Maharajah and Major Abhey Singh's brother played. They dined quietly at the palace.

Early the next morning Lord Louis, Edwina, and Patricia went out riding, returning in time to prepare for a visit to the

ancient and historic fort which stands on a rocky pinnacle 400
feet above the city.   Built of glowing Jodhpur stone, the fort
is a fine architectural feat, its great mass of masonry poised
delicately on a rocky eminence and all its façade, windows,
and balconies intricately carved.

After the first gate had been reached, the party abandoned
their cars and took to the waiting *dhoolies* (carrying-chairs),
which transported them up the steep, stone-paved causeway.
Massive doors were flung back to let them through.   Here
were courtyards, arcaded walls, more doors, more courtyards,
and, right in the heart of the fort, the Maharajah's treasury.
Here Edwina and her party were shown the State jewellery,
a collection of fabulous gems, which included some of the finest
pearls in the world.   After a tour of the armoury, the Mountbattens motored 30 miles to Sardar Samand, the Maharajah's
country palace, where they swam, sunbathed, lunched, and
dashed off to look at the lovely gardens on their way back.
At five o'clock Edwina inspected the well-equipped hospital,
and made a mental note that it would make 'a most excellent
training school for nurses', after which they called on a friend
and had a quiet dinner, which they must have needed, at the
Guest House.

The next day, Edwina, laden with magnificent gifts, presented to her and to her party by the Maharajah, emplaned
for Kandy, whence she intended visiting Singapore and
Batavia.   After a further tour of the internees' camps in Java
she went on to Singapore.   On Friday, November 23rd, she
was in Delhi.   It now became urgent for her to return to
England, and she flew to Karachi.   The only aircraft available
for the United Kingdom was a York freighter with no seats,
but Edwina was determined to get back, and decided to leave
in the York.

The return journey was hazardous in the extreme.   Twice
the York developed engine trouble, and at Cairo, Edwina
waited at the airport until she decided that she would change
aircraft and go on in another passenger machine.   At Castel
Benito the new plane developed obscure engine trouble, which
necessitated her spending the night in the R.A.F. transit
camp.

Nothing daunted, however, she was off next morning, and

at two-five B.M.T. the aircraft landed her at Lynham, Wilts, where she was met by her younger daughter, Pamela. That evening, at seven o'clock, she walked into the Dorchester Hotel. Since she had left London she had covered some 40,000 miles by air alone and had visited sixteen different countries. Her great test of courage and endurance was over. No matter how significant or insignificant her life might be henceforward, many thousands of men and women would remember always her smile, her cool handclasp and the loving compassion in her eyes.

CHAPTER XIV

INTERLUDE

In the New Year's Honours List Edwina was made a Dame Commander of the Royal Victorian Order. The pressure of work became ever more arduous. Her day was planned as exactly as a military campaign. It was cold, the skies were grey, and austerity was the watchword. Sometimes, when she was sitting in her office conducting interviews or doing her interminable paper-work, her spirits flagged a little and she thought of the East. Not of the desolate, war-torn areas she had recently visited, but of the East she had known so briefly in her youth and of which she had glimpsed tantalizing vistas when flying over princely states. There had been bred in her then a desire to know more of this land of beauty and contrast, and she promised herself that one day, when there was peace again, she would travel to India and there absorb something of its culture and philosophy.

Then, just as the stifling net of the daily round had closed about her, an opportunity came to go East with Lord Louis. A peace had recently been negotiated and signed between Great Britain and Siam, and Lord Louis had decided to further cement good relations by paying a visit to King Ananda Mahidol at Bangkok. On this occasion he went alone and the visit was an unqualified personal success. Lord Louis rapidly re-established amicable Siamese–British relations by typically elegant and individual gestures. He presented the King with a jeep and attended informally the dances at the Thai Officers' Club. He also negotiated a satisfactory trade agreement between Great Britain and Siam and was awarded the Order of the White Elephant, Siam's highest honour. No sooner had he departed, however, than the Prime Minister, Seni Pramoj, with whom he had concluded his agreements, fell from power, the King's jeep was stolen, and Lord Louis was informed that though the Foreign Office had given him authority to accept the Order of the White Elephant, he might not wear it in view of the strained state of relations existing between Britain and the former ally of Japan.

A month later, therefore, Lord Louis returned to Siam, unofficially with Edwina, and resumed his negotiations for rice with the new Premier, who promised him that the agreement would be kept. In the meantime, Edwina, though busy consolidating the work she had done on her previous tour, had fallen once again under the charm of the city the Siamese call Kreungtep—'the abode of the Gods'—with its golden pagodas, upswept architecture, and tropical creepers and flowers. But she was not to be permitted to linger here. She was swept off to Singapore, where Lord Louis had a delicate mission to accomplish. Earlier in the year, when the Supreme Commander was visiting the Viceroy of India in New Delhi, the latter had told him that Pandit Jawaharlal Nehru, President of the Constituency of the Congress Party, hoped to visit the Indian community of Malaya, and since he would in all probability become the first Prime Minister of India, it was politic, from every point of view, to accord him every facility and courtesy during his visit. This was not the view of the Poona pundits and British military authorities who feared Nehru might play up to the Indian National Army formed by the Japanese out of the Indian contingents that had surrendered after the fall of Malaya to fight against the British. The impending visit of Nehru, therefore, was ignored by the British Administration at Singapore, whose sole gesture of welcome was to post M.P.s at strategic points should there be rioting. No dispositions had been taken to meet Nehru at the airport, and indeed a suggestion that a car be put at his disposal was strongly vetoed.

Lord Louis was away until two days before the arrival of Nehru. When he discovered what the official view of this visit was, he made it abundantly clear that, since the President of the Constituency of the Congress Party had been invited to Singapore, every courtesy and facility accorded to distinguished visitors should be given him; including a car, passes to the leading members of the Indian community who were going to the airport to welcome Nehru, and trucks to bring Indians from country areas. Lord Louis was not countermanding official arrangements without careful thought. He was well aware that Nehru's coming might well have the

effect of touching off the enmity that existed between the
British and the Indian National Army, in which case, he felt,
conciliation was the one weapon which might avert disaster.
In fact, his hunch was correct. Whatever Nehru's feelings
were on arrival, the reception arranged for him by Mountbatten soothed and warmed him, and it was with the greatest
friendliness, if not gratitude, that he lunched with the Supreme
Commander, high-ranking officials, and prominent civilians at
Government House. He left Government House for a drive
through the streets to a Red Cross Indian Recreation Centre,
where Edwina was waiting to receive him. In the car with
him was Lord Louis. This, to his staff, was the final straw,
for, as they said when they heard what he intended doing, it
was almost certain that he would be assassinated by one of the
Indians lining the street. There was every opportunity for
these dire prophecies to be fulfilled. The car drove at a snail's
pace through the streets lined with Indians deliriously shouting
their welcome to Nehru and their pleasure at seeing him in
such noble company.

At the Recreation Centre, Edwina heard the distant roar of
voices, and then, as Lord Louis and Nehru joined her, the
Indians, in their anxiety to get near Nehru, pressed forward
and, like a wave of the sea, totally engulfed her. Knocked
off her feet and submerged, she was in danger of being trampled
on, but concerted action on the part of Lord Louis and Nehru
saved her. Nor was there time to make any speech of thanks.
The Mountbattens and Nehru had to push, almost fight, their
way to the one exit of the Centre, where they drove back to
Government House together.

This meeting with Jawaharal Nehru was an important one
for the Mountbattens, for whom it was the beginning of a
friendship which has endured through the years. Nehru at
that time was the new hero of India. If Gandhi was its voice,
Nehru was the stirring of its pulse. Handsome, healthy and
brilliantly intelligent, the son of an ancient Brahmin family,
he was educated at Harrow and Cambridge. He returned to
India more of a Western liberal than an Indian nationalist.
He practised at the Bar at Allahabad, and, becoming president
of the municipality, came under the spell of Gandhi. At this
time he became an agitator against British rule. Soon he

became a leading member of the Indian National Congress, and under his influence Congress declared that the goal of the Indian masses was to be complete national independence, 'and for the illiterate peasants of India, this liberal minded product of Western education, this believer in democracy and socialism, crystallized into the classic type of Indian hero—the rich youth who renounces the pleasures of the world to devote himself to poverty and asceticism for the public weal'.

As a result of his agitation against British rule, many years of his life were spent in prison. During his periods of incarceration he wrote his autobiography, read, meditated, and for his amusement tamed mice and spiders. His periods of imprisonment did not embitter him. But each time he emerged fortified to continue the battle for his beliefs.

Sensitive and humane, he is a man of great personal charm. Tagore compared him to the spring of eternal youth, and according to one of his biographers: [1] 'He loves mountains, clouds, rivers, and the laughter of children. He is a great admirer of sheer physical courage. Tyranny in any form, anywhere, moves him deeply.'

Here, then, was a man who could guide Edwina's mind towards an understanding of the East and of the Eastern mentality, a man who, by virtue of personal bereavements—his beloved wife Kamala had died in 1935—was lonely and withdrawn. The radiant vitality of Edwina's personality, her physical courage, intelligence, and hatred of oppression, made a deep impression on Nehru. With her, as with his sister, he could be himself.

.   .   .

At this time the Governments of Australia and New Zealand had invited Lord Louis and Edwina to make a tour of these Dominions. Edwina was already well known to many Australians who had been prisoners of war in the camps she had visited, and the 'Aussies' took both her and Lord Louis to their hearts. They landed at Canberra, where they were besieged by enthusiastic newspapermen, photographers, and autograph-hunters. Equally enthusiastic was their reception in Melbourne, Sydney, and Brisbane. The newspapers waxed

[1] *The Rising Star of India*, by Anup Singh (Allen & Unwin).

lyrical, and one banner headline said bluntly, 'He's a Beaut and she's even more of a Beaut'.

New Zealand welcomed them with less effusion but with equal sincerity. Throughout the tour gifts of all kinds, from freshly cut flowers to fresh trout and chocolates, were showered on the Mountbattens. Though most of the boxes of chocolate were sent to Edwina, she had little opportunity of sampling them, for the Supreme Commander, who has a sweet tooth, generally made serious inroads on the boxes.

By the end of the tour the Mountbattens were exhausted. But they had done an excellent public-relations job. Their goodwill visit had indeed strengthened the bonds of loyalty and admiration which bound the Dominions to the Mother Country. Lord Louis had to hurry back to Singapore, while Edwina remained to carry out an extensive itinerary of hospital inspections for the Red Cross and St. John organizations.

A fortnight later she joined him and accompanied him on a visit to Nepal, where its King decorated the Supreme Commander with the Grand Cross of the Star of Nepal. But Edwina's final and most vivid memory of this brief visit to India was of a short holiday at Kashmir, where, as guests of the Maharajah, the Mountbattens spent some days at Srinagar.

Watered by the turbulent Jhelum, Srinagar is known as the Venice of the North. As unique in its fashion as its statelier counterpart on the Adriatic, Srinagar of the seven crooked bridges has suffered many earthquakes, all of which have given to the city a strange and dishevelled charm. Ornately decorated balconies perilously straddle the water and flat-roofed houses built of brick and timber in shades of caramel and mushroom lurch amiably and preposterously towards the vast snowpeaks of the Vale of Kashmir.

Everywhere there is an exotic beauty. In the rugs and carpets of Kashmir, the saris of the womenfolk, in the strange and massive ornaments from Tibet and the materials and shawls from Persia. Edwina shopped in the narrow back-streets of the city, and went boating on the lake in a small barge, with a velvet dais and a splendid red-and-gold canopy, paddled by honey-coloured boatmen wielding heart-shaped paddles. But long after the dream had faded she remembered the loveliest of Jahangir's gardens, the Shalimarbargh ('The Abode of

Love'), with its long terraces, tapestries of flowers, grave ave-
nues of chinar where round a central pavilion of black marble
pillars 150 fountains made crystal music.

. . .

The life to which the Mountbattens returned in London
lacked the excitement, glamour, and element of risk which
always electrified them into achievement. For the Supreme
Commander the canvas of his activities had narrowed. His
most immediate concern was to attend the Senior Officer's
Technical Course at Portsmouth. Having divested himself of
two grades of rank, he was cheerfully preparing for further
service in the Royal Navy as Rear-Admiral in command of the
First Cruiser Squadron.

Created Viscount and Viscountess Mountbatten of Burma,
Lord Louis and Edwina stepped gratefully out of the limelight
to concentrate on domestic matters which had for long been
neglected. Broadlands was still a hospital, but there were all
manner of problems connected with the estate which needed
personal attention. Some of Edwina's pictures had suffered
damage after an air raid during which the firemen's hosepipes
had flooded the vaults in which they had been stored. One
of these pictures was Franz Hals' famous 'Portrait of a Lady',
whose surface varnish had been reduced to a milky slime. The
picture was later so skilfully renovated that it was impossible to
discover any trace of its immersion.

If the lives of the Mountbattens at this moment were static,
momentous happenings were astir in that of their immediate
family. Patricia had become engaged to Lord Brabourne,
whom she had met in Singapore when he was one of Lord
Louis' A.D.C.s, and their nephew, Prince Philip, carried about
with him everywhere in his battered valise a photograph of
Princess Elizabeth.

Patricia was to be married in October. Soon wedding
presents began to arrive and the small house in Chester Street
was filled with expensive gifts. One night burglars attempted
to force an entry. They were unsuccessful, but the incident
so preyed on the mind of the butler that for days afterwards
he had violent nightmares. Waking in the middle of one particularly vivid and unpleasant dream he found that, in his
agitation, he had reduced his room to indescribable disorder

and beyond the door could be heard raised voices and the trampling of feet. Peering out, he saw Lord Louis in his pyjamas, leading a posse of policemen, who were tearing through the rooms in hot pursuit of the intruders. Lord Louis had heard piercing screams and had instantly summoned the police. When a complete search of the house had been made without any trace of the burglars being found, the police withdrew, and Lord Louis returned puzzled to bed. The butler could have told him whose screams he had heard, but he deemed it expedient to remain silent then and later to buy a nerve-tonic.

Lord Louis, then on leave, took the greatest interest in planning the organization of the wedding. The King and Queen were to be present, and the Princesses Elizabeth and Margaret were to attend Patricia as bridesmaids. Over a thousand guests had been invited to attend the wedding in Hampshire. With his customary attention to detail, Lord Louis had worked out an original ingenious scheme for the parking of the guests' cars. So unusual was it that he woke one night realizing that utter chaos would ensue unless the instructions to chauffeurs and owner-drivers were not immediately changed. The secretaries were roused, and the work of amendment was instantly put in hand. Towards dawn, when the work was completed, Lord Louis placed the vast stack of envelopes in his car and drove off to post them himself.

The organization worked perfectly. Guests left London in the Bournemouth Belle, had luncheon—provided by their hosts—on the train, were met at Southampton and transported to Romsey. Patricia, like her mother, was married in Romsey Abbey, and the reception took place in the dining-room of Broadlands. Afterwards their Majesties accompanied the wedding party to Crosfield Hall, Romsey, to participate in a celebration given for all the Mountbatten and Brabourne tenants and staff.

This was a momentous occasion in the lives of the Mountbattens, for while, with the departure of their beloved elder daughter to her new and happy life, the walls of the warm, close family circle were breached, it was also the beginning of a closer alliance with the Royal Family. For the first time, Princess Elizabeth and their nephew, Prince Philip, were photographed arriving together at Romsey Abbey.

Vice-Regal Portrait

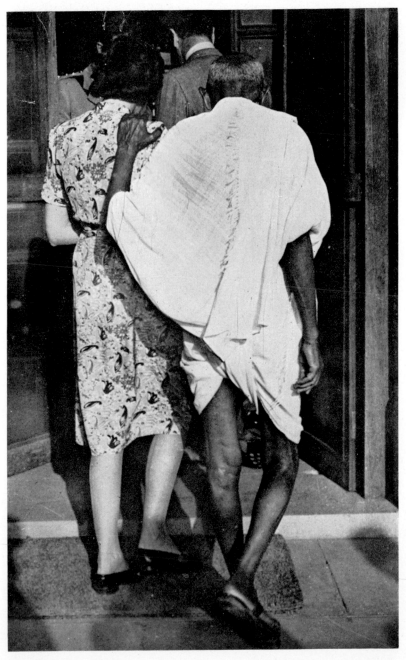

Famous photograph taken by Max Desfors at New Delhi of Gandhi with
his hand on Edwina's shoulder

In January 1947, two days before Princess Elizabeth left on her tour of South Africa, she accompanied her parents to a dinner-party given by the Mountbattens at Chester Street. Among the guests were the newly married couple, and also Lord Milford Haven and Prince Philip. Clearly this intimate gathering had great significance, and though the engagement was not announced until the return of Princess Elizabeth from South Africa, there were no doubts in the minds of those present that the King and Queen warmly approved their daughter's choice. Champagne was taken by the guests, and from the walls the eyes of the woman in the Franz Hals portrait which for centuries had watched the rise and fall of history looked down benignly on the young couple who were so deeply in love.

CHAPTER XV

THE LAST VICEREINE

THE GREEK writer who first recorded a description of India in the sixth century B.C. said that the Skiapodes were a race with feet so large that they were able to use them as sunshades, while others had ears of immense proportions in which they could enwrap themselves when they were cold. Herodotus added further embellishments to these tales, and Megasthenes offered it as his contribution that India was inhabited by a race of mortals with 'gentle manners, who had no mouths and existed on the fumes of roast meat and the scent of fruit and flowers. So delicate were their nostrils, that they dwelt mainly in the countryside to avoid the stench of cities.'

Down the centuries myths and travellers' tales formed, in the mind of the West, the Indian legend, and all that was related to the East was shrouded in mystery and wonder. India was the land of marble palaces, of fabulous jewels, and of sacred animals; a country so distant that it might well have existed only in the imagination of the scribes. European visitors to the Indies in the sixteenth and seventeenth centuries added their reports of palaces which eclipsed Versailles in grandeur, gardens of unbelievable beauty, and wealth beyond the dreams of avarice, and with the coming of the Western traders legend became fact. India was indeed a fabulous land. The Portuguese, Dutch, French, and English established themselves in small settlements along the Indian coast, which they rapidly expanded as they acquired lands and trading facilities from friendly native princes.

The main stations established by the British—at Madras, Calcutta, and Bombay, governed by a council of merchants, were controlled from home by the powerful East India Company. The interests of England in India were from the outset ably directed by men of courage and vision. Robert Clive and Warren Hastings led the way. They were followed by a succession of Governors-General and Viceroys, supported by an Army and a Civil Service, who first conquered, then pacified, ruled, and educated India for 200 years.

But the nineteenth century saw the dawn of a desire for independence in India. Education had widened the horizon of many Indians, some of whom had gained in Europe a democratic and legalistic view. As education developed, self-consciousness grew until finally it assumed a political form and a desire for freedom. 'In the early years, British Indian officials accepted and propagated the ideas of self-government on the basis of Indian acceptance of western ideals.' [1]

In 1818 the Governor-General of India, Lord Hastings, gave promise of 'a time not very remote . . . when England will, on sound principles of policy, wish to relinquish the domination that she has gradually and unintentionally assumed over this country and from which she cannot at present recede.' Several generations were to pass, however, before this promise was to be implemented, although during these years tentative efforts were made to associate Indians with the task of responsible government. Practical procedure in this respect differed considerably from the teachings of the schools and universities which were progressively influencing the Indian middle classes. Educational establishments, ignoring national tradition, fostered the British system, and therefore succeeding generations of Indians were imbued with the principles of democratic parliamentary rule.

So long as there was no immediate prospect of even the most limited form of self-government there was no militant nationalism, and therefore no sectional conflict, as later developed between Hindu and Muslim when the transfer of power became no longer a mirage, but a foreseeable reality. The question as to who should or would take over the government of the country once the transfer had taken place became the all-important issue.

In 1855 the Indian National Congress had come into being with the avowed aim of pressing its claim for Indian self-government. Later this claim was extended to cover absolute independence. The Indian National Congress never received full support from the Muslims, who recognized and resented that it was fundamentally representative of the Hindu. This

[1] *India, Pakistan and the West*, by Percival Spear (Oxford University Press).

resentment took on a tangible form when the All India Muslim
League was formed in 1906.

Though Hindu and Muslim are both Indians sharing the
Indian temperament and love of country, their dress, customs,
food, codes of conduct, and ideals are radically different.   The
growing and mutual distrust was evidenced by the frequent
and sanguinary clashes which occurred in the years following
World War I.

During all these years the British were seeking a formula for
a new Constitution.   The Simon Commission was followed by
the Round Table Conference, and this in turn was succeeded
by the Joint Select Committee of Parliament, and finally the
Government of India Act of 1935.

This set out to share the responsibility of government between the British Indian provinces and the Princely States in
a single government with the Viceroy as its head, together
with a Council of Ministers broadly responsible to the Legislature, and to create in the eleven provinces autonomous governments completely responsible to elected legislatures.   The
latter objective of the Act of 1935 was achieved, and the main
functions of Provincial Governments were placed under the
direction of Indian Ministers.   The primary object of the
Act did not come to pass in spite of untiring efforts defeated
by the outbreak of war in 1939.   Nevertheless the final outcome was the transfer of considerable power from Britain to
India.

Jinnah had broken with Congress by October 1937, whose
policy he considered to be purely Hindu.   He was now concentrating all his energies in strengthening and expanding the
Muslim League, and a year later he felt able to state that the
Muslims of India were represented by the League.   His
avowed intention was to partition India so that the Muslims
should rule in the areas where they were numerically pre-
dominant.   Thus Pakistan was the ultimate goal.

With the outbreak of World War II, India found herself
ranged in the ranks against Hitler.   The majority of Indians
were satisfied that this should be so.   The leaders of the Muslim
League, however, showed lukewarm support and endeavoured
to bargain that their contribution to the war effort was con-
ditional on their subsequent freedom to decide their own major

issues. The Princes had declared their support in favour of
the Allies. Congress, while supporting the ideals of freedom,
declined wholehearted support, on the grounds that India
herself did not enjoy such freedom.

In 1942 Sir Stafford Cripps was sent by the British Government to India with proposals for the participation of Indians
in the Government of the country for the period of the war.
This became known as the Cripps Offer, and contained provision for the subsequent stages by which India could be granted
constitutional settlement. This draft declaration obviously
removed many of the objections of both Congress and the Muslim League, but the stumbling blocks were many, and finally
the negotiations broke down completely, and Cripps returned
to England.

Summarized, the result of Sir Stafford Cripps' visit was that
Congress demanded immediate independence with no conditions attached, while the British Government reiterated that
the Cripps Offer was the only basis for negotiations.

The 'Quit India' resolution of the Working Committee of
Congress resolved on July 14th, 1942, was approved on August
7th by the All-India Congress Committee with only slight
modifications.   Despite the real possibility of invasion of India
by Japan, animosity towards Britain had hardened to such a
degree that the continuing success of Japanese arms was almost
welcome.

In the early hours of August 9th, Gandhi informed the All-
India Congress Committee that he would place their resolution
before the Viceroy. The matter was taken out of his hands,
for within a few hours Gandhi, together with Nehru, Mrs.
Naidu, and others, were dragged off to prison by the British,
who had decided to act in the face of Congress's threat to start
'a mass struggle on non-violent lines on the widest possible
scale' under the leadership of Gandhi. This mass arrest of
their leaders sparked off a chain of violence.

Jinnah, as spokesman of the Muslim League, exhorted the
Muslims not to follow the lead of Congress, and promised the
British Government full support in their war effort. As a
quid pro quo he wanted a promise that his Pakistan scheme
should be put into effect. A position of deadlock had been
reached, with Congress demanding independence on a United

India basis and the Muslim League also demanding independence with a settlement involving partition. This situation continued until the end of the war. Nonetheless Britain was committed to granting independence to India, and the immediate problem was to agree on the future form of self-government.

In 1945 the leaders were released from prison, and a tremendous effort was made to achieve a unitary solution. In March, the then Viceroy, Lord Wavell, flew to London for discussions with the Coalition Government. The proposal he submitted on his return was again rejected by Congress. When the Labour Government came into power in Britain the situation in India was getting out of hand, and there were both uprisings and communal unrest. The Government dispatched three Cabinet Ministers to try to achieve some settlement on the spot. These ministers were Stafford Cripps, Pethick-Lawrence, and A. V. Alexander. They produced the Cabinet Mission Plan, which was the final effort to achieve a United India with a weak central government and wide local powers. The mission failed, and it was against this tangled background that the final card was played—to send a new Viceroy to make a settlement inside a time limit: the object of the time limit being to induce a settlement.

Thus in the year 1947 the India of which Victoria of England had been Queen Empress, and which was populated by 200 million Hindus, 100 million Muslims and Sikhs, 50 million Depressed Classes, and 80 million inhabitants of the Princely States, speaking a variety of tongues, read or heard by word of mouth that the Queen Empress' great-grandson had come to free them from their shackles.

On February 20th, 1947, Parliament learned the nature of the appointment of Lord Mountbatten as Viceroy of India. In making the announcement the Prime Minister, Mr. Attlee, stated that he would 'be entrusted with the task of transferring to Indian hands the responsibility for the government of British India'. He added that there was to be a time limit for achieving agreement if possible, and for transferring power in any case by June 1948.

The first sailor and last Englishman to become Viceroy of India, Lord Mountbatten, had been chosen as the instrument to effect a voluntary resignation of power for which history has no precedent. Nor was he in any way anxious to undertake this complicated and delicate task, for when he was first invited by Mr. Attlee to succeed Lord Wavell as Viceroy he 'put up a stiff fight against the Prime Minister's pressure and blandishments' and the interview ended on a note of indecision.[1] His sole desire and long-interrupted personal ambition was to resume his career in the Navy. Finally, however, at the express wish of the King, and on the understanding that his return to the Navy would be guaranteed, Lord Louis accepted the Viceroyalty and the task of transfer.

Before the final decision had been taken, however, Lord Louis and Edwina, who had been looking forward to a long-planned family holiday in Switzerland, left for Davos.

Four days after their arrival in Davos, Lord Louis was recalled to London. He and Edwina were driven to Zurich, where a special aircraft was waiting for them. As soon as they reached London, Lord Louis went immediately to see the Prime Minister, while Edwina, who for the first time in many years was feeling ill, went disconsolately to Chester Street.

The next few weeks were full of tension. Apart from the magnitude and difficulties of the mission awaiting him, Lord Louis had personal anxieties. His mother, who had been taken ill at Broadlands, was recovering, but was far from well, and Edwina, who had not long been reunited with her family and friends, was loath to leave them again.

Once the die was cast, and the date of departure for India fixed, Edwina, with her customary verve, began making arrangements. In the intervals of meetings and interviews she went shopping to buy materials for Pammie and herself, an expedition which was, she said, 'a nightmare'. There were fittings, photographs, more interviews, more people to see. One particularly hectic day ended with the Prime Minister, his wife, and Prince Philip dining at Chester Street.

She was still feeling ill, and finally, having consulted a specialist, was told that she must have an immediate, if minor operation. Vastly annoyed at having to lose time, she nonetheless went into a nursing home, where the day after her

[1] *Mission with Mountbatten*, by Alan Campbell-Johnson (Robert Hale).

operation she was sitting up in bed, writing letters and going through her folders. The following day, feeling very shaky, she went home. This did not prevent her from going to the office, taking tea with Queen Mary, and on her return being invested with the Crown of India by the Duke of Gloucester, who had come to Chester Street for this purpose. Later, in the intense cold, she visited a V.A.D. who had had a baby at Queen Charlotte's Hospital.

By March 18th, the entire household at Chester Street was nearly demented as frenzied, last-minute packings took place. Yet there was still time and energy to organize a successful cocktail party at the R.A.C. Seven hundred guests came to bid farewell to the Mountbattens, among them the Duke of Gloucester, the Duchess of Kent, Queen Ena of Spain, members of St. John and the Red Cross, Government servants, and the caretakers from the St. John offices.

On the morning of the departure, Thursday, March 20th, 1947, Edwina rose at an unearthly hour, dictated last-minute letters, said farewell to her assembled staff, and with Lord Louis was driven in one of the Royal cars to Northolt. Prince Philip, Malcolm Sargent, and other close friends had come to say adieu. Travelling with Lord Louis and Edwina were their daughter Pamela, Captain R. V. Brockman, personal secretary to Lord Louis, Muriel Watson, personal assistant to Edwina, Elizabeth Ward, her private secretary, Charles, Lord Louis' valet, and a maid, engaged for the specific task of attending to the Vicereine.

That evening Lord Louis and Edwina spent the night at Admiralty House, Malta. Edwina insisted on driving up to look at the house where, but for India, they might have lived. The take-off was scheduled for ten a.m. the next morning and the York flew smoothly towards Fayid. Here it was hot, and suddenly, as Edwina contemplated the pinkly glowing sands of the desert, her spirits began to lift. Another adventure, the greatest of her married life, had begun.

The York flew through the night, reaching Karachi in the late afternoon. Here the party were given refreshments before they flew on to New Delhi. They touched down at Palam Airport, where they were met by members of the Interim Government, among them Pandit Nehru, Liaquat Ali Khan,

important officials, and a posse of journalists and photographers.

All that afternoon preparations had been in train in the main
courtyard and up the steps leading to the Durbar Hall of
Viceroy's House.   The Mountbattens motored to the entrance
gates of Viceroy's House, where they transferred to an open
landau and, escorted by outriders, bowled magnificently up
to the red-carpeted steps, at the top of which stood Lord and
Lady Wavell waiting to receive them.   Lord Louis bowed
his head and Edwina curtsied to the Viceregal couple, while
the camera-men below were ardently taking shots of their
meeting.

The next morning Edwina and Lord Louis escorted the
Wavells to the airfield.   It was very windy, and it was with
sadness that the Mountbattens watched the departure of their
predecessors.   On their return to Viceroy's House, Edwina
was presented with a sheaf of Indian Sunday papers.   One
of them, *Dawn*, featured a magnificent photograph of Elizabeth
Ward and Captain Brockman describing the arrival of Their
Excellencies!

Edwina was well aware that there would be little time in the
future to take stock of her new home, and now, escorted by
Pamela and Elizabeth Ward, she decided to make a tour of
inspection of the palace, which occupied five acres and was a
hive of activity.   For the number of people housed and fed on
the Viceregal estate, including wives and children, totalled
some 5,820 souls.   Viceroy's House was sanctioned in 1914, as
Vice-regal Lodge, Old Delhi, had been built only as a temporary abode for the Viceroy when the capital was moved from
Calcutta to Delhi in 1911.

Sir Edwin Lutyens was the architect selected, and in 1914
work was begun on the present Viceroy's House.   The outbreak
of war in August of this year brought the work to an almost
total halt, and no further progress was made until April 1920,
when it was continued.   The building stands partly on rock
and partly on firm ground, and though it has four floors, it is
constructed in such a way as to appear to have only two.
Divided into five main blocks, the building consists of a large
central block and four wings.   The State rooms were situated
in the central block.   The Durbar Hall was designed on a large

circular plan under a 180-foot dome. At each of the four corners of the Durbar Hall, and to the west of it, was the long State drawing-room. In the west front was the ballroom and the State dining-rooms. The table in this room was made to seat 104 guests. Under these west-front rooms were five semi-State rooms facing the formal Moghul Gardens.

The exterior of Viceroy's House is faced with red or white stone. In the interior every variety of marble and stone in India was used with great effect. From Makrana in Jodhpur came the white marble used in the Durbar Hall and adjoining corridors. Black marble was brought from Dhuslana in Patiala. The columns in the Durbar Hall were made of yellow marble obtainable only from Jaisalmer State. In some of the rooms and loggias green marble was used. Most of the marble floors were inlaid in complicated and traditional patterns.

The furniture was made by carpenters imported from the Punjab, of woods brought from Indian forests. Every imaginable variety of wood was used: teak, toon, poon, haldoo, ainee, rose-wood, shisham, and walnut. The majority of the materials for upholstery and curtains were obtained from various textile centres throughout India.

On the lower floor was a fully equipped cinema theatre, and the basements accommodated a modern printing press, pump-room for air-conditioning machines, carpenter's workshops, electrical workshops, mason and stone-cutter's shop, P.W.D. stores, office staff canteen, painter's shops, armoury, house-keeper's storeroom, house laundry and many other workshops, offices, and storerooms.

In addition to the main block of buildings, comprising Viceroy's House itself, the principal members of the Viceroy's staff, such as his private secretary, military secretary, comptroller, surgeon, bodyguard officers, etc., were all granted special houses built within the main estate.

Four large gardens were controlled by a superintendent, who kept a staff of one garden overseer, six foremen, ten sub-foremen, two clerks, 350 gardeners, and fifty boys. The up-keep of the garden amounted to between £23,000 and £26,000 per annum.

The Viceregal gardens were divided up into Indian formal Moghul Garden, the Purdah Garden, and the Circular Garden, together with the Viceroy's court, staff house gardens, utility gardens, cricket-grounds and parks and a nine-hole golf course, making a total of 175 acres.

The gardens were laid out by Sir Edwin Lutyens and are formal, designed in the Moghul and Italian style, with grass squares, flower-beds, and bridged waterways at three different levels. Waterways and beds were framed with rose-coloured Jaipur stone, and the flower-beds, though not large, were so designed that when they were in full flower the whole setting resembled a splendid carpet.

Twenty gardeners were employed only to decorate the State rooms, tables, and private rooms with cut flowers; while fifty boys had supervised the ten working bullocks and acted as bird-scarers.

Also contained within the Viceregal estate was a fresh-water swimming-pool placed in its own enclosure amid lawns and gardens. A squash court was also incorporated in the changing-rooms to the swimming-bath. A pack of hounds of the Royal Delhi Hunt were accommodated in kennels adjoining the Viceregal stables, and stabling for hunt horses and accommodation for hunt servants was also found.

Apart from the staff employed in the offices of the private secretary, which totalled 200 persons; in the office of the military secretary who employed a personnel of 124 and the aides-de-camp; the Comptroller's Establishment was a complex organization. All servants were under the orders of the comptroller, assisted by the deputy comptroller, catering assistant, and housekeeper.

The head *khansama* was the head table servant and the most senior among the butlers, *abdars*, *khitmatgars*, silvermen, and *massalchis*. He was generally a man with over thirty years' service. Assisting him was a second *khansama*. The head silverman was responsible for the safe custody of silver and cutlery in the house. He had under him eleven silvermen. The head butler was responsible for the pantry and all fresh food, e.g. fruit, milk, butter, coffee, tea, etc., which might be ordered both at meal-times and between meals. Two butlers assisted the head butler. The head *abdar*, assisted by eight *abdars*, was responsible for the 'ready-use cellar' and for all drinks consumed in the house. The *khitmatgars* were table servants, who might, in an emergency, be called upon to perform the duties of *abdar*. Forty-four *khitmatgars* were permanently employed in the Viceregal establishment, and the normal complement of liveried servants on duty for large luncheons or dinners in the State dining-rooms was 112. The head *massalchi* and his twenty assistants were responsible for all the washing up of china and glass in the service rooms.

The most highly paid servant in Viceroy's House was the head cook. Like his assistants, he was a *mugh* from Chittagong district in East Bengal. Separate cooks were responsible for cooking soup, meat, fish, eggs, vegetables, and savouries. Nine cooks were employed under the head cook.

The head baker and his five assistants came from the Hooghly district in West Bengal. The head kitchen coolie—or head kitchen-maid—assisted by ten coolies, was responsible for the cleanliness of the bakery, kitchens, and sculleries. Low on the list, but an important personage, was the chicken-cleaner. He was solely employed in plucking and cleaning poultry. As approximately 150 chickens were consumed daily by the Viceregal establishment, he was fully employed.

The household establishment comprised storekeepers and their assistants; tinmen, tailors, a carpenter, a barber, a head *tindal*, or 'head housemaid'. Under him were three assistants and a staff of seventy-five men, whose occupations were as fascinating as their names. These were: *khalassis* and hot-water bearers; *jemadar* sweeper, working under the order of the head *tindal*. He and his staff were responsible for the cleaning of all indoor floors and lavatories. Two tennis-markers were responsible for the tennis and squash courts and their equipment and for the discipline of seventeen tennis-boys, who also served as ball-boys and caddies.

Eight inquiry-office boys or pages were employed at the inquiry office. This office was situated outside Viceroy's House and it was their duty to take messages from the inquiry office, or to conduct visitors to offices in the house. There were only two lifts in the house, which were not automatic, and these were worked by six lift-boys.

The rickshaws were looked after by the *mate jampani*. The laundry *jemadar* was in charge of the laundry and maintained discipline among the pinmen and washerwomen. He was responsible for the issue of washing materials and for all the laundry equipment. The head *dhobi* and his staff were in charge of all the washing and ironing of household linen and the clothes of everyone living in the house, also of the staffs of household, garage, hospital, and stables.

The camp *tindal* was in charge of all tent equipment, camp furniture, umbrellas, *dhurries*, and flags. He was assisted by a camp polisher. There were also eleven camp *khalassis* under the camp *tindal*.

One of the most-sought-after positions in this vast domestic hierarchy was that of *daftery*. Three *dafteries* were responsible for seeing to all writing-tables and for providing stationery throughout the house. The men chosen as *dafteries* could read English, and were normally promoted from among the senior *chaprassis*.

Full dress for the staff consisted of scarlet tunics faced with gold braid and blue overall trousers with a gold stripe on the seam. For ordinary daily duties a blue undress uniform was worn.

The surgeon to the Viceroy worked with a fully equipped dispensary, operating theatre, and hospital ward on the Vice-regal estate. In his establishment were two assistant surgeons, three *peons*, and one lady house visitor. Also in his charge came the anti-malarial and sanitary establishment.

The A.D.C. in charge of invitations had an office consisting of one head clerk with two clerks as his assistants. One A.D.C. was responsible for the Viceroy's stables, which were apart from the body-guard stables. State carriages, victorias, and barouches were kept in his charge, together with postillions, liveries, and State harness. To assist him in the proper main-tenance of the stables there were *risaldars* of cavalry and a stable staff of four postillions, three *sikligars* (harness-cleaners), a coachman, a farrier, and no fewer than forty *syces* or grooms. A total of nine carriages were maintained, and in the garage were a Rolls Royce for the use of His Excellency, a Humber for Her Excellency, nine passenger automobiles, and two lorries.

Lord Willingdon (Viceroy of India 1931–36) acquired the first Viceregal plane in 1932. A larger plane, the *Star of India*, was purchased some time later. Lord Louis was to introduce the four-engined York in addition to the Dakota which was used by Lord Wavell.

Former Viceroys had their own band recruited from serving units, most of whom came from British units in India. The band was never idle. It played at State banquets, dinner-parties, and large luncheon-parties. At least once a month it played for a dance, usually attended by Their Excellencies. In addition it gave orchestral concerts and light programmes in aid of various charities. In 1942 the band was broken up and its members were placed at the disposal of the Defence Department.

The former chatelaines of this immense establishment, though they might make minor changes in the menus, the arrangement of furniture, or in flower decorations, had little real control over the running of the household. Successive Vicereines, having vainly tried innovations, had fallen in with the old and established order. In any case, it was understood that the social and charitable duties of the Vicereine left her little time for purely domestic affairs.

Edwina, however, had no intention of being a figure-head. From the beginning she took a personal part in the running of the establishment, taking particular interest in the welfare and accommodation of the indoor and outdoor staff. Also, with her individual ideas of the arrangement of rooms, she was constantly trying to move and re-group heavy teak-frame chairs and sofas, but could never complete her new scheme before a senior servant had noiselessly appeared and was staring in shocked and silent horror at the spectacle of the Vicereine exerting herself in manual effort. A former Vicereine, Lady Linlithgow, whose puppy had had a slight mishap on the carpet before a party, rang for a servant to repair the damage. But by the time a servant of sufficiently low caste had been summoned, the guests arrived to find the Vicereine vigorously mopping the carpet herself.

Always in the margin of spectacular historical events there watches an unobtrusive little man, who with pen or camera records the scene. So it was with the swearing-in ceremony of the last Viceroy and his Vicereine. This man, anonymous, elderly, and *blasé*, had photographed the cadaver of Il Duce, swinging high against the saffron sky of Milan; had attended the coronation of two kings of England; and quietly, for over thirty years, had recorded the facets of life and death, of national sorrow and rejoicing all over the world.

Now, as he took his place with the other pressmen and camera-men, who, for the first time, were being allowed to cover the ceremony in the Durbar Hall of Viceroy's House on the morning of March 24th, 1947, he was conscious of the impressive beauty of the scene and of its historic significance.

From where he stood he could see the audience who had come together to fill the vast circular hall.   On one side were the senior ruling princes, splendidly bedecked with jewels.   One fourth of the coat of one maharajah was entirely covered by diamonds; another carried a diamond-hilted sword in a purple velvet diamond scabbard.   On the other side sat the Viceroy's Executive Council in their national dress.

Of the leaders of free India, Pandit Nehru sat impassively, his eyes fixed on the two empty thrones set on a gold-carpeted dais beneath a canopy of scarlet and gold.   Tall and straight, and clad in their traditional dress of scarlet and blue, stood the Viceroy's body-guard.[1]

At nine twenty-nine the time of waiting came to an end as a fanfare of silver trumpets thrilling from the dome of the Durbar Hall announced the arrival of the Mountbattens.   As the notes of the trumpets died away, the crowd rose, and the A.D.C.s, splendid in scarlet, led Their Excellencies towards the throne.   The Viceroy, the Viscount Mountbatten of Burma, wearing the pale blue robe of the Grand Master of the Star of India over the full-dress uniform of a rear-admiral of the Royal Navy, 'looked superb with the dark-blue ribbon of Knight

[1] The body-guard was formed at Benares in September 1773 by Warren Hastings.   The official designation of the unit at this time was 'The Governor-General's Body-guard'.   This title remained the official designation, although after Lord Canning became the first Viceroy in 1859 the body-guard was usually called unofficially the Viceroy's body-guard.   The corps was originally recruited solely from amongst the Moghuls.   Hindus were added in 1800.   Seventy years later the composition consisted of Mohammedans, Brahmins, and Rajputs.   In 1883 Sikhs were enlisted for the first time, and in 1887 Punjabi Mussalmans were admitted.   The recruiting of Brahmins and Rajputs ceased in 1895.   The composition up to August 15th, 1947 was half Jat Sikhs and half Punjabi Mussalmans of the Tiwana, Awan, Moghul, and Rajput tribes.   Recruits were not accepted unless 6 feet tall and in possession of educational qualities above the sixth standard.

of the Garter and the overwhelming array of orders and ribbons across his chest. In addition to the Garter, they were
headed by no fewer than three Grand Crosses.'[1] Walking
beside him was the Vicereine, whose outward composure was
remarkable. Her gown of parchment brocade was slashed
by the dark sash and the star of the Order of St. John, and she
wore proudly her new Order, the Crown of India, together
with her war medals and other decorations.

Their Excellencies ascended the dais and took their places
on the golden thrones. Sir Patrick Spens, the Lord Chief
Justice of India, administered the oath, and Lord Louis repeated it after him. The whole ceremony was over in a quarter of an hour, the address taking four minutes. As the new
Viceroy and Governor-General regained his seat, the Viceregal
flag was unfurled on the flagstaff above Viceroy's House, and
his guards of honour in the forecourt gave the royal salute
simultaneously with similar guards of honour mounted by
every garrison throughout India.

The waiting audience then watched the resplendent figure
of the Viceroy as he rose to address them. 'This,' he said, 'is
not a normal viceroyalty on which I am embarking. His
Majesty's Government are resolved to transfer power by June
1948; and since new constitutional arrangements must be
made, and many complicated questions of administration
resolved—all of which take time to put into effect—this means
that a solution must be reached within the next few months.'
And he concluded his speech with these words: 'I shall need
the greatest goodwill of the greatest possible number and am
asking India today for that goodwill.'

Once again the silvery notes of the trumpets sounded from
the dome, and as they died away Royal Artillery at the top of
Kingsway fired the viceregal salute of thirty-one guns. Their
Excellencies, having made an unforgettable impression on those
seeing them for the first time, left Durbar Hall to organize their
new lives.

The arrival of the Mountbattens in India had caused much
fluttering in the dovecotes of the pukka sahib class. Until
then, with a few notable exceptions, the majority of European
women, wives of administrators, civil servants, and others,

[1] G.C.S.I., G.C.I.E., and G.C.V.O.   *Mission with Mountbatten.*

had considered Viceroy's House as the one citadel which would never be invaded by Indians, who, apart from the Indian Princes, many of whom had been educated in England, were considered by them as *persona non grata*. Though the Colonel's lady and Judy O'Grady were sisters under the skin, it was felt that Indian women, no matter how cultivated, could not enter the charmed circle. India, of course, belonged to the Indians, but Viceroy's House and its entourage belonged to the pukka sahibs. It had always been thus, and thus it would remain until such time as 'India was given away'.

These matrons had reckoned without the Mountbattens. They had asked India for goodwill, and in return were prepared to try to efface the memory of two centuries of subjugation and slights. They asked for co-operation and gave co-operation, and help where it was most needed. This policy, therefore, earned them the determined antagonism of those who refused to recognize the march of history, to make any compromise, or to understand the difficulties and subtleties of the task undertaken by the Mountbattens.

Now all they could do was to mourn the days of vanished splendour, the era of garden-parties, dinner-parties, and balls. The Viceroy and Vicereine were quite aware of the fact that they were the representatives of 'H.I.M. The King Emperor', and that they were expected to live in the pomp and splendour in which the Viceroys of India had always lived. Under more normal conditions they would no doubt have kept up the traditional round of entertainments, but the conditions under which they were living were far from normal and time was short.

The situation was serious. Hindu–Muslim animosity was beginning to take violent form. There was fighting and counter rioting. These were particularly acute in Bihar and Bengal. Inevitably the area of disturbance widened, and the Muslim League leader, Mr. Jinnah, informed Lord Louis that, very shortly, the situation would be completely out of hand. Lord Louis had been well aware from the outset that this mission would be a delicate one, but it was only now, when he had deliberated with the Indian leaders, that he realized that unless speedy and effective action was taken the British Raj, and indeed the whole of India, would be blown sky high in the eruption of the volcano of partisan hatred.

M

The Mountbattens had one thing to offer India: a gift that had been long withheld from the Indians—friendship; and this they gave, not as a social gesture, not as a diplomatic sop, but from their own reserves of kindliness and humanity.

While Lord Louis was tackling his side of the problem, Edwina was trying to adjust herself to her new existence. So swift had been the transition from her normal life that as she walked through the endless marble corridors of the palace that was her temporary home, a sensation of complete unreality overcame her and she began to suffer from a form of claustrophobia, feeling that she was completely cut off from the familiar outside world, and it was not until she had arranged the routine of her personal work, held a few meetings and dictated letters and reports, that the sense of unreality began to fade.

Her plan of campaign was simple and effective. She must gain the friendship of the wives, sisters, and daughters of the Indian leaders. The plan was simple; its execution was more complicated. The majority of these women were passionately anti-British and highly suspicious of the intentions of the representatives of Britain. All of them were intelligent, cultivated, and closely associated with the work of the leaders of India. They had watched the arrival of the Mountbattens with deep misgivings and now, silently, they awaited developments. Among Edwina's first visitors was the remarkable Rajkumari Amrit Kaur, for many years Gandhi's secretary.[1] From the beginning the spark of friendship was struck between them and endures to this day. The Indian Princess was well qualified to brief the Vicereine on the activities of the Indian woman in every field, and it was now that Edwina learned of the appalling handicaps that confronted the nursing profession in India, and of the desperate and urgent need for the establishment of an Indian Nursing Council, both from the domestic and international point of view. A Bill had been initiated in 1943, but had regularly been by-passed. With the forthcoming division of India it was obvious that a relentless battle must be waged to secure its legislation before partition.[2]

[1] After the transfer of power, Rajkumari Amrit Kaur became the first woman to hold Cabinet rank as Minister of Health, a post she held for nearly ten years.

[2] A week before Partition, the Nursing Council Bill was sanctioned by the Cabinets of India and Pakistan.

The days began to assume a familiar pattern.   In the morning there was a staff meeting, dictation, and interviews.
Edwina was ably assisted in her work by Muriel Watson, for
many years a St. John colleague, and a tower of strength in
every emergency.   Equally indispensable was Elizabeth Ward.
These two stalwarts were joined by Mr. Banerjee, an Indian
secretary who for many years had helped previous Vicereines
with their welfare contacts and work.

The first garden party given by the Mountbattens was
attended by the delegates of the great Asian Relations Conference, which had been meeting near the Red Fort in Old
Delhi during the last week in March.   Seven hundred guests,
many of whom had never set foot in Viceroy's House, walked in
the Moghul Gardens and circulated in the State rooms.   This
gathering was of immense significance to hosts and guests.
Alan Campbell-Johnson noted in his diary, 'As I mingled with
the guests I gained no sense of hostility, but only of reserve
struggling with suppressed curiosity.   The Mountbattens did
much tonight to break down this reserve.' [1]

It was not until the end of March that Edwina found time
to drive round Old Delhi and to make a sentimental journey
to the University, the former Viceregal Lodge, in which she and
Dickie had become engaged in 1922.   Much had changed in
India since that time, New Delhi had come into being, but Old
Delhi was still a city of mystery and enchantment.   Town
planning had had no part in the fashioning of the narrow alley-
ways and congested dwellings.   Yet mystery lingered behind the
stout teak doors, and behind the lattice-work over the windows
long, dark eyes stared thoughtfully down into the bustle below.

In the bazaars cross-legged craftsmen in their tiny booths
carried on their ancient skills.   Wood and ivory turners,
blacksmiths, coppersmiths, gold-beaters, and carpet-makers
worked with delicacy and precision.   Everywhere there was
colour and the smell of ghee and spices mingled with the scent
of smoke and pungent oils.   Golden children played in the
gutters and dignified old men, deaf to the noise and the lusty,
bursting life about them, played chess.

Yet in the midst of this apparently happy and uninhibited
throng stalked poverty, disease, and frustration, and the tale

[1] *Mission with Mountbatten.*

of misery and unrest could be told only by those who had long
been associated with it. They were many—European and
Indian women, whose lives had been dedicated to welfare work
in many fields. It was to these women that Edwina listened,
appalled by a long history of negligence, disinterest, and mis-
understandings.

One after the other the leading women of India responded
to her invitations. They came, coldly at first, but left warmed
by Edwina's friendliness and her perceptive understanding of
the problems with which they had battled for so long. Mrs.
Vijaya Lakshmi Pandit, brilliant sister of Nehru, soon became
a warm friend, and the shy daughter of Vallabhbhai Patel,
Maniben Patel, came to call, and to her surprise found herself
inviting the Vicereine and her daughter to visit their home.
One of the most welcome of Edwina's visitors was the aged
poetess and stateswoman, Sarojini Naidu. She had been at
school with Edwina's mother, and the tie of amity had endured
throughout Maud Ashley's brief life. Mrs. Naidu had never
forgotten Maud, and now she gave to her daughter the same
tender and affectionate friendship.

Early in the afternoon of March 31st the Moghul Gardens
outside Lord Louis' study were packed with press-men and
photographers. In the dark, air-cooled study a momentous
meeting was taking place. Mahatma Gandhi was paying his
first call on the Viceroy and Vicereine before beginning his
series of political interviews with Lord Louis.

After a brief interval the waiting camera-men saw Gandhi,
escorted by the Mountbattens, coming out to them. The impressive old man in whom beat the heart of India was in excellent humour. Obediently he posed, his toothless gums
stretched in a benevolent smile. The whiteness of his clothes
was dazzling in the brilliant sunlight. One man stood apart
from the rush of agitated camera-men. This was Max Desfors,
the Associated Press of America photographer. As Gandhi
turned, to return to the study, he placed his hand on Edwina's
shoulder. The shutter of Desfors' camera clicked. He had
secured an historic picture. Indians seeing this photograph in
their papers immediately understood its immense significance.
The Mahatma by this gesture was offering the Mountbattens
spontaneous friendship.

Later, in the study again, Edwina sat listening to the sage describing his early life and experiences in South Africa. For an hour and a quarter she listened to the gentle, lisping voice, which for more than half a century had been preaching *Satyagraha* (truth-force) and practising desirelessness. Thinking back on some of the subjects he had discussed, she remembered that he had said that originally the West had received its wisdom from the East: Zoroaster, Buddha, Moses, Jesus, Mohammed, Krishna, Rama, and lesser lights. He said, too, that the message of Asia was not to be learned through Western spectacles or through the atomic bomb. The message to the West must be the message of love and the message of truth. When Edwina rose to leave her husband and Gandhi to begin their political discussion she felt something of the regard and veneration which touched all those who approached the Mahatma.

Edwina's schedule was tight and there was little time for leisure. However, whenever possible she rode in the very early mornings with Lord Louis and Pamela. Sometimes she preferred to walk in the gardens with the old English gardener who for thirty years had cared for the Viceregal gardens, and with Mizzen, her old Sealyham. To the surprise of all, Mizzen had not only adapted himself to the exigencies of the climate, but, under the care of a devoted kennelman, appeared to have taken on a new lease of life.

While Edwina and the head gardener strolled together, Mizzen ambled gaily along, sniffing the delicious scents of freedom. From early January to late February the gardens were a delight of massed colour. Among the exotic and opulent flowers bloomed English annuals, sown the previous year, in a temperature of 110 to 118 degrees. Butterflies, like bright flower-petals, drifted through the air, which was scented with verbena, jasmine, and stock.

Lord Louis was anxious for Edwina to meet Mrs. Asef Ali, one of the aggressively anti-British Indian socialist leaders whose husband had just gone to the U.S.A. as Indian representative there. A courteous invitation was dispatched to her. This was courteously but firmly declined. *Impasse.* Edwina wondered what her next move should be. She did not have long to wait. Gandhi came to talk with Lord Louis. With him was Mrs. Asef Ali. 'I heard she wouldn't come,' he said, 'so I brought her with me.' During the whole time the Mountbattens were in India Pamela did Trojan work and was a tower of strength to her mother and father.

On April 19th, Pamela celebrated her eighteenth birthday. She, like her mother, had been swept up in a spate of work. She worked regularly at an improvised free dispensary, functioning in tents, where poor people from the towns and villages around Delhi who could not afford proper medical treatment or were unwilling or unable to go into hospital and to medical practitioners could receive free treatment.

The Mountbattens gave a small party for Pamela. Held in the walled garden by the swimming-pool, it was an enchanted evening, long remembered by the guests who danced, dined, and swam under a velvet sky and with the sound of fountains plashing, and the night perfumed with the scent of the myriads of red roses which climbed against the walls.

As the thermometer rose, most women and children left for the pure, cool air of the hills, but the Vicereine, disregarding the mounting heat, remained in Delhi to carry on her work.

Each day there were visits and inspections to hospitals and health centres. There were State ceremonies, banquets, investitures, formal luncheon-parties, informal luncheon-parties, cocktail parties, and dinners, and on each and every occasion the Vicereine was required to appear, exquisitely gowned, a model of charm and *savoir faire*, even if her head was bursting with migraine and her feet aching from having walked through endless wards and hospital corridors. Not all visitors had a flow of small talk. Some were shy, some disapproving, some over-awed, and some frankly difficult to unfreeze. All had to be encouraged and cajoled, and, in the main, even the dullest guests left Edwina's ambience feeling that he or she had positively sparkled in the Viceregal circle.

.   .   .

Towards the end of April the Viceregal party set off for Peshawar. On arriving at Government House, the Governor, Sir Olaf Caroe, informed them that they had flown in at a moment of extreme crisis. An immense Moslem League demonstration was taking place less than a mile away, which, with the intention of placing its grievance before the Viceroy, was preparing to march on Government House. At least 70,000 demonstrators who had come from the remote parts of the Province had made their way to this focal point.

It was decided that Mountbatten should go to them before they set off on their march, and without more ado he got into his car. Edwina, without hesitation, joined him. Cunningham Park was packed solid with fanatical demonstrators, among whom were many women and children. Waving green flags with the white crescent of Pakistan, their voices rose in a slow, impressive chant, 'Pakistan Zindebad'.

Members of the Viceregal party who had clambered up on to a railway embankment overlooking the crowd watched with apprehension. They had been told that the local police and military would be quite powerless to halt the demonstrators should they decide to march on Government House.

Lord Louis and Edwina, dressed in the bush shirts in which they had travelled, appeared. The chant of 'Pakistan Zindebad' continued, and the flags waved more wildly than ever. Within a few minutes, however, a few faint cheers could be heard. Thousands of pairs of dark, brilliant eyes stared at the Mountbattens. Then the cries of 'Pakistan Zindebad' died away and suddenly an outburst of cheering was followed by triumphant shouts of 'Mountbatten Zindebad'. For over half an hour Lord Louis and Edwina stood waving at the demonstrators. By the end of this time all tension was over and the multitude began good-humouredly to drift away. Officials, thinking on what might have happened, wiped their dripping foreheads, and the Mountbattens drove off towards Government House and a much-needed and belated luncheon.

The following day six cars carrying the Viceregal party drove up into the hills for a tour of the Khyber Pass and to attend a *jirga* [1] at Jamrud. As a girl of nineteen, Edwina had made this journey, at that time a venture not to be lightly undertaken by a young European woman. Always she had retained a vivid memory of the wild North-west Frontier scenery, and now she marvelled at finding nothing changed of what she so well remembered.

For all those years, while she had been undergoing her apprenticeship of life, while she had darted uneasily hither

[1] *Jirga*=Tribal meeting.

and thither seeking the answers, many of which still eluded her, the sun had beaten down upon this desolate country; there had been bloodshed and sickness, and in the stone-built villages, guarded by their watch-towers, women had borne their children while their superbly arrogant men had fought and died in tribal skirmishes.

The day was clear and sunny, every detail in the pure and limpid air was precise, yet there was a dreamlike quality to this hour as she watched once again a tribe of nomad tribesmen making their way slowly to their homes in Afghanistan. Having wintered in the Peshawar valley, they now moved steadily up the pass. Prodding and pushing the livestock were the lean tribesmen, and in the arms of the women were babies, many of whom were blue-eyed and fair of skin. They travelled steadfastly towards the high places in which they had their homes, and when they had passed along the ancient caravan route, the dusty track was silent and hostile.

From the top of the Charbagh Pass a superb panorama was spread beneath them. Beyond the Afghan border the mountains of the Hindu Kush merged into the snowy horizon. When they had looked their fill upon the promised land, the party drove down to Landi Kotal, where Lord Louis met the tribal *jirga* of elders. Once their business with him had been satisfactorily transacted, coffee was served; after which the party drove down to Peshawar, where they had luncheon. As soon as this meal was over, the Viceregal party emplaned for Rawalpindi, and on arrival almost immediately they set off on a motor journey to Kahuta, which had been devastated during recent riots between Muslims and Sikhs.

That evening Edwina attended a dinner in her honour. She had little appetite, for the sights she had seen that day were indelibly imprinted on her mind. She had seen thousands of refugees living like animals. She had walked through the rubble and ruins of towns and villages which appeared like blitzed areas at their worst, and in the hospitals she had looked upon tragic, pain-ridden human creatures, among them a Muslim child whose hands had been hacked off.

On the following day Lord Louis returned to Delhi, while Edwina took off for Amritsar, in the Punjab, to continue her tour of the riot areas. This lasted for three days, during which

she covered nearly 1,500 miles by plane, as well as great dis-
tances by car and on foot.   She had hoped to finish her tour
at Multan, in the Western Punjab, but, due to a heavy dust-
storm, the aircraft was unable to land.   The visibility was bad,
and the plane circled for some time before Edwina, much to the
relief of her companion, agreed to return to Delhi.

She was, however, determined to get to Multan, and some
days later set out at five a.m.   The dust was defeated, and a
satisfactory landing was made.   Of this visit she wrote:

> 'I was able to visit hospitals and refugee centres and see
> the riot areas, talking to a great many of the victims.   One's
> heart ached for them.   Many families had been completely
> wiped out, and their houses and property destroyed, whilst
> those who had survived lived in permanent fear of further
> aggression.'

Multan itself has a forty per cent Hindu community, and
one amusing note was that during the rioting, the Muslim
Police and Hindu troops had worked in such complete co-
operation that they had a dinner two days after order had been
restored to 'cement relations'.

It was rare for Edwina to complain, but the misery she had
seen on her tour, combined with blistering heat and humidity,
moved her to express her feelings on the subject: [1]

> 'This summer has, according to the experts, been the most
> trying on record, the temperature varying from up to 114
> in the shade (with a night temperature for many weeks rarely
> dropping below 95), to the middle nineties where it now
> seems to have settled, but with humidity rising all the time.
> . . . This has made active work, particularly out in towns
> and villages where there are often no such things even as
> fans, very trying indeed, and I have often found myself
> wringing out my hair two or three times in the day, in fact
> one forgets what it is to be dry.'

The thought, therefore, of spending a few days in the hills
was a welcome one.   With a large number of staff, equally
anxious for a breath of cool air, Lord Louis, Edwina, and

[1] Letter/Report to St. John.

Pamela flew to Ambala, and thence motored to Simla, via
Kalka, in an open touring Buick. Edwina enjoyed the drive
from the dusty plains up into the splendour of the mountains.
Viceregal Lodge, she said later, was 'hideous, but the gardens
lovely and the inside was comfortable'.

Viceregal Lodge, Simla, was built in 1887 as a summer residence for the Viceroy. Ignoring the vagaries of the climate,
an annual rainfall of sixty inches, and frost and snow from
January to March, the architects had chosen porous grey stone
to construct an edifice which resembled a baroque Scottish
residence. The State rooms were impersonal and pretentious,
though the private apartments were comfortable, and the magnificent views and gardens more than compensated those who
had to live, even briefly, in what a former occupant had called
'a Victorian hydropathic sitting on a peak'.

The gardens covered an area of fifteen acres and were laid
out on the contour of a hill with large lawns of English grass
surrounded by herbaceous borders leading to a circular rose
garden, terraces, tennis-courts, and a rock garden. Forty
gardeners found permanent employment in tending the gardens, while ten watchmen kept guard on the activities of the
monkeys which abounded in the hill station and whose mischievous habit of damaging bulbs, plants, and shrubs, and
entering houses on the estate, kept the watchmen busy for fourteen hours a day.

From the terraces of the garden was a view across the in-
tervening hills to the distant ranges of the snow-capped Hima-
layas.

The staff were lodged in houses on the estate, the oldest
having been built in 1876 and the most modern dating from
1935. Edwina, grateful for the respite from the heat of Delhi,
sunbathed, played the gramophone, wrote letters, and made
friends with the head gardener, with whom she walked through
the grounds while he enlarged upon the misdeeds of the
marauding monkeys.

On the anniversary of VE-Day 1945, Pandit Nehru arrived
to spend a few days with the Mountbattens. Though the
schedule was packed with conferences and talks, the party
found time to drive in the open car to the Retreat at Mashobra,
which had been lent to Alan Campbell-Johnson and his family.

This gem of a house, the week-end cottage of the Viceroy, was reached only by a rickshaw path. Situated near some thirty acres of fruit-orchards, its windows commanded a sublime view across the mountains to the distant lands of Tibet. Tea was served in the garden. To the surprise of Mrs. Campbell-Johnson, Pandit Nehru produced his own sugar (there was a sugar shortage at the time). After tea the party walked through the orchards, which, as they were built on terraces, entailed some stiff climbing. Nehru easily outdistanced the others, and while everyone was breathing somewhat heavily, seemed quite composed. This, he said, was due to his own technique for hill-climbing, which he demonstrated by walking uphill backwards, which he said made breathing easier at high altitudes and rested the calf-muscles.

During the week-end, Krishna Menon joined the guests at the Lodge. There were non-stop conferences, and Edwina, though doing her best to fit in with everybody's plans and demands, confessed to being slightly overcome by the high altitude. Nor did she feel any better when she was told that they were returning almost immediately to Delhi.

The journey back to Ambala was again made in the open touring car, but half way down the blazing sun forced them to raise the hood, and the tortuous, bumpy road brought the neuralgia back in full force. It was almost unbearably hot in Delhi—115 degrees in the shade. Edwina was longing to go to bed, but instead she went to work, everything having piled up during her absence. In the evening there was a dinner-party, and the next morning she was called at four-thirty a.m. to take off for a tour of the riot areas.

The weather became increasingly trying. Day after day Edwina noted: 'sweltering day with thermometer rising all the time'. One morning she and Pamela went round the Viceregal estate quarters to see the staff quarters. Some of the houses filled her with horror, so lacking were they in everything. Out came the notebook, and plans were made to 'do something about it', but before she could take any effective action she had to prepare herself to accompany Lord Louis on a brief and vital journey to London. He took with him the draft of the partition plan in its amended form. His hope and intention was to obtain the revisions and to point out to the Government the urgent necessity for passing the India Independence Bill during the current session.

The Mountbattens arrived at Northolt at midday, after a fast and gruelling flight. They were driven to Buckingham Palace, where they were the guests of the Royal Family. The days were indescribably hectic; every second was taken up with work and family reunions. It was cold—so cold that Edwina, sitting in her chilly office, thought longingly of the suffocating heat of Delhi.

India was never out of her thoughts as with determination she followed up with the various authorities' questions which were of urgent importance to India, and over which England proved of real help. These included contacts with the Royal Institute of British Architects, the Institute of Hospital Almoners, and the Royal College of Nursing.

She had a great longing to see Broadlands, but so heavy was her schedule that it seemed almost impossible that this could be arranged. However, by dint of rationing sleep and making an early start, she managed to get down for a night. Nostalgically she noted that the place was at its most beautiful with buttercups, lilacs, magnolias, and azaleas at their best. Prince Philip drove down to join his uncle and aunt, and on this evening he confided to them a deep secret. He had become engaged to Princess Elizabeth.

The last days flew by. There was a luncheon at Buckingham Palace to celebrate Queen Mary's eightieth birthday; more interviews, a recording session for the Burma Reunion, later to be held at the Albert Hall; last-minute commissions for friends in India, and finally a few hours of mirthful relaxation spent watching the Crazy Gang at the Victoria Palace.

By Saturday, May 31st, the Mountbattens were back in Delhi. On the Tuesday, Lord Louis was to make his momentous announcement on the transfer of power which would decide the future of India. While the Viceroy and his staff worked at fever pitch, Edwina drove off to make another tour of the riot area in Gurgaon. She returned in despair, having seen burning villages and hospitals filled with riot victims hopelessly and helplessly awaiting supplies which were unprocurable.

During this period of stress and tension Edwina had been cementing her good relations with the wives and sisters of the leaders, and since their influence over their menfolk was tremendous, some of the goodwill which the Viceroy was able to build up with the Indian leaders was well supported by his wife's warm and imaginative approach to the feminine element. Her overtures of friendship were genuine, and even had the plan gone awry she would still have retained the respect and admiration of many of the women, who now considered her as being above political suspicion and interested only in the welfare of the sick and the under-privileged of India.

As the time grew near for Lord Louis to make his announcement the tension in Viceroy's House reached its climax. Meeting after meeting was held by Lord Louis with the Indian leaders. During this time the Press attaché, Alan Campbell-Johnson, was preparing releases, and planning with All India Radio world-wide transmissions which included Britain and America. 'I imagine,' he wrote, 'that the concentration of Press and Radio interest in today's events is heavier than any single development in Asia, since the surrender of Japan.' [1]

At the All India Radio, Lord Louis spoke with 'slow and deliberate diction. . . . His message was subdued and objective at the moment of personal triumph.' [2] After him came Nehru, whose address was moving and compelling. In his speech he said: 'We are little men serving great causes, but because the cause is great something of that greatness falls upon us also.' The third speaker was Jinnah. He was followed by Baldev Singh, who spoke for the Sikhs.

The following day some 200 representatives of the Indian and World's Press met in the Legislative Assembly to hear Lord Louis expounding on the plan. It was a brilliant *exposé*, and earned the admiration of the majority of pressmen attending the conference. The *Statesman* in its leader called it 'an extraordinary achievement of intellect and personality, and by it many lurking misconceptions should be removed from the public mind'.

Walter Lippman, famous American commentator, wrote succinctly in the *Washington Post*:

'Perhaps Britain's finest hour is not in the past. Certainly this performance is not the work of a decadent people. This,

---

[1] *Mission with Mountbatten.*   [2] *ibid.*

on the contrary, is the work of a political genius requiring
the ripest wisdom and the freshest vigour, and it is done with
an elegance and a style that will compel and receive an
instinctive respect throughout the civilized world. Attlee
and Mountbatten have done a service to all mankind by
showing what statesmen can do, not with force and money,
but with lucidity, resolution and sincerity.'

But there were still to be many dangerous moments between
the production of the Partition Plan and the actual transfer
of power.   Lord Louis had still to rule with an interim government composed of disparate elements, all of whom were determined to achieve victory for their adherents.   Much would
have to be smoothed out and accomplished before the plan
came into being.   Lord Louis' staff, on being presented with a
special calendar designed by him with each date-page announcing the number of days—seventy-two—before zero hour,
groaned inwardly.   This obviously meant that not only was
the pressure of work not to be eased, but that it was to be
intensified.

The events of the past few weeks had taken their toll of all
those concerned in the great developments, and it was apparent that a break, however brief, was indicated.   Lord and
Lady Louis decided to go to Simla for forty-eight hours.   It
was arranged that they would go from Simla to Kashmir,
where Lord Louis had matters of extreme importance and
urgency to discuss with the Maharajah.   One of his major
problems was to reconcile the native hereditary Princes with
the new plans for India.   There were 565 native States, each
with a separate treaty with Great Britain, whose tutelage they
had willingly accepted in the past.   Now it was Lord Louis'
uneasy task to convince them that they must, without delay,
accede to whichever of the two new dominions they chose,
thus integrating themselves in the constitutional framework of
the chosen dominion.   He obtained the authority of the future
governments of India and Pakistan to promise the Princes that
they would be generously treated, retaining all their personal
prerogatives, privileges, and honours and their great personal
wealth, which included a guaranteed privy purse.   These
promises were later implemented by the Governments of India

and Pakistan. Three of the Princes remained recalcitrant:
the Nawab of Junagadh, the Nizam of Hyderabad, and the
Maharajah of Kashmir. Both Gandhi and Nehru, hoping
that the Maharajah of Kashmir would make no declaration of
independence, had expressed a keen desire to visit the State,
but the Maharajah had pointedly not invited them, and Lord
Louis felt that by seeing the ruler first he might clarify the
situation and bring him into line with the other ruling Princes.

Lord Louis had obtained the concurrence of the future
Government of the Dominion of India to tell the Maharajah
that if he decided to accede to Pakistan they would understand
and their relationship would remain a good one, but if he
decided to accede to India they would be happy to accept the
accession. Lord Louis' main object was to get him to make
up his mind, for he was an old friend, and Lord Louis well
knew his weakness was that he could never make up his
mind.

It was arranged that Edwina should motor down to Ambala
to join Lord Louis and his party, and that they should fly from
there to Kashmir. She had left orders to be called at four-
fifteen a.m., but woke at three and worked until it was time to
leave. The drive down was cool and the views were surpassingly lovely. At Ambala the party emplaned for Kashmir,
and by eleven-thirty that morning they were flying over the
lovely land.

Lord Louis and Edwina were guests of Their Highnesses the
Maharajah and Maharanee. A programme of entertainments
had been arranged for the Viceroy and his wife, and there was
much motoring to beauty spots, a fishing trip, and a banquet
at the palace. Unfortunately, Lord Louis was unable to make
any headway with the Maharajah, who used the habitual
simple but effective delaying tactics and, while remaining an
excellent host, avoided as much as possible any political conversations. Towards the end of the visit, the Maharajah,
having mulled over Lord Louis' suggestions, agreed to a meeting on the final day, but when the moment arrived the Viceroy
was informed that the meeting would have to be postponed,
as the Maharajah was indisposed, and was, in fact, laid low
with the colic. As the banquet of the previous night had
similarly affected many of the guests, what could have been

interpreted as a *'maladie diplomatique'* could, in the circumstances, have been genuine. Nonetheless, Lord Louis was
extremely disappointed by his unsuccessful visit.

The Mountbattens returned to Delhi, now a veritable fur-
nace, to welcome Field-Marshal Montgomery. The highlight
of his short visit at Viceroy's House was a dinner-party for
eighty-six guests. That night, under the watchful eye of
Edwina, two of Britain's most distinguished sons, a great soldier
and a sailor-statesman, dined off the Viceregal gold plate, while
the scent of flowers with which the great table was decorated
mingled with the aroma of fine wines. As the Field-Marshal
took his seat his eye was caught and held by the insignia on the
front of the scarlet-and-gold uniform of the *khidmutgar* who
waited on him. All the Viceregal servants wore the Viceroy's
personal insignia, 'M of B', set within the Garter. Lord
Louis had paid Lord Montgomery of Alamein the delicate
compliment of changing the insignia worn by his *khidmutgar*
from 'M of B' enclosed in the Garter to 'M of A' enclosed in
the Garter. The Field-Marshal was enchanted by this subtle
gesture.

This banquet was to be followed by a series of dinner-parties.
The first, a small family affair, celebrated Lord Louis' forty-
seventh birthday, and was attended mainly by members of
the staff. American Independence Day was fêted with great
splendour at Viceroy's House, and 140 guests, including the
American Ambassador, American guests, Pandit Nehru, and
Mr. Jinnah, ate turkey with cranberry sauce.

The popular conception of the life of a Vicereine was one
which incorporated visions of this pampered being dwelling in
marble halls, where, fanned by *punkahs*, she read the latest
novels or was carried through the gardens in a palanquin
when an elephant and *howdah* were not available. This, in
fact, was the life led by the ladies of the zenanas, but the Vicereine had little time for such diversions. Her engagement
book was a nightmare to secretaries and maids alike, for there
was scarcely a moment during the day and night when she
was not on duty; and the Vicereine, having other matters on
her mind, was not vitally interested in her wardrobe. Her
cotton dresses were mostly run up by Indian dressmakers on
their old-fashioned sewing-machines, but in the evenings she

(*Above*) Independence Day in India. The Mountbattens being acclaimed by a joyous mob

(*Right*) On a visit to Lahore at the time of the partition of India, 1947

With Prince Charles and Princess Anne in Malta

was very splendid indeed in her elegant formal gowns, whose simplicity was a foil for her incomparable jewels.

. . .

On July 5th Edwina called on Mahatma Gandhi at Bhangy Colony. For three-quarters of an hour she sat on the floor of his little room having a wide discussion on many matters. She watched him spinning, and marvelled at the dexterity and beauty of his big, smooth hands. From him radiated gentleness and a firmness. He was old, he was ugly, and his eyes behind the gold-rimmed bifocals he wore were wise and profoundly sad. But his laugh was merry and young. There was friendship between 'Bapu' and Edwina Mountbatten.

When she left him she visited the Sweepers' Colony, in the midst of which Gandhi had his small house. She noted that the sweepers' quarters were inadequate from every point of view—lack of sanitation and water, and overcrowded, as are most quarters of this kind in India. Later on she visited the Harijan (Sweepers) Udyoghshala, where the children of sweepers are given training in different professions.

Her other varied activities in Delhi itself included planting a tree to inaugurate Ladies' Day of Tree Plantation Week, when an active programme for beautifying Delhi resulted in the planting of hundreds of flowering and fruit trees throughout Delhi Province, and the opening of the laboratory extension to the All-India Malaria Institute.

Early one morning Lord Louis, Edwina, and their daughter went riding. On the way home Pamela was thrown. She was carried back to Viceroy's House unconscious. Edwina was frantic with anxiety, but fortunately no bones were broken and there were no serious injuries.

On the next day, before beginning her day's work, she gave her daughter a blanket bath, entertained the Maharajah and Maharanee of Jodhpur to luncheon, worked all afternoon, had tea with Pamela, now slowly recovering, and in the evening was a gracious and charming hostess to the eighty-four guests who had been invited to celebrate July 14th at Viceroy's House.

The climax of this busy week was the celebration of the Mountbattens' Silver Wedding. This anniversary had great

N

significance for Edwina and Lord Louis. India had seen the
full flowering of their romance, and now, after twenty-five
years, they were once again together in the country which had
seen the beginning of their young happiness. Edwina, sitting
by Pamela's sick-bed, mused on the young couple who had
hoped to conquer the world. Indeed, the sweets of the temporal
world had been theirs. Of what had that young couple talked
and thought? Certainly spiritual issues had not at that stage
disturbed them.

She remembered the young naval officer with whom she
had danced at the ball at Claridges. At that first meeting she
had known, as she knew now, that this was her chosen companion and the one man with whom she wanted to spend her
life. This wish had been, in part, granted by the Fates. She
had watched Dickie emerging from the rank and file, and rise,
on his own merits, to great heights, and she had done her best
to stand by his side and help him. But always she thought
Dickie's head had ruled his heart, while her heart had ruled
her head, and in her impulses to right injustice, to heal, and
to alleviate suffering, she had made many errors of judgement
and many enemies. The critics would always be vociferous,
and always, because they did not understand, her motives
would be misinterpreted. But the one person who mattered
always understood, and he knew what the world so often failed
to realize, that in their union she was no grey eminence, no
power behind the throne; she was, and was content to be,
the wife of Dickie Mountbatten.

This memorable day began with an Investiture, the last
Imperial Investiture held by Lord Louis in the Durbar Hall;
and throughout the day messages, tributes, and gifts reached
the Mountbattens from all over the world. The family gave
them a beautiful cigarette box, while their staff presented them
with an inscribed silver salver. Their Indian friends and
thousands of humble citizens of India sent messages of goodwill. Among the letters most treasured by Edwina is a note
from Gandhi:

'Dear Sister,
          'So you are celebrating the silver jubilee of your
wedding amid a shower of congratulations and good wishes.

Let me add mine to them. I hope that your joint career here will blossom into citizenship of the world. I hope your daughter is fully recovered.

'Yours sincerely,

'M. K. Gandhi.'

The eventful day came to a close with a banquet, which included many of the Indian leaders of the Congress Party and Moslem League, as well as the senior Ruling Princes. After dinner, for the first time, there was Indian music and dancing.

.   .   .

On August 7th Edwina noted triumphantly: 'Great victory. After months of work by us, and years of work by others, an Indian Nursing Council (and also one for Pakistan) has now been approved by an Act. It is the biggest step forward in progress in nursing in India.' [1]

It was indeed a giant step forward, and those who had long fought for the passing of this Act were grateful to Edwina for her role in this victory, a part of the emancipation, of the renaissance of the Indian woman.

The woman of ancient India—of 2500 B.C.—produced an ideal of womanhood such as did not exist in any part of the civilized world. Woman trod the earth free and proud, as befitted the consort of a conqueror. No other age could have produced the concept of 'Ardha-Narishvara'—the Almighty himself was half man and half woman. In later times the status of woman slowly declined. India was no exception to the world-wide trend that kept women subservient to man throughout the Middle Ages and up to recent times. The Indian woman, like her sister in medieval Europe, was not a person in her own right. Yet quietly and unostentatiously the Indian woman of today has harked back to the status of her Vedic ancestress. Few movements of modern times have been so rapidly and quietly accomplished as the emergence of the Indian woman into public life. No militant feminism marked her entry into politics and the professions. Silently, in response to Gandhi's appeal, women of all classes of society came forward to take their places in the struggle for India's freedom. From the sheltering confines of *purdah* and

[1] Letter/Report.

restrictions imposed by tradition, the women came out to take their rights of equal citizenship with their men.

'The Women of India are really at last coming into their own [Edwina wrote],[1] and with Mrs. Pandit's appointment as India's Ambassador to Moscow and again heading the U.N. delegation; Mrs. Naidu as Governor of the United Provinces and Rajkumari Amrit Kaur as Member for Health, I feel Indian men will have to look to their laurels and the women of the West to theirs.'

. . .

The last week of British rule in India was hectic and exhausting. Everyone was working longer hours and under more trying conditions than previously, also crises of a different magnitude arose each day and sometimes two or three times a day.

On August 13th, Lord Louis and Edwina flew to Karachi, where Lord Louis was to perform his final official duty as Viceroy of a united British India, by conveying His Majesty's and his own greetings to the new Dominion of Pakistan. The Viceroy and Vicereine were pleasantly surprised to find the route from the airfield to the town fairly thickly lined by cheering crowds, but Edwina's pleasure at this warm welcome turned to anxiety when she heard that a plot had just been discovered to throw a bomb at Mr. Jinnah in the State procession which was to take place on the following day. Heated discussions were in progress as to whether the drive should be cancelled or the route altered, but the two main protagonists, Lord Louis and Mr. Jinnah, who would be driving together, were determined that the plans should go forward as originally conceived.

In the evening a State banquet of sixty was held, at which it had been understood that there should be two toasts but no speeches. Lord Louis, therefore, was dismayed when Mr. Jinnah stood up and delivered a lengthy oration from half a dozen closely typed sheets. Eventually he proposed the health of the King in 'charming terms'. Lord Louis had, in consequence, to make an impromptu speech, which he ended by proposing the health of Pakistan. The banquet was followed

[1] Letter/Report.

by a reception at which the host, Mr. Jinnah, was 'to be seen, with his silver hair and white ashkan, towering above most of his guests and talking to very few of them'.[1] Lord Louis and Edwina patiently shook hands with some 1,500 of the leading citizens of Pakistan.

The following day, the 14th, Lord Louis addressed the Pakistan Constituent Assembly, to which he and Edwina were driven in State. Before Lord Louis made his speech there was a slight *contretemps*, as Mr. Jinnah wanted to take the principal seat for himself, as President of the Constituent Assembly. Firmly and decisively Lord Louis pointed out that this was impossible, as he was still Viceroy and representative of the King. Eventually Mr. Jinnah gave way and Lord Louis made his speech.

Though the thought of the bomb plot was in everyone's mind, the State procession led by Lord Louis and Mr. Jinnah took place as arranged in open cars. Following Lord Louis and Mr. Jinnah were Edwina and Miss Jinnah, and in the third car sat the Prime Minister's wife, Begum Liaquat Ali Khan, and Pamela Mountbatten. The route was fairly thickly lined with crowds controlled by military and police. Subsequently, in a typical piece of understatement, Edwina commented to one of the staff: 'Mr. Jinnah was evidently most relieved when he got us back safely to Government House without any untoward incident and we were equally thankful that he too had suffered no harm.' So relieved was Jinnah that no tragedy had marred his hour of triumph that something of his cold reserve melted and his adieux to the Mountbattens were warmly emotional.

The Mountbattens returned from Karachi to New Delhi in the afternoon of the 14th. For months they had been carried forward by the impetus of the work which was to lead to the climax which would take place on the morrow, and during all that time they had seldom, if ever, been alone together. But on this, the eve of the transfer of power, they dined alone. After dinner Lord Louis returned to his study, and Edwina sat down at her desk to catch up with her work. The clocks in Viceroy's House ticked inexorably on. . . . The curtain was about to fall on a long and glorious chapter of British history,

---

[1] *Mission with Mountbatten.*

and in the Legislative Assembly the voice of Pandit Nehru
rose loud and clear. 'Long years ago,' said Nehru, 'we made
a tryst with destiny, and now the time comes when we shall
redeem our pledge, not wholly or in full measure, but substantially. At the stroke of the midnight hour, when the
world sleeps, India will awake to life and freedom.'

Just before midnight Lord Louis took off his reading glasses,
turned the keys on his dispatch boxes, and, with the help of
Alan Campbell-Johnson, tidied the room and stowed away the
outward and visible signs of Viceregal activity. When his
desk was cleared, he sat down before it. Part of his mission
was accomplished—his unenviable task was nearly completed.

At twenty minutes past midnight the President of the Constituent Assembly, Dr. Rajendra Prasad, and the new Prime
Minister, Pandit Nehru, arrived to tell Lord Louis that at the
midnight session of the Constituent Assembly they had taken
over power and had endorsed the request of the leaders that
he should become their first Governor-General.

At eight-thirty the next morning an official audience of some
500, including a number of Ruling Princes, waited in the Durbar Hall for the swearing-in ceremony to commence. The
silver trumpets which had heralded the last Viceroy's installation sounded again as the newly created Earl Mountbatten of
Burma, the first Governor-General of free India, entered. The
vast hall was a shimmer of gold: gold the thrones, golden the
carpets and of golden lamé the gown worn by the Countess
Mountbatten of Burma.

The couple ascended their thrones. There was a momen-
tary hush, broken by an explosion. Heads turned sharply,
only the Mountbattens, bathed in the full glare of the flood-
lights, did not move a muscle. The photographer whose
flash-bulb had exploded quickly replaced it. As the ceremony
ended, the bronze doors of the Durbar Hall were flung open,
and the historic moment came to a close to the appropriate
sounds of 'God Save the King' followed by 'Jana Gana Mana'.

The official guests, including ambassadors, princes, and the
Cabinet, then drove in procession from Government House
(ex-Viceroy's House) to the Council Chamber. Lord Louis
and Edwina were last, in the State carriage. Never in the
memory of those in the procession had such a crowd been

seen. Not only did they line every roof-top and vantage point, but they pressed around so thickly that finally they became quite unmanageable. Frenzied and hysterical, the crowd, estimated at over a quarter of a million, began trying to force their way into the Council House. Fortunately, for each individual member of the crowd was trying to shake the hands of Lord Louis and Edwina, the two Guards of Honour, joining with the police, kept the seething mass at bay long enough for the Mountbattens to get out of the landau and into the Council Chamber.

After the ceremony in the Council Chamber, the Mountbattens had again to fight their way through the crowds. Though two more Guards of Honour were out for the departure ceremony, they found it almost impossible to control the masses. Pandit Nehru went up on to the roof and waved to the surging people to make way and go back. They responded immediately, and it became possible to open the door. Even so, it took the Governor-General, his wife, and staff nearly half an hour to struggle back to their carriage. At one time they were held up for five minutes by the pressure of numbers. And all the time the crowd were yelling '*Jai Hind*, Mahatma Gandhi *ki jai*, Pandit Nehru *ki jai*', and finally, as the Mountbattens reached the landau, these cries were replaced by shouts of 'Mountbatten *ki jai*, Pandit Mountbatten *ki jai*' and even 'Lady Mountbatten *ki jai*'.

After luncheon the Mountbattens decided to pay an impromptu visit to the great Children's Fete being held at the Roshanara Park in Old Delhi. Five thousand school-children mobbed the party in an effort to shake hands with Lord Louis and Edwina. In the sizzling heat they visited the sideshows, watching small children climb up ropes which were non-existent and snakes swaying to the sound of gourd-pipes. Pamela Mountbatten found herself rooted to the spot with horror as she watched a fakir apparently biting the head off a snake. Before leaving, the Mountbattens handed out gifts of sweetmeats to the children, and it was to the sound of gleeful high childish voices that they drove away to change for the great event of the day, the salutation of the new Dominion Flag.

The ceremony was scheduled for six p.m. A parade had

been arranged of the units of the three Services and pages of
orders had been issued, rehearsals carried on for days, and
carefully allotted seats on raised platforms had been provided.
No one, however, had anticipated the enormous crowds who
would be present on this, the greatest day in Indian history,
which was a national holiday, and who would be far beyond
the control of enclosures or police. Nearly a quarter of a
million people had found their way to Princes Park. They
were in high good humour and had one idea in their minds:
to converge upon the central dais with its flag-pole.

As in the morning, the Mountbattens drove in state in an
open coach, and all along the route the crowds waved, cheered,
and shouted. At a slow walk the bodyguard, with their
admirable and patient horses, breasted a way through the
crowd to the appointed position opposite the grand stand at
the Parade. There was, however, absolutely nothing to be
seen of the grand stand, and although a row of brightly
coloured *pugarees* indicated where the troops had been engulfed,
there was no other indication of a military parade. Pamela
by this time had been completely swamped in the human sea.
Pandit Nehru, plunging into the fray, dragged her to safety
and then struggled along to the Mountbattens' coach to tell
them that their daughter was safe. After a hurried consulta-
tion with Lord Louis and the Delhi Area Commander, it was
decided that the only thing to do was to hoist the flag, fire the
salute, and abandon all other idea of the programme. This
was done amidst scenes of fantastic rejoicing and tremendous
emotion. As the flag broke, a brilliant rainbow appeared in
the sky, which was taken by the crowd as the best possible
omen for the future, especially as the new Dominion Flag of
saffron, white, and green greatly resembles the colours of a
rainbow.

Meanwhile the danger of a large-scale accident was becoming
so great that the Mountbattens agreed that the best way of
averting any tragedy was to try to move the coach on, thus
drawing a part of the multitude with them. Pandit Nehru
was to act as the bait and was invited by Lord Louis to sit in
the coach, which he did, perching on the front hood above the
seats. In the meantime, Edwina and Lord Louis had collected
a motley crowd of refugees inside the coach: the Polish wife

of a British officer who had been in danger of being crushed
under the wheels; four Indian women with their children,
while an Indian Press photographer had climbed up behind.
The bodyguard gradually opened a way through the crowds
and then the whole throng swung round and began to follow
the State coach.   During the whole of the three miles back to
Government House thousands of people ran alongside the
carriage, but at the gates, at a signal from Pandit Nehru, they
melted quietly away.

The finale of the day was a State banquet at Government
House.   At nine-fifteen p.m. 300 guests filed upstairs and were
individually presented to the Governor-General and his wife.
The guests wandered freely through the State rooms and drawing-rooms.   Outside the Moghul Gardens, festooned with fairy
lights, were floodlit.   There was among the guests a feeling of
relaxation and tranquillity as they savoured this long-awaited
moment when India should again belong to the Indians.

.   .   .

At four-fifteen the next morning Lord Louis and Edwina
were called, and by five-thirty they were flying towards Bombay, as Lord Louis and Field-Marshal Auchinleck were to pay
a twenty-four-hour visit to say goodbye to the first contingent
of British troops to leave India.   The rain pelted down as
Lord Louis, standing on a small soap-box, made his speech.
The party then went on to a luncheon-party at Government
House, and though no publicity had attended their arrival,
by the time they emerged from the reception at the Taj Hotel
some 50,000 people were waiting to greet their new Governor-
General.   These were but a spearhead of the vast masses who
accompanied the procession of cars back to Government House.
From the car in which he sat, Alan Campbell-Johnson could
see the Mountbattens standing up in their open Rolls, with the
police helplessly trying to prevent frenzied Indians from leaping
into the gubernatorial car to proffer their good wishes and
thanks to Pandit Mountbatten.

Lord Louis returned to Delhi, while Edwina began an
arduous non-stop tour of Bombay's health, education, and
welfare institutions.   Trailed by a legion of ragged, under-fed
women and children, she marched doggedly through the rain
and mud of Bombay's slums.   What she saw in the miserable

tenements angered and distressed her. In under three days
she visited seven hospitals, clinics, and dispensaries, four social-
welfare committees, three colleges, one remand home, and a
young women's hospital. In a report on this visit to the slums
she urged in trenchant language that immediate and fundamental changes be made in the welfare of the under-privileged
who 'lived under conditions which must be a constant reproach
to the citizens of the great and wealthy city of Bombay'.

When Edwina returned to Delhi she found that the wave of
optimism which had carried the Indian leaders through
Independence Day had now deposited them in perilous quick-
sands. The British were on their way out of India. Lord
Louis was invited by the Indian rulers to remain as the first
constitutional Governor-General of the Dominion of India.
Mr. Jinnah decided that he himself would become the Governor-General of the new Dominion of Pakistan. Pakistan
bisected India. Pakistan itself was bisected. There had been
serious trouble in the Punjab. Now even graver events began
to shape themselves. The people had risen up against their
leaders' acceptance of partition. In this communal irruption
twelve million Hindus, Sikhs, and Muslims were involved, and
migration of some nine million people began overnight in an
area the size of Wales. For Pakistan the immediate danger
was to the key province of the West Punjab which was being
flooded with poverty-stricken Muslims in lieu of wealthy Sikhs.
For India the gravest threat of danger was to Delhi, the focal
point of this mass migration. Before long some 400,000
refugees would be trekking towards disaster. They fled in
bullock-carts or afoot, carrying their children, their sick, and
their belongings, until fatigue halted them in their tracks.
Smallpox, cholera, and other diseases hovered about them, as
did the overfed vultures, waiting for yet another scrawny body
to fall by the wayside.

In the meantime Edwina and Rajkumari Amrit Kaur, the
new Minister of Health, set off for a tour of the danger areas.
Gentle Rajkumari Amrit Kaur had qualities of endurance,
will, and sacrifice which belied her gentle, frail exterior.

The small party set off in the Dakota. Owing to shortness
of notice and difficulties of communication in the Boundary
area, the local military authorities did not hear in time that

the plane was arriving earlier than expected, and the welcome party on landing consisted of a puzzled baby buffalo. The next leg of the journey to Jullendur was accomplished by jeep. Conditions in the camps were bad and there was a desperate shortage of nurses. In one of the hospitals penicillin and X-ray films were urgently needed. Though there was little time to linger on individual cases, one particular case was brought to the notice of Edwina and Rajkumari Amrit Kaur. This was the extreme anxiety of an old man for the welfare of two baby boys whom he had found in the street and adopted.

By this time Edwina had already formed the United Council for Relief and Welfare and had become its first Chairman. The Council was established to co-ordinate the efforts of all the voluntary societies undertaking relief and welfare work and to ensure that the service worked with the maximum speed and efficiency.

Conditions in the Muslim Refugee Camp at Amritsar were deplorable. Seventeen thousand refugees were existing on open swampy ground with no shelter, no adequate water supply, and no food except what could be scrounged by the military authorities. After a visit to the Victoria Memorial Hospital, which was short of supplies and filled with surgical cases suffering from stabbing, sword-wounds, or bullet-wounds, Edwina went through the city, which was like a place of the dead, completely laid waste in parts, and even where the buildings were intact many streets were utterly deserted.

At the close of this exhausting day news came through of a savage attack on a lorry of non-Muslim refugees from Sialkot. Immediately Edwina and the Minister of Health returned to the Victoria Memorial Hospital. Knives and hatchets wielded by a Muslim mob had severely injured those who had survived the attack.

On arriving back at Circuit House, where they were to spend the night, Edwina found Tara Singh, leader of the Sikhs, waiting to see her and Rajkumari Amrit Kaur. Tara Singh was full of unjustifiable grievances and allegations against the Boundary Defence Force.

The next morning, after a sleepless night, the party flew off to Lahore, arriving at seven-ten a.m. They went directly to the Muslim Refugee Camp at Walton Training School,

where 45,000 refugees were accommodated. After a tour oɪ
the Refugee Centre at the Chinese Camp the party had a
hurried breakfast before continuing their inspection. Their
next visit was made to the Hindu Relief Camp. This was
overcrowded and chaotic due to there having been no evacuation the previous day, plus a new arrival of refugees, so that
the numbers exceeded the available room. They went on to
the Mayo Hospital. Two of the wards contained all Muslim cases
with appalling wounds and mutilations. The children were
particularly heartrending to see, with amputated limbs and
slashed faces. Yet another hospital which was visited had
Hindu patients only. This hospital had been threatened with
attack and had been provided with a guard.

By one-thirty the party had emplaned for Rawalpindi,
where Edwina was taken to the Wah Refugee Camps for Sikhs.
She had previously visited this same camp in May. That
night was spent at Command House, and the next morning
they took off for Sialkot, where in drenching rain Edwina and
her party made another tour of inspection, visiting camps and
hospitals. They then embarked on a skiddy road to drive the
45 miles to Gujranwala, where there were several Refugee
Camps to be visited. In nearly all these camps there was a
great outcry for more food, security, and evacuation. The
majority of refugees were thoroughly panicky. They had
been through a very hard time, and incidents still occurring in
the area were increasing their anxiety—an incident of shooting
thirteen members of a family in the city the day before had
done little to reassure them. Medical supplies and food were
left wherever possible.

When Edwina returned to Delhi, the report she made on
the situation on both sides of the Boundary was alarming. It
was evident that the refugees were in the grip of a mass hysteria
and that immediate steps must be taken to overcome the
almost insuperable difficulties of organizing help for the millions
on the move.

Both Edwina and Lord Louis had hoped that they might be
able to spend a few days of rest in Simla, but no sooner had
they arrived there than disquieting news reached them of the
march of events in the stricken areas. To increase Edwina's
gloom, news came through of the acute distress of the household

treasurer, whose son and daughter-in-law had been killed in a stabbing affray in Delhi. He and his wife had insisted on leaving together for a funeral, and their train had been attacked by a mob of Sikhs.

The news became increasingly disturbing. Rioting had been going on in Delhi, and even in Simla itself. An urgent message came through to Lord Louis from Nehru and Patel asking for his immediate help and advice in what had now become a national crisis. Within the day Lord Louis, with Edwina and their by now jaded but ever loyal staff, returned to Delhi.

Once in possession of the facts, Lord Louis proposed the setting up of an emergency committee. This was agreed, and Lord Louis was invited to become its chairman. His first reaction to the crisis was to set in motion procedure which had been eminently successful at C.O.H.Q. and in S.E.A.C., and thus the first Emergency Committee met in the council chamber of Government House. Edwina attended these first meetings, as did most of Lord Louis' staff, and she was thus able to make an important and direct contribution to the framing of the Government's welfare policy.

Less than forty-eight hours after her return from Simla, Edwina was presiding over the first meeting of the United Council for Relief and Welfare, and using every ounce of her charm, tact, and psychology to weld fifteen different organizations into one enthusiastic corporate body. It was a tremendous tribute to the goodwill that the Mountbattens had built up with the Indian leaders that they should have been called in by them in this first grave emergency.

Apart from the problem of the riots and refugees, there were domestic crises which needed immediate attention. Edwina made a tour of the compounds of Government House. The Muslim servants were in a state of panic, for, fearing attack upon their relations, they were trying to bring them to safety in the compounds, and as they streamed in in their dozens, food had to be found for them. Supplies were running low, there was no milk, butter, sugar, or tinned food available.

The next days were lived at such a frantic pace and with so little regard to danger that Lord Louis' British and Indian A.D.C.s, deputed to attend Edwina, never knew what their tours with her would involve. On more than one occasion when she came upon dead bodies lying in the streets she insisted that they be removed and she herself helped move them.

Those who were with her in these days recorded an early morning visit to the T.B. Silver Jubilee Hospital, where panic reigned. Dead Muslim domestics killed the previous day were lying about. The staff and patients went in fear of their lives. Edwina soothed both staff and patients, had the bodies removed, and then went on to the Irwin Hospital, where victims were pouring in and where the wards were overflowing with the wounded. In the mortuary were 180 bodies. The situation was appalling. No trains were coming into Delhi, all transport was dislocated, and there was only a two days' supply of food in the city. Added to this there were urgent problems of fuel and medical and staff supplies.

Edwina, militant now, descended on the kitchens of Government House, and austerity became the order of the day. Resignedly the staff pulled in their belts, and nibbled secretly at dry biscuits to stay the pangs of night starvation; distinguished guests invited to dine ate dubiously through menus consisting of cabbage-water soup, a morsel of spam and potato, and a minute portion of cheese with one biscuit.

On December 7th, Gandhi arrived at New Delhi. The friends who met him were steeped in gloom. They drove him to Birla House. He knew already that Delhi was a city of the mad and the dead. His distress over the situation was acute. Despite his fatigue he immediately set out to visit a Muslim Academy which was in grave danger of attack. He drove out to the Academy alone, and spent an hour there talking with the principal, teachers, and boys. 'His presence hallowed the Academy.' After his visit it was no longer in danger of attack. After this, alone and without escort, he toured the riot areas, visiting refugee camps in and out of the city. At his prayer meeting one morning he said, 'I think of the poor refugee in Delhi, in both East Punjab and Western Punjab today while it is raining. I have heard that a convoy of Hindus and Sikhs fifty-seven miles long is pouring into the Indian Union from West Punjab. It makes my brain reel to think how this can be. Such a happening is unparalleled in the history of the world and it makes me, as it should make you, hang my head in shame.'

October 2nd was the date of Gandhi's birthday. He was seventy-eight. Edwina came to congratulate him. He was sad. 'Where do congratulations come in?' he asked. 'Would it not be more appropriate to send condolences? There is nothing but anguish in my heart. Time was whatever I said the masses followed. Today, mine is a lone voice. . . . I have lost all desire to live long, let alone 125 years. . . . I cannot live while hatred and killing mar the atmosphere.'

The 'lone voice' was the voice of conscience and it was heard, as it had been countless times before. The crisis in Delhi died down, but the work of salvage continued unabated. The United Council for Relief and Welfare was functioning admirably. Relief units, doctors, St. John Ambulance Squads, and welfare workers of the National Christian Council, the Y.W.C.A. School of Social Services, and other organizations were posted to refugee camps. As soon as Delhi returned to life, Edwina started off on another of her extensive tours of the East Punjab.

In one town, ringed by refugee camps, Edwina called a meeting in an hotel. The lobby was packed with welfare workers, all eagerly awaiting her speech. Just before she was due to begin, the lights failed, and two electricians sauntered in and started fiddling with plugs and light-switches. In the midst of the confusion Edwina was called to the telephone. It was Lord Louis ringing from Delhi. The line was bad, but through the sinister cracklings Edwina heard that their daughter Patricia Brabourne had just given birth to a fine son. Feeling highly elated, the new grandmother went back to address her meeting.

In his diary Campbell-Johnson wrote:

'Lady Mountbatten's extensive tours have made a very deep impression on the refugees and welfare workers alike. They are no mere formality. With her unique Red Cross and St John experience, she is providing the Government at the Centre with detailed and expert guidance based on first hand information on the most urgent of all its human problems.'[1]

[1] *Mission with Mountbatten.*

Yet another tribute was to come from the Governor of the United Provinces. The letter read: [1]

'To the Governor-General's Lady from a mere Governor,

'Greetings—I have been watching your work and am filled with a deep admiration for your untiring and infinitely fruitful spirit of compassionate and effective service. No woman in your place has ever put herself in touch before with the people. You have not been aloof and condescending in your well-doing. You have been gracious and intimate and personal. The last of the Vicereines is creating her own immortality in the hearts of suffering India. The Governor-General is proving himself a great statesman as well as a great human being with imagination, authority and determination. I sent him on the 7th of the month, a floss-bracelet or Raksha-Bandan which Hind women send from huts and palaces equally to men whom they honour and trust and rely on as friends. The Rajput Queens used to send these bracelets on the full moon night of the special month to Moghul Emperors etc.—one occasion when communal labels did not count.

'I don't know how long I shall be in these provinces, but my one real gift has been having full scope and bearing real fruit. My gift of friendliness. Men and women who have not spoken to each other for years meet under my roof every day in a more cordial manner after an initial moment of uncertainty. . . . O yes—the lions and the lambs lie down very pleasantly together in my green pastures. Each of us can only do our best, but as Browning says, "There shall never be one lost good". What comforting belief.

'I send you my love and also my benediction.

'Your affectionate friend,

'Sarojini Naidu.'

[1] After the transfer of power, Mrs. Naidu, one of the great Congress personalities was offered the Governorship of the United Provinces. A post of tremendous importance, as 'on the ability of the United Provinces Government to prevent the Punjab troubles spreading across its own borders largely depended the fate of Northern India.'

With the Queen and Prince Philip, April 1957. Taken on the occasion of the 350th Anniversary of the grant by King James I of the Charter to Romsey

Lord and Lady Brabourne with their children after the christening of their baby daughter Amanda Patricia Victoria. In the background are the Earl and Countess Mountbatten of Burma. The children are Norton aged 10, Michael 7 and Joanna 2½

CHAPTER XVI

THE WORLD IS A BRIDGE

O N NOVEMBER 11TH, a plane carrying the Mountbattens touched down at Northolt. Anxious as they were to attend the Royal Wedding, both Lord Louis and Edwina had been deeply concerned at leaving India, even for a few days, in this moment of trouble and danger. But after much reflection they decided that since their position in India was strictly constitutional it could not be argued that the Governor-General's presence was essential for the day-to-day conduct of affairs, and furthermore, it was important to them to be present on this great occasion, not only as relatives of the bride and groom, but also as representatives of free India.

This visit was to be even more hectic than previous 'flying' visits. No sooner had they arrived at the Dorchester Hotel, where they were staying, than pandemonium broke loose. The telephone never stopped ringing, special messengers arrived with letters, flowers, and more letters. Edwina rushed down to Hampshire to make arrangements for the stay of Princess Elizabeth and the Duke of Edinburgh, who were to spend the first part of their honeymoon at Broadlands. There was a family dinner of sixty at Buckingham Palace, with dancing afterwards, and there was the christening of Norton Louis Philip Knatchbull. The ceremony was performed by the Archbishop of Canterbury, who had officiated at the wedding of Patricia and John Brabourne. The handsome, plump baby was much admired by his grandmother, who, though fond of infants, much preferred them out of swaddling-clothes and equipped with some kind of repartee.

By mid-week Edwina was exhausted and was suffering from a bad cold, which did not prevent her from accompanying members of the Royal Family to view the wedding presents. She had two to contribute to the magnificent display: one entrusted to her by the Government of India, and the other a small piece of lace cloth woven from yarn spun by the Mahatma.

On the eve of the wedding the Mountbattens gave a large cocktail party, and while Lord Louis was attending Prince Philip's bachelor party, Edwina went wisely to bed with aspirin and hot milk.

Next morning Lord Louis and Edwina drove to the Palace, where they joined in the family procession. Pamela, one of the bridesmaids, went separately. At Westminster Abbey the aunt and uncle of Prince Philip were seated to the left of the altar with his family. The bridegroom wore the everyday uniform of a naval officer, the full-dress frock-coat and cocked hat being sacrificed for reasons of post-war austerity, and since, like others commissioned during the war, he possessed no sword of his own, the sword he carried was that once worn by Prince Louis of Battenberg.

After the ceremony the young couple emerged from the Abbey to be greeted by the cheers and good wishes of thousands of people, whose love for their radiant Princess was now to be extended to her husband. Edwina and Lord Louis drove back to the Palace for the wedding breakfast. Bridal and group photographs were taken by Baron. That afternoon the Royal train left Waterloo for Winchester, and Edwina's thoughts accompanied the young couple now speeding through the familiar landscape towards Broadlands and the peace and solitude of the ancient mansion in which she and Dickie, many years before, had begun their honeymoon. . . . She did not learn until some time later that the privacy of the Royal couple had been constantly invaded by curious sightseers, who hid in the trees or lay in wait in the grass to spy on them as they went by.

By the time the first week of the Royal honeymoon was ending the Mountbattens were back in India, where the situation was becoming daily more complex and difficult. Edwina plunged back into her ocean of work. She spent the morning of her forty-sixth birthday at a meeting of the Emergency Committee. Her birthday treat, later that day, was a flying visit to Fatehpur Sikri and Agra. Built by the Emperor Akbar, Fatehpur (Victory Town) was a monument to a famous Muslim holy man. A dream city, now fallen into desolation, it is dominated by the great Gateway of Victory, over which, at the Emperor's command, are inscribed these words:

'Said Jesus (on Whom be peace!) the world is a Bridge, pass over it, but build no house there. He who hopes for an hour hopes of eternity. The world is but an hour; spend it in devotion. The rest is unseen.'

At Agra, Edwina, as once before, looked upon the Taj by moonlight. She had forgotten the beauty of this poem in marble which Shah Jehan had built for Mumtaz Mahal, the beloved of his heart, and for a while she stood meditating upon the destiny of this woman whose legend transcended time and whose epitaph was carved wondrously upon her tomb.

. . .

The November winds swept mercilessly over the Punjab, victimizing the semi-starved refugees who, without woollen garments and bedding, were still streaming into the camps. By the end of this month it was estimated that the total number of refugees in camps all over India was about 1,250,000. All these camps were being supplied with food, clothing, shelter, and medical attention. Those organizations concerned with the welfare of the refugees worked with increasing fervour. The United Council for Relief and Welfare had undertaken many varied relief activities, including the administration and general welfare services in camps. In addition to providing voluntary workers in camps, hospitals, and refugee clinics, the Council established two First-Aid Posts and large quantities of supplies, including medical requirements, linen, and clothing. Milk and emergency foods had been collected and given to hospitals and refugee centres.

Edwina continued her work; she presided at meetings, was resourceful, tactful, forceful, and took no rest. She felt 'grim' and did nothing about it, and then, after a particularly strenuous week, she decided that she had better be X-rayed. This done, she promptly forgot all about it, and was reminded of it when the plates were presented to her. The result must have been satisfactory, for the subject of her health was not mentioned again.

Apart from her constant tours and visits to refugee camps, she accompanied Lord Louis on his official tours. The occasion of their visit to Jaipur was the Maharajah's Silver Jubilee, a magnificent affair in the most fantastic medieval city in India.

Here, for the first time since the war, Lord Louis played polo. On a glorious bright day Edwina and the Maharanee with the *purdah* ladies watched a Trooping of the Colour. They then drove out 40 miles for an alfresco lunch and duck-shoot. On their return she visited a girls' school and watched a charming and colourful pageant performance of village life. She dined with the '*purdah* ladies' and retired exhausted to bed.

Edwina returned to Delhi to welcome her daughter and son-in-law, Lord and Lady Brabourne, who had come to spend Christmas with her. John Brabourne had many close ties with India. His father had been Governor first of Bombay and then of Bengal and Viceroy for six months. He was much loved and his memory was revered by the Indian Nationalists. They, like his many friends throughout the world, had never ceased to mourn his death, which had cut short a brilliant career.

Apart from constant visits to refugee camps and the unremitting labour connected with the United Council for Relief and Welfare, Edwina accompanied Lord Louis on his official visits to the courts of the Princes. Everywhere the Governor-General and his wife received a warm welcome, and it was evident that infinite thought and care had been given to the planning of the entertainments offered them. Splendid indeed were the courts of the Maharajahs. There was colour and pageantry, polo, duck- and tiger-shoots, magnificently caparisoned elephants and always the sound of bells and music. There was, too, a good deal of welfare work to be accomplished; for wherever Edwina went she visited schools, hospitals, clubs, and clinics. At Gwalior she assisted at the opening of a new research laboratory, trotted round a leather factory on heels which, though usually normal, now seemed to have become abnormally high. An exhibition and cattle fair next claimed her interest, and the morning came to a close with the inspection of a pottery factory. By this time she felt as if she were on stilts. But after a brief siesta she rallied, and the rest of the day was free to attend a military display and torchlight tattoo, with a State banquet to round off the evening.

Now, because of the unrest, the inter-religious killings, and the complete negation of all his teachings, Gandhi began his last fast. It was an 'all-in fast' to death. He lost 2 lb. each day. On the third day his weight was down to 107 lb. He lay on a cot in an enclosed porch in Birla House. A white *khadi* cloth framed his face. All day long queues filed past the still figure. Many wept, all bowed their heads in humility and love. The Mountbattens called on the Mahatma. He was weak, his voice a thin thread. With a flash of humour he said to Lord Louis, 'It takes a fast to bring the mountain to Mahomet',[1] and rallied sufficiently to have a discussion on the possibilities of breaking it. 'Gandhi said he had laid down seven conditions, all effecting the basic security and civil rights of Moslems both in Delhi and India as a while, which would have to be implemented'[2] before he could be induced to break his fast. All India waited for the outcome of this self-imposed martyrdom. Finally, having obtained the pledges of peace for which he had asked, he ceased his fast. By this act he had put an end to religious riots and violence throughout both Dominions.

Some days later, being still in a weakened condition, Gandhi was carried to prayers in a chair. While he was speaking, the noise of a violent explosion was heard. A handmade bomb had been flung at Gandhi from an adjacent garden wall. Gandhi did not flinch. As soon as Edwina heard this news she hurried to visit the Mahatma. He told her he thought it was military practice and that no one should look down on the misguided youth who had thrown the bomb. 'He probably looks on me as an enemy of Hinduism,' he said. The youth's name was Madan Lal. He had become associated with a group of agitators who were plotting to kill Gandhi. Madan Lal failed in his efforts to destroy the Mahatma. His place was taken by Nathuram Vinayak Godse, the editor and publisher of a Hindu Mahasabha weekly in Poona. Godse was embittered: 'I sat brooding intensely on the atrocities perpetrated on Hinduism and its dark and deadly future if left to face Islam outside and Gandhi inside,' he said later, 'and I decided all of a sudden to take the extreme step against Gandhi.'

[1] Lady Louis had often called on Mahatma Gandhi, but Lord Louis never had, for it would have been against protocol for a Viceroy to do so. Now, however, that Lord Louis was constitutionally Governor-General, and Gandhi seemed near death, he decided to visit him.
[2] *Mission with Mountbatten.*

At five o'clock on January 30th, Gandhi hurried to a prayer meeting. The congregation bowed reverently. The deepest bow was that of Nathuram Godse, sitting in front, his hand clutching a small pistol. Gandhi blessed the congregation. Godse pulled the trigger. Two shots rang out in quick succession, blood splashed Gandhi's white clothes, and with a whispered '*Hey Rama*' (Oh God) he slipped to the ground. The murderer fired again, and the third bullet embedded itself in the Mahatma's lung. By the time the doctor reached him, he had been dead for ten minutes.

Lord Louis had returned from Madras that afternoon. Edwina had remained there to complete a tour of hospital inspections, and it was not until late that evening that the news of Gandhi's assassination reached her. She spent most of the night telephoning Delhi and making plans to fly back immediately. She did not go to bed at all. Leaving Madras at six a.m., she reached New Delhi by one o'clock. By this time the funeral cortege which had left Birla House at eleven-forty-five a.m. had inched its way to the Jumna River, where the cremation was to take place. Here over a million people waited for the approach of the army weapon-carrier on which, on a raised floor, lay the open coffin. Four thousand soldiers, 1,000 airmen, 1,000 policemen, and 100 sailors marched in the van and rearguard of the carrier. Aircraft flew over the procession, dipping in salute and showering flower-petals. The funeral pyre was made of brick, stone, and earth. Sandalwood logs impregnated with incense had been laid upon it. Lord Louis, Edwina, their staff, and guests made their way towards the pyre. A thin cordon of R.I.A.F. men separated the gubernatorial party from a solid mass of packed mourners. Looking around him, Lord Louis realized that if the people should surge forward suddenly those nearest the pyre would inevitably be pushed into the flames, and he therefore arranged for all nearest the platform to sit on the ground.

At four-forty-five p.m. Ramdas, Gandhi's third son, ignited his father's funeral pyre. Instantly the logs flamed and a great moan burst from the crowd. The flames burnt high and clear, and, as Lord Louis had anticipated, the crowd plunged towards the burning body. Nothing could now hold them back. Lord Louis, rising, indicated that it was time for his party to go, and led by him they linked hands and made their way through the seething throng.

For fourteen hours the pyre burned. When the embers had grown cold, the ashes and splinters of bone were collected in a homespun cotton bag, and later, after pinches of the ashes had been given to Gandhi's closest friends, the remains were immersed at Allahabad, at the confluence of the sacred Ganges, the holy Jumna, and the Saraswati. Encased now in an urn, ashes and splinters of bone were borne reverently downstream. The contents of the urn were then given into the keeping of the river, and soon the mortal remains of Gandhi were being carried towards the open sea.

The entire world mourned the passing of the Mahatma. Edwina, like thousands of others, was conscious of a sense of irreparable loss. She felt that they had lost a real friend and wise counsellor, as well as a world leader and supreme force for good and justice.

. . .

Time now was growing short and Edwina's days were crammed with work and tours of inspection. She was sad and tired. There seemed to be no end to the problems of misery and illness. The visit of her closest friend, Paula Long, acted as a tonic, but even friendship could not be allowed to interfere with work, and poor Paula saw her hostess but rarely. But Paula Long was possibly the only one of Edwina's friends who at this period understood her total absorption in her task and made no demands on her. Then and later the small social circle which had surrounded her in the past had less understanding of the forces working in the woman who had always been close and available to them. Often they were both disturbed and irritated by the barriers which seemed to have come between them. Edwina, they felt, was accessible to the needy and to her co-workers, but no longer to them, and since they had not followed Edwina's path, the change in her was incomprehensible to them.

In former days Viceroys during their five-year term completed an itinerary of tours which took them across India in leisurely fashion. Lord Louis, however, hoped that he might complete this vast programme in four months. Past tours, as has been recorded, were leisurely affairs. Scarlet-bound programmes were distributed to guests and staff of the Viceroy. The Viceroy had at his disposal two special trains, one for the broad gauge and one for the metre gauge. The carriages of both trains were painted white on the outside, while the inside of the various compartments were decorated either in pale apple-green or in other cool colours. At each end of the bogie containing the main drawing-rooms and dining-rooms were small observation verandas with highly polished brass railings. In pre-war days the Viceroy's party usually consisted of Their Excellencies, members of their family, and from ten to fifteen guests. Their Excellencies' personal staff, consisting of private secretary, military secretary, assistant or deputy private secretary, sometimes the comptroller, four or five A.D.C.s and also the political representative, if His Excellency was visiting an Indian State. In addition, there were approximately twenty members of the clerical establishments and 120 servants, and an advance party of clerical establishments and servants was always sent to assist Provinces or States to prepare for Their Excellencies' visits. The Superintendent of Police and the District Traffic Superintendent responsible for the railway along which the train was travelling always accompanied the train.

Their Excellencies, their guests, and each member of the personal staff had separate compartments with bathrooms to themselves. Meals were served on the train, which involved elaborate arrangements to ensure that sufficient provisions were available, particularly on long journeys. As many as 2,000 eggs a day, ten fowls, and 100 pints of milk had to be ordered and arrangements made to keep them fresh.

Whenever the special train arrived at the station where the Viceroy had to detrain, the engine-driver had to make certain that the train stopped so that the door of the Viceroy's carriage was exactly opposite the red carpet. The speed of the train was carefully regulated to ensure that the Viceroy arrived exactly on time, and this was not always simple, as it had to go slowly in the morning at the time His Excellency shaved. Tours by special train were invariably looked forward to by the staff, and journeys after a hectic three weeks in Indian State or Calcutta were a welcome relief, as there were few interviews, and the assistant A.D.C. had less to do.

The Mountbattens, vital, dynamic, modern, and pressed for time, made absolutely no use of the splendid trains. They travelled by aircraft—'they come on the wings of the wind', as one poetic ruler put it.

In March, the Governor-General and his party, consisting of fifty persons, set out on a nine days' tour to Calcutta, Orissa, Rangoon, and Assam. Their schedule, printed in four little booklets with differently coloured covers, was heavy enough to strike terror into the heart of even the most active individual. At Calcutta official function succeeded official function, and after a fifteen-hour day of non-stop activity the Mountbattens dined at the Royal Tolley Gunge, the oldest golf club in the East. Alan Campbell-Johnson, watching Lord Louis and Edwina circulating among the guests, wrote: 'After dinner the Mountbattens were at their phenomenal best during all the small talk, setting the conversational ball rolling with groups of a dozen people at a time, breaking down reserve and shyness without apparent effort.'

At Orissa, when their official duties were over, the Mount-battens visited ancient caves embellished with exquisite draw-ings, saw some Burmese dancing, bathed in the frothing surf, and, feeling more relaxed, took-off next day for Rangoon. This was a goodwill mission undertaken by Lord Mountbatten on behalf of the newly independent India to the newly indepen-dent Burma. As a symbol Lord Louis had suggested that he be allowed to hand back the throne of Thebaw, the last of the Kings of Burma, which the British had removed and taken to Calcutta. The highlight of the visit was the ceremony of the restoration of the throne of Thebaw. This throne, a vast structure over thirty feet high and approximately the size of a two-storied house, had been dismantled in Calcutta and the separate pieces sent off in cases to Burma, where they were reassembled.

After a hasty sightseeing tour which included a visit to the great Shiwe Dagon Pagoda, the principal shrine of world Buddhism, and in which eight hairs from the Buddha's head are preserved, the Mountbattens flew back to Calcutta, where Edwina was to record a farewell broadcast to the people of West Bengal. Just as she was setting out for All India Radio studios, a storm of unparalleled violence burst over the city, but Edwina, knowing that all arrangements had been made for the broadcast, set out, while thunder, lightning, large hailstones, and a deluge of rain slowed her on her way to the studios.

Having made a short visit to Assam, the Mountbattens returned to New Delhi, before setting off again for Kapurthala, Travancore, and Cochu. Travancore was picturesque, with thatched or tiled sloping roofs and tropical vegetation. During her stay Edwina was taken to see an enormous artificial lake, clotted with islands and a long guest-house set in a strategic position. The whole place was teeming with wild game, elephant, bison, and cheetah. Nothing ever stirred Edwina quite as much as seeing wild beasts in their natural habitat, and as she cruised around the islands she was able to watch elephants with their young feeding near the water's edge. She breakfasted on a tiny island overgrown with wild lilies, and walked through the jungle, coming upon a herd of bison. A fishing expedition was arranged which entailed much tiring walking. A tropical downpour soaked her to the skin. She caught no fish, but was ecstatic simply because everything in her responded to the beauty and solitude of nature.

Edwina had not wanted to come to India; now, as the days went past, she knew that she did not want to leave. Not only did her work claim her, but India itself had woven itself about her heart, and visits and moments which until then had been part of the usual routine, became precious. The political and historical aspect of her sojourn in India had often tormented her and dimmed some of the rare moments of relaxation she might have enjoyed. She was far too 'aware' to be anything but saddened by some of the events at which she had assisted, but at this point she tried to memorize and record only those days which would live in her memory. There was a drive 35 miles along the Tibet Road amid scenery of exquisite beauty. The snow-capped mountains all about were crystal clear, and the whole countryside was afoam with flowers. On the return journey the party stopped at a Tibetan village where a 'mela' (fair) was in progress. At Gaja(?), in Patna, there was a memorable visit to a unique library which contained a fabulous collection of early documents. At Mysore, Edwina and Pamela rode into the jungle on elephants. From the heights on which they were perched they saw wild elephant, cheetah, and countless long-tailed monkeys.

Back in Delhi, the usual routine continued, but, since there was so much to be done, at an accelerated tempo. There was much entertaining—later it was estimated that during the fifteen months the Mountbattens had spent in India they had entertained at Government House 7,605 guests to luncheon, 8,313 to dinner, and 25,287 to garden-parties, at-homes, and tea-parties.

For three weeks before they left they entertained non-stop. They invited all those who had helped them and worked with them, and the most memorable party they gave was for their indoor and outdoor domestic staff. Nothing had been omitted that could give them pleasure—a band, conjurers, a juggler, and a superb buffet—and they came in their hundreds, bringing countless relations and children of every age. Edwina and Lord Louis and their own staff attended to the wants of their guests. This was voted a great success, and was attended by many women, some of whom were out of *purdah* for the first time. On this same day, Saturday, June 19th, Edwina made a farewell broadcast to the people of India. She spoke with emotion and deep sincerity.

'My farewell message to the people of India on the eve of my departure from this great and much-loved country will be a personal and informal one—because that has been the whole basis of my partnership and friendship in these past historic months. From the moment I arrived I was touched by the generosity of spirit and the warmth of sympathy and understanding shown to me; and at the confidence and trust which each one of you so quickly extended. You accepted me and my husband and daughter as your friends and colleagues, and we felt grateful and humble. It has been a true privilege to serve India and to work side by side with so many of you in these recent testing times—from north to south, from east to west, in towns and villages, in mountains, hills, and plains. I have felt proud to share your joys and sorrows, your hopes and your disappointments, and I have valued above all else the fact that you have looked on me as one of you. I have joined you in

moments of supreme achievement and happiness, rejoiced
with you at India's long-awaited freedom and independence
and at the great things you have already accomplished.

'I have been with you also at the moment of the nation's
greatest calamity, when Gandhiji's tragic death numbed the
whole country and the entire world, and I felt cast down and
saddened like each one of you. I have seen also much
suffering and a scale of tragedy unparalleled except possibly
in a state of war. Evil things have happened and at times
a temporary madness has prevailed. But these things have
not been because of the will of the people, but as a result of
circumstances and inevitable upheavals. During all these
times I have marvelled at your courage, your devotion to
duty, and your fortitude in the face of untold misery and
beset by obstacles and difficulties which, I thought, would
have daunted even the bravest. But I have never seen you
fail. I have watched with pride the devotion of the Medical, Nursing, and Welfare Services, who have so nobly lived
up to the true traditions of their professions. I have seen
the ceaseless and uphill work of those entrusted with the
moulding of the characters of the future citizens of this
country. It is obvious that freedom confers immense
obligations no less than privileges, and a Himalayan task
faces the new India in building up her medical, nursing,
and educational structure. An early revolution in health,
education, housing, and general standard of living is
vital if the Indian people are to benefit from their newly-
won independence.

'Your magnificent leader and his colleagues are fully conscious of this and are ceaselessly struggling to that end. I
am grateful to you and to India for so many things—for
the example of high courage, selfless devotion, and true
service; for giving me glimpses of your glorious heritage of
culture; for your natural courtesy and hospitality, and the
wondrous beauty of your country and the spirit and bearing
of your people. . . .

'At this moment you stand between the past and the
future, beset, of course, by problems and even perils on a
gigantic scale—but so does the whole world. You face all
manner of them, but here in India I know there will be no

lack of faith or unity of purpose in your determination to overcome everything that stands in the way of justice and progress. You could never depart from your brave ideals or your high hopes and constructive plans. Even if sometimes you are beset by feelings of frustration, disappointment, and even despair, these are only natural and transitory, and I know you are bound to triumph and that you will never lose your confidence.

'In these last days I have been immeasurably touched by the number of people of all communities and creeds who have come to me from many parts of India bearing messages and gifts as tokens of their friendship. The gifts made by refugees, by social workers, and by my many colleagues and friends of the last months will always be among my most treasured possessions, and I thank them from the heart for their thought of me at this moment and my appreciation and good wishes for the future goes out to each one of them.

'Although in a physical sense my husband, Pamela, and I will be leaving India so soon, we shall always be with you in spirit, and I think you know you will have our affection, our gratitude, and our prayers at all times. The close links of comradeship that have been forged between us are such that can never be broken, and I know that it is inevitable that I shall return. So this is not farewell, but only au revoir.'

On their last day in India the Mountbattens drove through the streets to the Chandni Chowk to receive a farewell address from the Delhi Municipality. The streets were packed with cheering crowds who flung garlands into the open car. At the Gandhi grounds a quarter of a million people had gathered and on every side there were tears and lamentations at their departure.

There was a final visit to the refugee camps at Kurukshetra and Panipat, and here again Edwina was mobbed by the refugees, who struggled to touch her, crying out that she was their father and mother and must not leave them.

On the night before their departure they attended a State banquet given by the Cabinet. Pandit Nehru paid tribute to the Mountbattens, and when he turned towards Edwina, he said:

'The gods or some good fairy gave you beauty and high intelligence, and grace and charm and vitality—great gifts —and she who possesses them is a great lady wherever she goes. But unto those that have even more shall be given: and they gave you something that was even rarer than those gifts—the human touch, the love of humanity, the urge to serve those who suffer and who are in distress. And this amazing mixture of qualities results in a radiant personality and in the healer's touch.

'Wherever you have gone you have brought solace, and you have brought hope and encouragement. Is it surprising, therefore, that the people of India should love you and look up to you as one of themselves, and should grieve that you are going? Hundreds of thousands have seen you personally in various camps and other places and hospitals, and hundreds of thousands will be sorrowful at the news that you have gone.'

      .   .   .

The night of June 21st was one of great sadness for Edwina. She spent most of the night trying to write and work. At six a.m. she was called. The last farewells were exchanged with the servants and staff. All were visibly much affected. For the last time Edwina walked down the main steps of Government House, and after Lord Louis had inspected the Guard of Honour they were both driven in a State coach, accompanied by Pamela, through the main gates, and later transferred to the car which was to drive them to the airport.

The aircraft stood waiting. Pandit Nehru and other friends of the Mountbattens had come to say farewell. It was a tense and sorrowful parting for all those assembled there, and then the adieux were said, and the sounds of the powerful engines filled the air. Soon the plane was a speck in the sky. The Mountbattens were on their way home.

CHAPTER XVII

'PARTIR C'EST MOURIR UN PEU'

THE FLIGHT back was a nightmare. Besides Edwina's sadness at leaving India, her unfinished work, and her friends, the first leg of the journey was a continual anguish. Travelling with her for the last time was her twelve-year-old dog Mizzen. Knowing that he must undergo six months quarantine in order to re-enter England, she had decided that rather than inflict this torture upon her beloved old companion, she would have him put down. On arrival at Malta this was done. She stayed with him until all was over, and then, sick at heart, resumed her flight.

The next few months were difficult ones for her. She had to readjust herself to living an ordinary, instead of an extraordinary life. The house in Chester Street now seemed to have shrunk to the size of a sardine tin, out of which she and her belongings bulged. And though the relief of re-entering her own life was great, her spirit ached at having had to abandon the many projects of work which, together with the Indians themselves, she had been engaged.

Only at Broadlands did she find any peace. The month of June was particularly clement that year, and the sunny days and green loveliness of the English countryside soothed her nerves. She was suffering from a deep depression, brought on by years of overwork, of living at a tremendous pace, and, more than anything, she missed Mizzen. The ghost of a small, gallant Sealyham walked always by her side.

Slowly she gathered up the threads of her former life. She plunged headlong into a sea of work and attended to estate and family matters. Her grandson was a great joy to her, for, though she did not belong to the school of grandmothers which is publicly puffed with pride at the exploits of their grandchildren, she felt that Norton was an exceptionally beautiful and intoxicating child.

On the twenty-sixth anniversary of their wedding day Lord

Louis was installed a Knight Companion of the Garter. The ancient and beautiful ritual took place in the Royal Chapter of St. George at Windsor.

In the meantime there was much surmise as to what the future occupation of the ex-Viceroy was to be. It was rumoured that he had been offered the post of Ambassador to Moscow or Washington; that he was to be the next Minister of Defence; that he was to return to South-east Asia as Special Commissioner. There was much nodding of heads and whispers emanating from various sources. Lord Louis kept his own counsel. His only desire was to return to service in the Royal Navy. This wish was granted. He was appointed to the Mediterranean Fleet as Rear-Admiral in command of the First Cruiser Squadron. This appointment, when it became known, caused a great stir. How, it was asked, could the recent ruler of a sub-continent adapt himself to playing a minor role on a small island under a Governor, a Commander-in-Chief, and a number of senior admirals? Was it possible for his wife, the ex-Vicereine, to take her place as 'junior wife' to Lady Power, the wife of the naval Commander-in-Chief? Everyone was assailed by doubts and fears. The Supremo, they said, was too used to issuing orders to welcome having to obey them, and Edwina would find life in Malta dull and restricted. Only the couple concerned had no doubts about the outcome of their return to Malta.

In the time before they left, Edwina found that life had once again become a mad rush, and thus she liked to live, and was once again hectic, vital, and pressed for time. In August the Mountbattens spent a short holiday in Ireland. Edwina, who, like everyone else, had been leading an austere, food-rationed, and coupon-governed existence, was ecstatic about her first luncheon in Dublin. Having partaken of lobster and of a large steak, she went happily off to Mullaghmore. Here they put up in Mrs. Hannon's small inn, which was, as it had always been, scrupulously clean and comfortable. Classie-bawn, which had been in need of attention, had been excellently restored by a local contractor and was now in the hands of decorators. The Mountbattens and their daughters made the most of their holidays. The days were perfect, with brilliant sun and sapphire- and emerald-coloured seas. The countryside was as enchanting as ever, with its whitewashed, thatched cottages, with their hedges and gardens of wild fuchsia, hydrangea, and montbrettias. And all around were the rugged hills and the mountains. Here, in this familiar and loved spot, Edwina found something of the carefree simplicity of her childhood. She could drift dreamily through the long, sun-stricken days engaged only in pursuits of her own choosing—shrimping, fishing, picnicking, and paddling in tide pools, walking along the beach and, on occasion, going up to the castle to watch the decorators at work.

On the last day of their stay the weather broke, and in the teeth of a gale she struggled up to Classiebawn to say a long farewell to the old place. The next day she was in the plane on her way to Canada. She and Lord Louis were to open the Canadian National Exhibition in Toronto.

In early September the Mountbattens were back at Broadlands. They were to leave for Malta in October, and their last month in England was a frenzied one. Norton, now aged eleven months, was so engaging that Edwina had him to stay at Broadlands whenever she could tear herself away from her work.

In mid-September the Mountbattens made a sentimental journey to the South of France. The Riviera for them was filled with nostalgic memories of a pre-war world, and they hoped that in these few days they might recapture something of this vanished epoch. They were successful, in that the sun shone and the landscapes were familiar and beautiful. From the heights of Mougins, where they were staying, they motored along the coast, finding small deserted beaches where they could sunbathe, swim, and laze. Edwina had hoped to do some shopping, but was shocked at the exorbitant prices charged. Meat was 600 frs. a kilo, while butter had rocketed to 1000 frs. a kilo.

One morning the Mountbattens drove down to the Villa de la Croe to have luncheon with an old friend. The Duke of Windsor, they found, was in excellent form and with all his old charm and looks.

Before returning to England, Edwina made a special trip to Nice to see her mother's old maid.

Just before their departure for Malta, Pandit Nehru arrived

P

in England for the Dominion Conferences. Edwina and Lord
Louis, delighted to be able to return some of the hospitality he
had shown them in India, invited him to Broadlands, where
one evening, in the midst of great hilarity, they taught him to
play Racing Demon.

.   .   .

'I had forgotten how attractive Malta is,' Edwina remarked
to her daughter the day of their arrival, as they walked into
Valetta to make a series of 'useful and nonsensical purchases'.
The charm of Malta and the warm welcome offered her by
her old friends combined to restore Edwina's courage, which
had been slightly frayed by the prospect of starting a new
existence here under conditions which were certainly at vari-
ance with the life she had led for some time.

Since their old home, the Casa Medina, had long since been
converted into flats, the Mountbattens stayed at the Hotel
Phoenicia. But they had to have a home, and houses were
difficult to find. It was so long since Edwina had been an
ordinary naval wife that she had forgotten the many frustra-
tions of having to cope with the domestic architecture of living.
Now, therefore, the ex-Vicereine turned her great talents for
organization to good use. She found a house. True it had
long been uninhabited and was shabby and derelict, but once
they had rented it and taken possession, Edwina cleared one
room, which she used as headquarters, and from here she
issued orders, and saw to it that they were implemented as she
wished.

Compared to her life in India, her day-to-day existence in
Malta this time was hardly hectic. But, as always, her innovations created a stir. Instead of going to the club fre-
quented by all naval wives, Edwina and Pamela, much to the
surprise of these ladies, betook themselves to a Maltese café,
where they had their elevenses consisting of Expresso coffee and
Maltese pastries. Here, in the pleasant sunshine, they could
watch the small, colourful, and amusing street incidents which,
put together, made up the pattern of Maltese outdoor life.

Edwina 'supported' Lord Louis at cocktail and dinner-
parties, watched him playing polo, and kept a vigilant eye on
the slow progress of the decoration of the Villa Guardamangia.
Watchful critics, eager to report any attempts at pompousness

on the part of the ex-Vicereine, found nothing to say. She was tactful, attentive, and modest—in fact all that a naval wife should be.

It was inevitable that she should be asked to take part in the local welfare organizations on the island. Since she was an international authority in her own particular field, her experience and advice were constantly sought in medical, nursing, and health schemes which were being introduced in Malta. A tremendous event was the celebration of the St. John centenary, in which Edwina was greatly involved. Her personal staff being so reduced as to be practically non-existent, Pamela became her mother's personal assistant and secretary, and as the volume of work increased, so did she render invaluable services to her harassed parent.

On her birthday Edwina and her family took a picnic lunch and drove out to a famous beauty spot. In the evening they dined in *Newcastle*, Lord Louis' flagship, and afterwards were shown a film, *The Best Years of Your Life*. The title of this film must certainly have provided Edwina with food for thought, and when they returned to the Hotel Phoenicia, she thought of her previous birthday, when, standing before the moon-drenched splendour of the Taj Mahal, she had communed with the shade of the beloved of Shah Jehan.

On December 29th, Edwina announced that the villa was now ready for occupation. Lord Louis, who was suffering from a heavy cold, moved straight from the hotel into his new bedroom. Edwina and Pamela, having attended a children's party aboard *Newcastle*, moved in later that evening. Despite an overpowering smell of paint, Edwina was delighted to walk into her own home. The next day, however, she was a little disenchanted. It was bitterly cold, and when Lord Louis' bath was emptied the water ran straight into the kitchen beneath, nearly drowning the cook and flooding everything.

Slowly, however, the house began to take on real charm and character. Edwina surveyed her work and found it good. It had been no easy matter to reinstate a derelict and shabby house. The year ended on a note of nostalgia as the Mountbattens thought back on the last New Year's Eve spent in India.

. . . . . .

The Villa Guardamangia was, the following year, to house
two illustrious guests.   In October, the Duke of Edinburgh,
who shared his uncle's passionate love of the Navy, arrived in
Malta to take up his appointment as First Lieutenant in H.M.S.
Chequers, leader of the 1st Destroyer Flotilla, and later in the
year, his wife, Princess Elizabeth, flew out to join him on the
first of the many visits she would make him while he was
stationed at Malta.

This was her first unofficial visit abroad, and it was one of
the happiest holidays she had ever spent.   For the first time she
lived the life of an ordinary naval wife, drove her own car, and
dined and danced with her husband at the Phoenicia Hotel.

The Mountbattens were ideal hosts and cicerones, and whenever it was possible the two couples would go swimming and
sunbathing.   Both Lord Louis and his nephew were enthusiastic water-skiers, and the former was particularly interested in
under-water fishing.   Edwina did not share her husband's
love for this sport, but she followed him faithfully on these
expeditions, her head enclosed in a glass box and suffering
agonies from claustrophobia.

It was at this juncture that a serious problem presented itself
to the Mountbattens.   Their financial affairs had become increasingly involved by the draconian conditions of the Cassel
trust, and by the ever-increasing expenses of Edwina's voluntary work.   The cost of her tours in this country and her
travels overseas which she bore herself (and indeed still does)
themselves ran into thousands a year.   She was connected
with over sixty voluntary organizations; she held a number of
posts in the St. John Ambulance Brigade, was patron of eleven
funds and associations; honorary president of ten hospitals
and nursing associations, patron of eight, vice-patron of another eight, chairman or a member of many councils and
committees, and a governor of Westminster Hospital.

In addition, the mission to India had substantially depleted
the coffers.   As already stated, they had entertained some
41,205 people, and it was largely owing to this approach,
which was without precedent in Viceroy's House, that such
good feeling between the British and the Indians was so firmly
established.   The allowance of a Viceroy—£13,000 per annum
—could not possibly suffice for the vast scale of their extra-

official activities, entertainments, and journeys.   On the return
of the Mountbattens to England they had to find a very large
sum, certainly well into five figures, to meet their over-spending
in India.   With income tax and sur-tax at 19s. 6d. in the
pound, and with no possibility of touching capital, the only
way such heavy expenditure could be met was either to ask
for a Government grant or a Private Bill to enable Lady Louis
to draw on her own capital.

The latter course was the only possible solution.   In addition, the K.C. whom Edwina consulted, pointed out to her that
public legislation, if it could be introduced, would assist all
married women placed in her position under the anachronism
of law affecting their property and which made it impossible
to anticipate income on trust.

With this in view, Edwina agreed to the measure going
forward as a Private Bill.   The reaction was disastrous, and
arrows began to pring from bows which had long been poised
at the Mountbattens.

> 'It is a bad principal when the law is pointedly altered
> in one case [said one paper bluntly].   And the suspicion
> will remain that this exceptional treatment commends itself
> to Mr. Attlee and his colleagues because the advanced views
> of the beneficiaries also commend themselves.'

These attacks were singularly unfair, for, had the Press bothered
to investigate the truth, they would soon have discovered that
the object of the Bill was to save the country from having to
find a large sum of money to pay for the deficit on their Viceregal period in India.

The Bill passed its three readings in the House of Lords
without any opposition, but when a group of Conservative
Members of Parliament decided to oppose its passage through
the Commons on the grounds that the principle, if applied,
should refer to all heiresses in similar circumstances, the
Private Bill was withdrawn.

The Labour Government, however, introduced the Married
Woman (Restraint Upon Anticipation) Bill, which became law
in November 1949 by a substantial majority.   Edwina, now
again a wealthy woman, could continue to give financial aid
and support to the many causes which relied upon her.

While Lord Louis was away on his Fleet cruises, Edwina dedicated her time to consolidating the work begun in various parts of the world.   She visited India, where, as patron of the United Council for Relief and Welfare, she toured the refugee camps and was able to have on the spot meetings and discussions with the health and welfare authorities concerned.

In 1949, Lord Louis' appointment as Fourth Sea Lord was announced, to take effect from the following June, and the family began to plan their return to London.   It was clear that though the house in Chester Street was an excellent *pied-à-terre*, it was too small as a permanent town house, and Edwina began to look for a more adequate residence.   When it became known that the Mountbattens were house-hunting, a number of vast and cumbersome mansions were proposed to them.   But Edwina, remembering the number of staff required to keep Brook House going, made it clear that she wanted an unpretentious house that would be easy to run.   Her final choice fell upon a house in the Regency style in Wilton Crescent.   A narrow town house, its somewhat unprepossessing façade does not do justice to the large, well-proportioned rooms behind, and indeed the restful and spacious interior is due to careful planning, designed to accommodate the beautiful furniture, pictures, and bibelots which fill the handsome rooms.

By May 1950, the Mountbattens were installed in their new house.   The birth of a second grandson marked their return, and soon life had fallen into its usual pattern.   It was no ordinary routine, for the multifarious ramifications of Edwina's work took her often out of England.   Early in 1951, she undertook an extensive tour, primarily for St. John, but also for the St. John and Red Cross Service Hospitals' Welfare Department, of which she is chairman.   The committee provides women welfare officers for service hospitals wherever there are British personnel serving.   She began with a circuit of the West African territories—the Gold Coast, Nigeria, Sierra Leone, Gambia, visiting military hospitals and making a survey to see where the St. John organization could be established if it did not already exist.   In East Africa she was able to see some of her own personnel, and also in Tanganyika, Kenya, Zanzibar, Uganda, and other parts.

Invited to finish her tour with a visit to India and Burma,

she was still in New Delhi when, having made a date with a Duchess, she flew 6,000 miles almost non-stop to keep it. The Duchess was Britain's newest warship—H.M.S. *Duchess*, seventh of the new Daring class destroyers. Edwina had promised Thorneycrofts, the builders of the warship, that she would name the ship and send it gliding into the Solent, and, true to her word, she was there.

Edwina, a little frailer-looking than of yore, but with her vitality and enthusiasm unimpaired, entered again into her life of work and entertaining in London. She was so busy that she had little time to think about re-converting Broadlands from a hospital to a private home again, and only the intimation of the visit of the late King George VI and Queen Elizabeth spurred her to instant action. For years the house had been geared to wartime austerity. Plywood masked the saloon walls; the sculpture which adorned the pillared hall was crated, the pictures were stored, and a six-months plan had been made to get the place in order.

Operation Broadlands, however, took place in less than two months, and by the time Their Majesties arrived they were able to enjoy a Broadlands completely restored to its pristine order and beauty. Their hosts, however, were not yet to settle down to a peaceful existence spent between London and their country home, for in May 1952 Lord Louis took up his appointment as Commander-in-Chief Mediterranean in Malta.

Admiralty House was situated in a narrow street in the middle of Valetta. It was one of the few houses in Malta with no sea view, and despite having a ballroom and a large reception-room, had only five bedrooms, with the result that it was difficult to accommodate guests. Happily, there was little to do in the way of re-decoration, for the previous occupant had employed soft pastel colours. Edwina liked particularly a pale clear green, which, in this country of harsh sunlight, was always cool and restful. Inevitably the house was filled with flowers and with pets. Pamela had brought her mongoose Neola, who, now a seasoned traveller, settled down surprisingly well in her new home.

The chief function of the Admiral's wife was to entertain, and since Edwina did this surpassingly well, it was no hardship to her to hold three official dinner-parties a week for about twenty-six guests, while official luncheon-parties, attended by all the members of the Allied Headquarters, the British Forces, and the Maltese people generally, were numerous.

Some days after she arrived in Malta, Edwina gave a women's luncheon-party. This was to be closely followed by an official deputation of welfare workers. The luncheon guests had just departed, leaving their hostess to run round collecting heaped ash-trays. Unfortunately, there were no wastepaper baskets or fireplaces available, and Edwina, hearing the approach of her visitors, wrapped the stubs in a piece of paper and flung them out of the window—into the street. Two minutes later an affronted Maltese steward burst into the room. The Marine sentry beneath the window had accused him of emptying an unsavoury parcel of cigarette-stubs over his head. Edwina admitted her guilt and sent for the sentry to reassure him of the steward's innocence.

During the two and a half years Edwina was to stay in Malta she visited surrounding areas in the Mediterranean and Middle East, carrying out inspections and visits in connexion with the St. John Ambulance Brigade—she was chairman of St. John and Red Cross Service Hospital Welfare Department and the Save the Children Fund.[1] She visited service and civilian hospitals, child clinics, and medical and welfare units in all these areas, and also went on an extensive tour to Korea and the Far East.

When the Greek earthquake occurred in the summer of 1953, Lord Louis decided to leave immediately for the scene of the disaster. Edwina accompanied him, and they were among the first to reach the stricken population. Edwina immediately began organizing relief and comforts, and on her return to Malta a Greek Relief Fund was formed, of which Edwina was the patron, and which fund worked ceaselessly to send aid to the victims of the earthquake.

Edwina's work in Malta meant that she was in her office every morning by eight-thirty a.m. at the latest, and that, as always, she worked well into the night. During her long

---

[1] Save the Children Fund: a world-wide organisation, founded in 1919 by Eglantyne Jebb. Doctors, nurses, teachers, and welfare workers in a dozen different lands—from Britain through Europe, to Africa, Malaya, and Korea, are labouring to save children from suffering and to raise standards of child-care throughout the world.

experience of Malta she had always been most conscious of the vital help which was needed in the islands of Malta and Gozo among mothers and children. She always felt, however, that any attempt at improvements and the giving of help should be organized by the Maltese themselves, and it was for this reason that on May 18th, 1953, Edwina, as President of Save the Children Fund and President of Honour of the International Union for Child Welfare, formed a branch of the Save the Children Fund in Malta, and she is still today their International President.

Approximately eleven clinics were formed for the care of the children and their mothers, and these clinics gave such valuable help that when the time came for the Government of Malta to take over this organization, they decided to increase the number of clinics. There are now forty-four throughout the islands of Malta and Gozo.

Among other activities with which Edwina was connected in Malta were the Naval Wives' Voluntary Service; the Allied Wives' Club (formed after the Allied Headquarters was set up by Lord Louis); Service Families Nursery and Convalescent Home; Malta Memorial District Nursing Association; Sea Rangers, and Girl Guides Association.

It will always be remembered in Malta that, no matter how busy Edwina was, she somehow found time to visit the various service clubs, not only those dealing with welfare, but also the various social clubs organized by the service wives. Here she talked with other sailors' wives.

During this period Lord Louis was invited to become the Allied Naval and Maritime Commander-in-Chief Mediterranean, and to set up the headquarters for the six N.A.T.O. countries involved—Turkey, France, Greece, Italy, America, and Great Britain—thus carrying out the two appointments, British Commander-in-Chief Mediterranean and Allied Commander-in-Chief Mediterranean.

In this capacity he was invited to visit the Emperor of Ethiopia. He sailed for Eritrea, where he was re-joined by Edwina. Here they were met by the Duke of Harar, who escorted them to Addis Ababa. The official programme arranged for the three-day visit was full and varied, and significant features of the itinerary were visits to institutions,

which included a tour of schools, clinics, and other welfare
centres.   This visit was recorded in great detail in the Ethio-
pian papers, the only omission being the gift of two monkeys
to the distinguished visitors.   Edwina was greatly rejoiced by
her new pets, and lavished much care and sympathy upon the
creatures, who did not, at the time, reciprocate her attentions.
Indeed, both she and Lord Louis returned to Malta with their
faces severely scratched.   The monkeys were installed on a
sunny veranda, where they promptly devoured every green
plant within reach.   Nonetheless, Edwina cherished them and
refused to part with them.

Towards the end of 1954, while they were still stationed in
Malta, a distinction which they particularly prized was accorded to the Mountbattens, when the Freedom of the City of
Edinburgh was conferred upon them.   The ceremony, attended by some 3,000, took place in the Usher Hall, Edinburgh.
On the same day the University of Edinburgh 'capped' them
as honorary Doctors of Law.

Sir James Miller, the Lord Provost, in handing over the
burgess rolls, described the Mountbattens as having 'a Renaissance quality'.   When he handed Lord Louis the silver casket
containing his 'Burgess ticket' and Lord Louis had replied to
his speech, the Lord Provost addressed himself to Edwina.
Having outlined her career, and stressed her work for hospitals,
nursing, and the St. John Ambulance Brigade, he presented
her with the casket containing her 'Burgess ticket' and concluded his address with these simple words: 'It is given to you
by the City of Edinburgh in recognition of your humanitarian
work and devotion to the nursing and welfare services, in the
relief of suffering and distress.   Our citizens are proud this
day to add your name to their Burgess Roll.'

Lord Louis terminated his appointment in Malta in December 1954, when he returned to England, and in the New Year
he took over his appointment as First Sea Lord and Chief of
the Naval Staff, the first time a son has followed his father in
this appointment.   The wheel had come full circle.

Edwina had faithfully 'followed the flag', and now the
sailor was home from the sea.   Lord Louis had fulfilled part
of his destiny, and certainly his dearest ambition.   But if
Edwina thought to rest, she found that now she was enmeshed

in the toils of her many activities. The burden she had assumed was a monumental one, and since she was aware that if she ceased her association with even one of the many interests involved, the whole pattern of what she was trying to create might be affected, she simply cut down on her private amusements and interests and, assuming new responsibilities, tried to weld the whole machinery of her working life into one cohesive whole. She was, and is, fully aware that to carry out her responsibilities to St. John and Red Cross and the other voluntary organizations she is actively concerned with as well as to achieve her ambitions for the nursing profession, she must be ruthless where personal, even close friendships are involved. Her vitality is great, her reserves of strength are not, but since her faith is profound and her desire to help suffering humanity transcends all other considerations, she continues to do what she considers is not only her duty but her privilege and pleasure. 'I would give my life to save one child from suffering,' she once said, and though the world which for a quarter of a century has cynically observed the lives of the Mountbattens might smile at such a phrase and seek for the motive underlying it, this statement is truly her manifesto of love and service.

CHAPTER XVIII

CANDID CAMERA SHOT

ALL PUBLIC figures are in time the victims of their publicity. Since their legend is built mainly upon the contribution of photographers and pressmen, inevitably it is the mask, and not the face which beams upon the world. The candid camera-shot is rare—and often devastating. The subject off-duty may stoop, wear glasses, be lined, weary, or dyspeptic—may indeed be human; but legendary figures are not human: the public does not wish it to be so. The sacred monsters walk eternally in the flash of light-bulbs, and their faces from youth to senility are smooth as glass.

Yet, contradictorily, it is the element of curiosity—the abasement of idols—which causes the public to strip their heroes of privacy in order to establish by means of gossip, hearsay, and the columnist's printed word that their favourite film star, entertainer, or public figure, when at home, reacts exactly like themselves. It is consoling to think that heroes and heroines must all go to the dentist, suffer from corns, unrequited love, and an overwhelming greed and desire for cream cakes, candy bars, and/or strong drink. Facts such as these are slippers on the feet of clay. They build up the picture, create an intimacy, and make approachable the loved, the envied, and the hated.

To the biographer of a living person a singular task is given. It is his duty to angle the lens of the mind so that the candid camera-shot is given its place in the gallery of splendid and glossy arranged photographs, and it is perhaps these candid camera-shots which are the real and revealing clue to a character and personality.

The great, the noble, and the historic occasions—the hand of Gandhi placed on the shoulder of Edwina Mountbatten; the Vicereine and Viceroy together are recorded. It is those other moments—the slipping off of too tight shoes, the grandmother playing with her daughter's baby on the floor, the

mature woman of the world laughing, with head thrown back,
like a young girl; the grave President of St. John, wearied by
a morass of papers, pushing them aside and taking the dog for
a walk—it is with such candid camera-shots that the vital,
irresistible, warm Edwina comes to life.

The library at Wilton Terrace is a charming and intimate
room.   The walls are white, the curtains grey, with swagged
and tasselled pelmets.   The carpet is silvery.   The whole room
has an iridescent quality, like the inside of an oyster-shell.
The alternation of glazed alcove with shelves and tiers of books
at the end of the room is well contrived.   The alcoves are filled
with Chinese carvings.   Above the mantelpiece is Raeburn's
fine portrait of David Haliburton of Bushey, and on another
wall is Romney's portrait of Mrs. Herbert.   Among the many
photographs scattered about the room is one of the Queen.
Taken in Malta in 1949, it shows the young, newly wedded
Princess, her face trapped in a mesh of sunshine.   There are
photographs of the Duchess of Kent, of Roosevelt, and of
Churchill.   On the desk is a portrait of Mrs. Pandit, and two
volumes of the short stories of Somerset Maugham, together
with a catalogue of a current exhibition.   There are great
vases of mixed sweet peas, gladioli, and carnations.   This is a
gentle, cool, and feminine room.   Only the utilitarian switchboard of the telephone indicates the multifarious activities of
the mistress of the house.

Elizabeth Ward materializes before me.   She has a habit of
doing this which is sometimes disconcerting.   She is tiny and
slim, and her wistful, elfin little face gives a misleading impression of softness.   In fact she is made of tempered steel, is
highly intelligent, and is fanatically dedicated to Edwina.   She
works at high pressure and cannot be bull-dozed and bluffed.
She looks slightly distracted at this moment:

'Lady Louis isn't in yet, and she has guests to dinner.'

I murmur something about having just seen the elusive lady
at a fete at Marlborough House, where she was accompanying
the Queen Mother.

'That was then,' says Elizabeth Ward, flying towards the
telephone; 'but where is she now? You've no idea how difficult
it is to pin her down.   I leave urgent notes for her all over the
house.   Here's one.'—She grabs it off the telephone pad and

stuffs it in her pocket.—'I must get hold of the guests and stave them off a little. She's been at it all day——'

She vanishes abruptly, and I resume my contemplation of the room. I admire a pair of splendid eagle console tables, and a small gold chocolate cup, one of a pair, made from burial-rings for the first Lady Palmerston. The maker was John Lechartier, and the handles have Latin inscriptions appro-priate to burial ceremonies.

The door opens. Edwina erupts into the room. She is warm, welcoming, and vital. She is wearing a print suit and a magnificent cluster brooch with matching earrings. She offers me a drink, pours one for herself, kicks off her high-heeled shoes, and sits down. On this occasion our talk is about books. She reads widely: anything from Shaw to T. S. Eliot. Sometimes she re-reads Shakespeare or Proust. She prefers books on travel or books about personalities to love-stories or long historical novels. She has a great admira-tion for the books of Freya Stark and has a particular liking for the works of Dylan Thomas.

Edwina is a profoundly cultured human being. Reading is as important to her as is music, and music is very important indeed. Her favourite composers are Bach, Scarlatti, Purcell, Schumann, Schubert, and Elgar. She does not much care for modern music. Choral music she loves, and thinks Han-del's 'Messiah' almost unsurpassed in beauty. She likes Negro spirituals, but does not, in general, care for the human voice. For this reason she is not a great lover of opera. Nor does she much care for the violin, unless it is played by a master such as Yehudi Menuhin, who for many years has been a great friend.

Edwina is an incurable tidier-upper. During a conversa-tion she will rise, is an abstracted way, and scoop up and empty any brimming ashtrays in view. Her family are resigned to this gentle mania, as they are to her incurable habit of writing herself little notes to remind herself of this and that. Her greatest achievement in this field was the note found by one of her daughters at Broadlands. It was a brief and simple list. It ran: 'Kill cockerel, empty dustbins, write Queen.'

On another occasion we talk about historical characters. Edwina says that she would like to have been Florence Nightin-gale. She says, 'I should like to have been a pioneer in the

alleviation of suffering. I want to help and comfort people.'
We discuss the influence that people have on one another.
She says, 'I think that perhaps Gandhi had the greatest in-
fluence on me.'

It is winter and cold. The library is a bower of hot-house
flowers. The room itself is exceedingly chilly. It would seem
that the heating is not functioning. Edwina, wearing a cin-
namon-coloured wool jersey dress, comes in. She does not,
at first, appear to notice that I am huddled in my coat. We
begin talking, and suddenly she too realizes that the temperature is arctic. A bell is pressed and the butler appears.
Edwina announces brightly that she fears that something may
have gone wrong with the central heating. Collier eyes me
coolly and in a hushed voice imparts some information to
Edwina. Later she informs that on the morrow there is to
be an official party, and that the butler has decided to turn
off the radiators to keep 'his' floral decorations cool and fresh
for the guests the next day. However, strange gurglings
announce a welcome change of temperature, and soon I am
able to peel off my coat. We talk about ₁ood. She is not
inordinately interested in food, though she enjoys planning
interesting meals for her guests. Her own tastes are fairly
orthodox. Her favourite menu might include potato-and-
onion soup or ministrone. Then sole or Lobster Newberg.
She does not care for meat, but when she has it, it has to be
cooked until it is leathery. She likes cottage pie, Irish stew,
and steak-and-kidney pudding. But she also enjoys strange
and exotic foods, curries, spices, most foreign foods, and particularly Chinese food. She herself is not a good cook, but
she enjoys watching a really skilled cook at work. As a child
she spent as much time as she was allowed with her grandfather's old chef, Brinz. A naturalized Austrian, he was one
of the heroes of her childhood. Edwina treasures many
photographs of herself when small, seated on the austere
Brinz's knee.

'Most chefs,' says Edwina, 'are artists, and therefore tem-
peramental. Our present chef, who is excellent, arrived with
an ancient parrot whose language was anything but delicate.
Chef loved his parrot, and as long as the bird was happy and
contented our meals were superlative. The moment the

parrot was off colour there was a marked deterioration in the quality of the cuisine. Once, returning from our holidays, I found the kitchen plunged into silence, with chef in deep mourning. There was no sign of Polly. I did not dare ask what sad fate had overtaken him, but I was considerably relieved when faint twitterings were heard again in the kitchen quarters. Chef had acquired a budgerigar and all was peace and harmony'.

Brillat Savarin and Edwina would not agree on the subject of entremets. She loves all the old English nursery favourites: roly-poly pudding with golden syrup; open treacle tart; spotted dog. Slim as a reed, diet has no meaning for her. Whenever possible she likes to indulge in pastas. She has, too, a passion for mushrooms, asparagus, and plover's eggs, and all exotic fruits, such as mangosteens and grenadillas. She seldom eats chocolate nowadays, preferring boiled sweets, peppermint lumps, and acid drops.

Edwina, as it has been told, loves animals—all animals—but particularly her dogs. Her Sealyham, Snippet, is her constant companion. Officially Snippet sleeps on a chair in Edwina's bedroom. In fact the dog sleeps on her mistress' bed. Snippet was once the unwitting heroine of an amusing and complicated drama between a well-known firm of caterers and a temporary butler. As is usual when an official reception takes place at Wilton Crescent, a number of chairs and certain glassware are hired. On this particular occasion, once the party was over, the glasses were placed in the basement to await collection next morning. When the butler went down next day to repack the glasses, he found Snippet, then a puppy, sitting amidst a debris of broken glass. He immediately jumped to the conclusion that the pup had swallowed quantities of broken glass and was just about to breathe her last. An urgent summons was phoned to the vet. In the meantime, Edwina asked the butler to ring the catering firm and to check the number of glasses which had been sent. This the butler proceeded to do. But he was so upset by the whole episode that he merely succeeded in asking the catering manager how many glasses had been sent, as a number had been smashed, and the pieces swallowed by her ladyship!

Edwina inspires friendship—and jealousy. Those who care

for her are almost fanatical in their devotion. Dozens of men and women throughout the world have cause to remember her kindness and thoughtfulness, and many simple little letters testify to their gratitude and regard for her. Those who do not know her personally are prepared to criticize. I have never heard her pass unkind judgement on anyone, even on those who at times have maligned her.

Her sense of humour prevents her from ever being pompous, though always she has dignity. Over the years I have noticed that she exhausts herself in fulfilling commitments which she might reasonably have avoided. But the more humble the charity, the school, or the function concerned, the more punctilious she is to implement her promise to make a speech or simply be present. Once she has given her word, nothing can make her break it.

Edwina keeps regular office hours. She works in her office at St. John Ambulance Headquarters. Her office is a small room, severely functional, and furnished with pieces which appear to have been retrieved from dentists' waiting-rooms in the provinces. The walls are cream, the carpet is of green haircord. The window looks out on to a patch of sky dented by chimneys. On the somewhat battered desk are two telephones. On the mantelpiece are personal photographs. On the walls hang a coloured photograph of Princess Margaret, Commandant-in-Chief St. John Cadets, a map of the world, and a painting by Anna Zinkeisen from which were reproduced the appealing 'cadet recruiting' posters.

Edwina works in her office from Monday to Friday (taking the bulk of what she has not got through during the day home with her at night). Often Snippet accompanies her. Before Snippet there were other beloved dogs, and the gnawed wastepaper basket bears mute testimony to the boredom that overcomes puppies subjected to an office routine.

Miss Maud Harrison, Secretary of St. John Ambulance Brigade, like all those who work with Edwina, has the greatest admiration for her vitality. 'She has,' says Miss Harrison, 'the most prodigious memory for facts, people, and places. She has no use for inefficiency, but she is scrupulously just, and makes allowances for mistakes. She likes to have flowers about her. When she is working she smokes very little, but

she is a squirrel with pencils.' Edwina collects and loses
pencils. Her hoard of pencils includes slim gold ones—these
vanish immediately—and hardier specimens, stubs of which
are sometimes to be found in the depths of her handbags.
Plots are made to equip her with jumbo-sized pencils fitted
with patent devices intended to be firmly attached to her desk.
These, too, vanish mysteriously.

Edwina's appointment as Superintendent-in-Chief is made
by the Grand Prior of the Order of St. John of Jerusalem and
is confirmed every three years. She is responsible for the
women personnel of the St. John Ambulance Brigade both in
the United Kingdom and Overseas. These women include
those from the Commonwealth countries, and also Chinese,
Indians, West Africans, and Malays.

Edwina spends nearly all her week-ends going up and down
the country carrying out inspections and making speeches.
During the week there is organizing and paper work. To most
people the tedium and the strain of this self-chosen, highly
exigent existence would be insupportable. She takes an active
part in a long list of charitable organizations. No figure-head
she. She is a born organizer, and no matter what the circumstances of her birth and environment, she would by virtue of
her prodigious drive, have risen to the top. She is a power
behind the scenes, yet, in her lifetime, there will never be any
true evaluation of her work. Obviously, therefore, the motive
power is not self-glorification.

Edwina Mountbatten is a mystery to many of her contemporaries. One woman says, 'Well, I don't know her personally, but people who are born with a golden spoon in their
mouths have no political convictions; they only have theories.'
I tell Edwina this. She says, 'We are all politicians at heart.
All thinking people are. Only I have no aspirations or ambitions. Simply a desire to serve. I am concerned with politics
only insofar as they further the cause of the people by raising
the standards of health, education, housing, and social welfare
in general.'

People really matter to her. She thinks every single human
being is worth giving her life for. She believes that every
individual is entitled to the benefits of progress. She, like her
great grandfather, Lord Shaftesbury, is a reformer.

Years ago, on returning from a trip to South Africa, we discuss racial discrimination. It saddens her. She has never been able to understand a colour bar or racial discrimination. She judges individuals entirely on their merits, regardless of race, colour, or creed. Racial discrimination, she feels, is a virulent form of injustice, and she feels passionately about injustice.

Edwina has no vanity. One afternoon we are sitting talking when Elizabeth Ward suddenly materializes at Edwina's elbow and announces that the car is waiting to take her to some function. She is still in the suit she has worn all day. In a trice she has retrieved the shoes she had taken off and placed on a console table, and with these in her hand she vanishes. In about five minutes she reappears fresh and glowing, a cascade of silver foxes flowing from her arm. I admire her hat, a little nonsense of osprey and black velvet. 'Dickie says it makes me look rather like a Maltese terrier peering through the feathers.'

Over the years Edwina has made many friends. It is indicative of her own standards that her closest friends are themselves remarkable women in their different fields. One of these is Nan Pandit.

Mrs. Ranjit V. Pandit, High Commissioner for India in London and Indian Ambassador to Ireland, is small and singularly impressive. She generally wears saris, and her tiny feet are shod in high-heeled shoes. Her face is serene and unlined, and soft silver hair waves back from a broad and classic brow. Her hands are exquisite. She is friendly, welcoming, and feminine. There is nothing militant about the brilliant Nan Pandit.

She first met the new Vicereine of India on her return from consultations in Moscow. They met at her brother's house. According to Mrs. Pandit, the arrival of the new Vicereine was in the nature of a shock to all the Indian leaders present that day, for unlike former Vicereines, she was informal, natural, and as unlike an official's wife as it was possible to be. Immediately, said Mrs. Pandit, she identified herself with India and Indian welfare problems, and with the life of the country. It was obvious that in India she found a spiritual climate which suited her and from which she drew some benefit, 'for you cannot give without taking'.

'In the past,' said Mrs. Pandit, 'it was customary for Vice-roy's ladies to have formal little parties at which everyone sat stiffly. Edwina plunged headlong into informality, inviting different groups of women, and, having found out what their interests were, she brought them together, and when they had been together for a while the ice melted, and everyone became friendly. Politics were forgotten and women discussed women's problems. It is difficult,' she continued, 'for Western women to penetrate the mind of an Indian woman who has not been westernized, and who comes straight from her traditional back-ground, but Edwina had the perception to penetrate beneath the surface and to find out what made people "tick", and this at one of the most crucial periods in the history of India. The people of India love Edwina, and the work she began then, she consolidates with every tour.'

'On one occasion,' said Mrs. Pandit, 'I was obliged to go to Leeds on some official mission. I travelled with my secre-tary and three other officers. I had a speech to make. When this was over I started back for London. I was tired and rather cross. I was travelling in a reserved compartment, and just before we left the Inspector came and asked me whether I should mind if Edwina, who was travelling in the same train but had not made any reservation, could join us. Naturally I said that I should be delighted. Looking out of the window I saw Edwina staggering down the platform (she had been making a tour near Leeds) weighted down by her suitcase. She came and sat with me. She was radiant and full of vitality. There was some trifling sum to pay, and she opened her bag to pay it. I then realized that I never paid anything, that I had forgotten what it meant to handle money. There was always someone to pay for me. I thought, then: here am I, a middle-class Indian woman with a retinue, while this great lady, with her background and wealth, carries her own suit-cases and deals competently with the realities of life, and I was ashamed.

'During the trip she was full of gaiety. Just before we arrived I said, "I can't wait to have a hot bath and to fall into bed, I'm completely exhausted." To this Edwina replied, "I shall be driving down to Broadlands tonight. I've a speech to make in Southampton early tomorrow morning."'

After this little anecdote Mrs. Pandit sat for a while smoking reflectively. She was thinking of Edwina. 'It is difficult to describe just where her appeal lies. She has so many facets. She has what is, I think, known as "star quality", and I mean that in the nicest possible way. She has, too, a sense of humour which prevents her ever becoming pompous. She can take a joke against herself.

'At one of the Commonwealth Receptions, during which the Mountbattens were present with Her Majesty the Queen, a little incident took place which gives point to what I have just said. Edwina looked chic and soignée in a new creation of black-and-white lace. It had been made for the occasion. Some little while later Sir Anthony and Lady Eden arrived. Lady Eden was wearing a model identical with that worn by Edwina. This was, of course, a situation that could not fail to amuse the feminine element present, but nobody smiled or made any comment. Edwina, completely unruffled, chuckled, took the incident in her stride, and said, "It suits Clarissa so much better than it suits me," but Lady Eden's evening was obviously ruined.' When asked which couturier had made the *gaffe*, Mrs. Pandit gave a diplomatic smile. 'That,' she said, 'I cannot remember.'

Edwina Mountbatten possesses magnificent family jewels, but she likes semi-precious stones, topazes, aquamarines, and amethysts. One of her favourite pieces of jewellery is a gold necklace recently given her by her husband to celebrate their thirty-fourth anniversary. Lord Louis designed the necklace himself with the years woven into it in Roman numerals.

Though she does not rank among the world's best-dressed women, Edwina is interested in clothes, or rather she was, like all great mondaines, interested in them. She now has little time to spare for fittings and long consultations with couturiers. Also, she is often in uniform, which becomes her well. She likes simple, tailored clothes, and dislikes what she calls 'button-and-bow' creations.

Her outdoor recreations are riding, swimming, and sunbathing. She loves concerts, a good play, and a good book. She constantly laments the fact that she has so little time to read. She is essentially modest about herself. When asked to qualify her limitations she said, 'I haven't really any academic qualifications. I find this a tremendous handicap. I should have liked to have had some definite background for the development of my brain. There are so many things I should like to have done. I should like to have mastered a few languages, to take down 200 words a minute in shorthand, to have taken my State nursing. When you have great responsibilities, I feel you should be equipped to cope with them. I feel the lack of training very much. Sometimes I wake up in the middle of the night and think of the things I should know.'

When asked whether she was patient in her approach to people, she said, 'I think so; I attach tremendous importance to friendship. The few intimate friends I have, have given me such loyalty and service. Probably my greatest weakness is being more interested in the human aspect and human contacts than in the detailed workings of an organization. Paper work oppresses me, and I had rather deal with the verbal side, except in cases of snap decisions. I am a great believer in decentralization and I decentralize as much as I can.'

I remember that on one occasion I accompanied Edwina to Broadlands, in whose grounds she was to address the Romsey Townswomen's Guild on their twenty-seventh anniversary. She is their president, an appointment she has held for some nine years.

By nine-thirty one morning I was in the drawing-room at Wilton Crescent, admiring the beautiful Empire chairs with their rosy fawn velvet seats and backs. From them my eye wanders to a portrait of Lady Hamilton by Romney. Her lovely, wilful face looks down upon a decor which harmonizes with the colours in the portrait.

Edwina came in. She is as crisp as a new lettuce. She sweeps me downstairs. In the hall she collects an armful of folders, all tagged with red labels on which are printed 'Today', 'Now', and 'Urgent'. She pounces on Snippet, who is coming with us, and directing a stream of instructions to whoever is standing in the hall, makes for the car.

We speed through the suburbs. Almost immediately she buries herself in her files. Finally, because concentrating in a fast car makes her feel queasy, she puts aside the files and her glasses. Without them she is as blind as a bat. She talks about Broadlands saying that it becomes more and more important to her. She says, 'Broadlands has always been home to me. I suppose that there are always places which are directly connected with a line of thought and action. Possibly Broadlands may subconsciously have had a powerful effect upon my life.'

We drive through the gates into the grounds. The parkland is serene and lovely. Edwina looks with contentment upon the perfect representation of an eighteenth-century painting, complete down to the decorative cows cropping the juicy grass, while horses wander freely beneath the great trees. Something of the perpetual tension which animates Edwina seems to vanish here. Mysteriously she softens, becomes absorbed only in matters which concern the chatelaine of Broadlands.

We have an early lunch in the splendid dining-room designed by Henry Holland. Four magnificent Vandykes glow upon the walls. In an alcove hangs a portrait of Lady Hamilton. Encircled by a pretty and conventional wreath of flowers, she is the epitome of freshness and beauty. The picture has an interesting history. Sir Joshua Reynolds once purchased a canvas on which was painted a wreath of flowers by Jean Baptiste Menoyer. After spending several days at Broadlands as the guest of the second Lord Palmerston, he decided to make his host a gift, and having painted an amiable motif in the wreath of flowers, dispatched it with his compliments to Lord Palmerston. Milord admired the wreath of flowers, but cared not at all for Sir Joshua's subtle compliment, which was a life-like study of a large eye, supposedly the eye of friendship. However, he accepted the gift with good grace; but the moment he heard of the passing of Sir Joshua he commissioned Thomas Lawrence to paint over the 'eye of friendship'. The result was the inspiring portrait of Nelson's Egeria. It was only recently, when the painting was cleaned and sprayed, that the 'eye' was revealed beneath the rosy curves and draperies of Emma.

From birth Edwina has been surrounded by exquisite objects and priceless pictures. Her appreciation of them is acute, and in order that others may enjoy her possessions she lends pictures and *objets d'art* to exhibitions all over the world. She herself is not a collector in the great tradition, though she finds it difficult to resist a fine piece of Ming or Worcester. At one period she collected drawings. Among them were some by Salvador Dali. One of her favourite portraits of herself is by Dali. She says, 'It has a great significance for me. It is, in a fashion, a complete character analysis.'

The Dali drawings have pride of place in her bedroom at Broadlands. Overlooking the Test and the green sweep of the park, it is a deliciously feminine room, light, gay, charming, and restrained. It is decorated in off-white and pink, and the curtains are perpetually abloom with great magnolia flowers. On the chaise-longue are scattered a profusion of lacy, frilly pillows. On low tables are displayed jewelled snuff-boxes and pill-boxes. Edwina attaches great importance to small personal things—photographs, books, and bibelots—regardless of their value. Other favourite drawings in this room are two crayon portraits. One of Edwina as a child with her grandfather, and one of her father, Lord Mount-Temple, by Sargent. On the dressing-table among the tortoiseshell brushes, combs, and mirrors are snaps of Lord Louis and the Mountbatten girls. There never was such a family for collecting and displaying photographs of one another. Their deep family feeling and devotion to one another are expressed by this plethora of snaps (not always flattering ones) and studio portraits, placed on all the surfaces on which their eyes might possibly rest, and just as Edwina surrounds herself with photographs of her loved ones (including departed dogs and exotic pets), so does Lord Louis have snaps of his wife, his daughters, and their and his favourite horses, in his quarters.

Luncheon is served by Charles Smith, who has been with the Mountbattens for over twenty-five years. Charles was originally Edwina's footman, and accompanied her on many of her early travels. He is now Lord Louis' valet, and the keystone of the staff at Broadlands. He no doubt regrets the vanished yesterdays, for the staff is sadly depleted. However, having married an efficient and accommodating wife 'who can turn her hand to anything', he has a willing A.D.C.

Coffee is served in the drawing-room. In this gracious, spacious room, with its Louis Quinze *boiserie* chairs hang some notable portraits. There are two by Thomas Lawrence, one of the second Lord Palmerston, and one of his wife aged nineteen when she was Emily Cowper. Here, too, are masses of

flowers in white pots, exquisite trifles on tables, and photographs and books piled high on a table.

We sit quietly savouring the peace and the silence. This
does not last long, for within five minutes Edwina is on the
move again. It is time to go to the fête. Edwina puts on a
decorative little hat and gloves. We stand in the doorway
looking up at a glowering sky. It begins to pour. Charles
appears with a vast, striped golfing umbrella. This Edwina
ignores. Bravely she goes off, her high heels digging into the
lawn. We go towards the Orangery, in which the fête is being
held. In the distance, sensible raincoated figures can be seen
streaking along towards the rendez-vous. The ladies of the
Romsey Townswomen's Guild have turned out in full force.

The Orangery is packed to capacity. Owing to the rain,
some of the stalls which had been set up outside have been
transferred inside, though a few stout-hearted ladies have
covered their wares to shelter them. The pervasive smell of
wet macs and potted plants fills the air. In the distance, on a
trestle table, are arranged the tea-urns and mounds of buns
and home-made cakes and scones.

Edwina is escorted to her seat. A whimpering child is
hushed. The ladies gaze attentively at their President. When
she stands up to speak there is complete silence. She talks
with tremendous sincerity, of familiar things—of persons and
events familiar to her audience—and it is obvious that there
is a bond between them and herself. When she sits down there
is a great burst of clapping. As soon as the speeches are ended
there is a rustle and a bustle as the ladies rush to the stalls.
Edwina admires rows of home-made jams, preserves, and
pickles, chats with an old friend, exchanges a joke with someone who knew her as a child; asks after the aged father of one
stall-holder and soldier son of another. Gradually her arms
are filled with the fruit of the diligence of the ladies of the
Romsey Townswomen's Guild. All appears to be going to
plan when a crisis occurs. Cups of tea are being returned to
the stalwart manning the tea-urns. It would seem that some
horrible chemical reaction has taken place, causing the tea in
the urns to 'turn'. Charles is summoned from the house and
spends the rest of the afternoon rushing to and fro with kettles
of boiling water. Edwina is seemingly indefatigable. She

Q

samples buns, rock cakes, and tea. The incident of the urns becomes a matter for laughter. It is then that I discover one of the sources of her perennial gaiety. She is really, sincerely enjoying herself.

At some time towards the end of the writing of this book I spent hours going through the weighty albums which date back to Edwina's infancy. Here, recorded by the camera, is a pictorial history of Edwina Mountbatten. In the posed, studio portraits was the plump child with the silver-gilt curls and wide, candid eyes. Here is another portrait: Edwina with her mother, Maud Ashley, her cheek close to the silver-gilt hair. Here are snaps of Edwina and Mary with governesses and favourite dogs and ponies. Edwina is thin and leggy and the curls are now plaits. I turn the pages, discovering Sir Ernest Cassel, sad, remote, and uncompromising, gazing into the camera. I come upon snaps of the adolescent Edwina with plump, curly-haired cousin Marjorie. About them is an aura of gaiety, of shared confidences, of school-girl secrets and of the curiosity inspired by standing at the gates of adult life.

The cavalcade flits past: Edwina and Dickie with bright untarnished faces. Young and in love. . . . Wedding pictures, honeymoon pictures, the round, unlined faces touched with rapture. Then comes snaps of the trip to America, and large, skilful photographs of places of interest on the first tours abroad. Then Adsdean, the puppies, the lion cub, and then the children: Patricia first, and then Pamela. There are snaps of Edwina with friends whose faces are part of contemporary history. Each album tells the history of a decade, and as the years pass, the playgrounds and beaches of the international set are superseded by grim photographs of Edwina in uniform, of Edwina travelling by air, jeep, and on foot on her errands of mercy.

Late that afternoon Edwina discovered me surrounded by albums and steeped in gloom. In a few moments, however, my sadness was dispelled, for she does not allow the past to weigh upon her spirits. It then flashed through my mind that the secret of her astonishing vitality is that she lives intensely and urgently in the present. There are no recriminations, no regrets, only a great curiosity, a great compassion, and a tremendous and dynamic reverence and love for life.

INDEX